THE
WORD
IN THE ENGLISH
CLASSROOM

THE WORD IN THE ENGLISH CLASSROOM

Best Practices of Faith Integration

Editors

Jamie Dessart
Brad Gambill

 Abilene Christian University Press

Abilene, Texas

WORD IN THE ENGLISH CLASSROOM
Best Practices of Faith Integration

Copyright 2009 by Jamie Dessart and Brad Gambill

ISBN 978-0-89112-536-5

Printed in the United States of America

Scripture quotations, unless otherwise noted, are from The Holy Bible,
New International Version. Copyright 1984, International Bible Society.
Used by permission of Zondervan Publishers.

LIBRARY OF CONGRESS CATALOGING-IN-PUBLICATION DATA
The word in the English classroom : best practices of faith integration / editors, Jamie
Dessart, Brad Gambill.
    p. cm.
Includes bibliographical references.
ISBN 978-0-89112-536-5
1. American literature--Study and teaching. 2. English literature--Study and teaching.
3. Faith--Study and teaching. 4. Faith in literature. 5. Christianity in literature. I. Dessart,
Jamie. II. Gambill, James Bradley, 1964-
 PS42.W67 2009
 810.9--dc22

                        2009025135

Cover design by Rick Gibson
Interior text design by Sandy Armstrong

For information contact:
Abilene Christian University Press
ACU Box 29138
Abilene, Texas 79699-9138

1-877-816-4455 toll free
www.abilenechristianuniversitypress.com

09 10 11 12 13 14 / 7 6 5 4 3 2 1

CONTENTS

THE HEART ON THE TABLE:

Or Everything I Know about Faith Integration I Learned in the Classroom

JAMIE DESSART (WAYNESBURG UNIVERSITY)

For some, Christian higher education begins early with an undergraduate career at a Christian school. For others, there is an awareness of Christian higher education throughout their entire academic lives. For me, I had little to no idea that my personal faith could have anything to do with the body of knowledge I was learning in graduate school. I could talk a good game on testimony night, having been raised Southern Baptist as a child, but I could not have articulated a connection between my role as a college professor and my identity as a Christian. So, when I began my first job at a Christian school, I found myself struggling to learn what the phrase "integration of faith and learning" meant.

My school begins our fall term every year with a faculty convocation filled with professional development opportunities, which usually include faith and learning issues through a selection of wonderful speaker/leaders. This seemed like the best place to begin my own personal journey in defining faith and learning. So I was surprised when, after one fall convocation, some older colleagues pulled me aside to ask a very serious question: What exactly does integration of faith and learning mean? We had just heard a wonderful presentation by Susan Gallagher, the co-author along with Roger Lundin of *Literature Through the Eyes of Faith*,[1] and had spent the whole day immersed in this very important concept for Christian higher education. My colleagues were serious; they truly did not know what this "integration" would look like in their classrooms. They were asking me, they said, because I seemed to know. Turns out, what they were asking was a question that many faculty members have asked and are still asking—even faculty who have worked for years at Christian schools. Beyond the theory and discussion of terminology, they said, what are the practical applications of integration? What do I *do* in my courses?

This question is not always answered in the excellent literature we read at professional development workshops and other venues. Susan Gallagher and Roger Lundin's book is a wonderful introduction to the discussion of faith in the English field and an overview of integration. Arthur Holm's *The Idea of a Christian College*[2] lays out a very clear plan for faculty at Christian schools and is a book new faculty should read. Brian J. Walsh and Richard Middleton's *The Transforming Vision*[3] gives faculty an understanding of the term worldview for both themselves and their students. Many other books are standard reading fare to understanding the paradigm of integration. But what many faculty members are looking for, myself included, is the next step, the point where practical application meets theory, the praxis of integration. What do you *do* when you walk in the classroom door?

My colleagues had a number of very basic concerns and misconceptions that I have come to realize are common. Was all this talk pointing to reading a devotional and/or praying at the start of the class? It would be a simple and easy answer if all I needed to do was download the daily lexionary and read the morning Psalm in class, but a few minutes of the Bible followed by textual instruction doesn't sound like integration at all. Neither does mentioning how Jesus is the Word at the beginning of each semester, as that is not truly living faith. Paul says in Romans 10:9 that "if you confess with your mouth 'Jesus is Lord,' and believe in your heart that God raised him from the dead, you will be saved." Simply saying it isn't enough; it's a package deal. Would they be asked about church attendance, faculty wondered? Some schools do require faculty to adhere to the tenets of certain denominations, as well as their students. Yet many of us have wandered away from the Church at given times; I ran far away from organized religion after my father's death, but I never strayed from God. If faith and learning means I'm at my church whenever the door is open, I don't think I'd ever get any papers graded. So exactly how much would be expected of faculty: Bible studies, statements of faith in class, temperance?

At our school, with no denominational requirements outside a Christian statement of faith for faculty and no such requirements for students, we were charting unfamiliar waters. Waynesburg University,[4] affiliated with the Presbyterian Church U.S.A, was primarily a secular school until about two decades ago when the decision was made by the Trustees to hire a President who would bring the school back to its religious roots. I was a member of one of the early groups of faculty who had to write a faith statement prior to hiring, and during my tenure, faith and integration was added as an area of review for tenure and promotion procedures. With that background, the questions by faculty, especially those who had twenty or more years at the school, were understandable; we were, and are, in the process of crafting a unique type of school. Negotiating integration while reinserting faith was bound to be difficult. Although it was clear that simply counting church attendance or utilizing opening prayers was not what the administration was suggesting, many faculty had little concept of the harmonizing of personal belief and academic discipline.

What I realized was that the praxis of integration was a complex entity, one that is more than listening to a lecture or reading a well-written book. It was a living, breathing creation that changed constantly, not confined to lecture halls, but taking place in offices, across tables in the cafeteria, and at the coffee pot in the break room/storage area. What we were doing was creating our own support groups, modeling, without knowing it, the early church. After hearing the speakers, we talked about listening to our friends denote specific lessons and student reactions to various pedagogical methods. The small group break out sessions during those workshops often started and ended with stories of triumphs or disappointments, with which we could all commiserate. Others were negotiating a way to bring knowledge and belief together, we were excited to learn, and we hoped that we would have an "aha" moment for our own classes.

Beyond these convocations and in an effort to further my own understanding, I began attending workshops and conferences, talking to others, and searching for help. What I quickly discovered was that those who had long been acquainted with Christian higher education, and those who had been at Christian colleges as students, also struggled with integration. I remember attending one well-meaning conference where numerous thinkers of varied disciplines strove to move beyond the paradigm of integration. This paradigm, faith and learning, has been around for years and, as many can attest, does not come close to an adequate explanation for what we are currently trying to accomplish. After further conversation, I came away to realize that the variables of integration were much more complex than I ever thought. For example, denominational backgrounds clearly matter when using terminology of faith and learning; one of the main speakers at that specific conference wanted to replace the old term of integration with the idea of "testimony," by which he definitely didn't mean the Southern Baptist tradition of testifying to my journey with Christ. I was confused at first as I tried to reconcile how he, as a Calvinist, used what I saw as the very Baptist term of testimony. Fortunately, those literary theory classes I took in graduate school served me well; I knew what ambiguity was and the way in which signs and signifiers could be slippery when in use. This was a perfect example.

When I began to attend conferences with others from Christian schools, I discovered that colleagues at all types of institutions had very similar questions. Between arranged sessions with speakers, we would find places with comfortable chairs and share our experiences, bringing home other people's handouts and syllabi to utilize for our own ideas. Whether it was cross-discipline or just English faculty, the connections were made in friendly settings. At a particularly wonderful conference I attended at Seattle Pacific University, one of the most meaningful discussions I had occurred late in the evening after we had all been to a movie. In the sessions and panels, I did take away many ideas that I have incorporated into my own teaching, but it was, and is, often the impromptu moments where the "aha" occurs. The theory and abstraction of the concept becomes meshed with the practical in those chats. It's like when I first met gender theory; reading Helene Cixous put the ideas in my head, but it was a few years later, driving down the interstate between adjunct jobs, when a billboard advertisement showed me, in a concrete way, what Cixous meant by writing the body.

Numerous times I have read about a Christian worldview, but it has often been off-the-cuff discussion in class where I came to truly understand that there are different ways of viewing the world. One memorable example was in a class where I was teaching a short story by Issac Asimov about a robot who, when turned on for the first time, immediately asks who his creator is. How else, I asked, beside believing we are created with a purpose by God, could we view our beginnings? A student's blasé response opened a whole dialogue about believing we are products of a cultural assembly line. His point, that we are random parts assembled and sent forth into the world without purpose, engendered amazing discussion among the students and sent me back to my own office afterwards to really contemplate a world where there was no divine creator. In that classroom, on that day, faith integration moved from conceptual to concrete or, at least, robotic.

My personal thoughts on the integration of faith and learning, it turns out, *were* formed in the very secular schools that I had believed taught me nothing about Christian higher education, and I imagine the same is true for many professors at Christian colleges. While learning Lacan's theory of the Imaginary and the Symbolic, I was being prepared for understanding the

Word as God in the Garden. The first time I heard of the phrase "integration of faith and learning" I was reminded of the end of Geoffrey Chaucer's *Troilus and Criseyde,* when Troilus, after his death, learns the truth of the world from his place in the afterlife. To a medieval mind, to speak of a separation between faith and knowledge would be an impossibility, for knowledge, the music of the spheres, comes straight from the mind of God. It is us, in our fallen state as sinful mortals, who enforce a separation between the very fundaments of our nature. I distinctly remember a workshop where I kept insisting that there was no need to integrate the two halves because there was no distinction between the two; being the only medievalist there, I'm sure many wondered if I was from another world. Medieval philosophy paved the way for me to move beyond the basic paradigm of those first forays of readings and lectures, and I discovered that I needed to remind myself what I had always known: any attempt to name or describe something, as Chaucer teaches us, is fleeting and random, broken wind in the face of God's permanence. Chaucer's metaphor of the *House of Fame,* where one word is a stone thrown in a pool sending ripples out and back across the surface, has helped me come to the place where I can now enter my classroom with the strength to try something new, open my very soul to the students, and deal with the ripples that come back at me in return.

Parker Palmer, in *The Courage to Teach: Exploring the Inner Landscape of a Teacher's Life,*[5] says that when we enter the classroom, we walk in, slash open our chests, and heave our heart onto the table for the students to see. To truly learn to teach, and have the courage to do it, we must truly know ourselves first. Shakespeare had it right—*to your own self be true.* When I quit trying to parrot the pedagogy and walked into that classroom as nothing more than Jamie, who loves to sit on the desk with a soda in one hand while enthusiastically talking about the origin of words, I became a teacher. And the same, it turns out, is true for this imperfect term called the integration of faith and learning. When I quit trying everyone else's ways to engage my students, some book's notion about how to introduce a Christian worldview, or patterning myself after what a great speaker suggested, that was when I allowed myself to become the totality of my self—including my faith in its naturally, integrated role. I opened the door to my Southern Baptist roots, struggled to hear God's voice amid the world's chatter, and my students responded to the heart on the table and the Spirit in the room.

The genesis of this book came from such a heart-on-the-table conversation. Why can't someone write this down, somebody wondered aloud. Can we post all the information from the classes on the web? Can't we share with each other how we found what worked for us? And, we thought, what if we could put together a collection of those moments with each author sharing their best practices? Could we just talk to each other about what worked and what didn't, as if we were sitting around a virtual table of faculty in Christian higher education? We could include a cross-section of colleagues from different schools with varied denominational background. We could get creative writers, composition instructors, and literature specialists from British, American, World, and any time period. It would be a coffee klatch of scope and breadth.

This book is envisioned as that conversation, a collection of colleagues. Imagine them sitting in your office, sharing your table in the cafeteria, or talking around the microwave, sharing their struggles, and listening as you speak in turn. Most of our contributors are currently teaching at a Christian school; the colleges and universities run the gamut of denominational affiliations. From all around the country, the authors share specific ways in which they negotiated faith and learning in the classroom, both intentionally and accidentally, what worked, and what didn't. We hope the reader gains ideas and insights from others' struggles and triumphs, while understanding that many of us are in the same boat, trying to steer our way on the path God has laid before us. It's my hope that this book gives courage and sustenance to those of us standing with our hearts out in front of the classroom as both teachers and professors of faith.

Endnotes

1   Susan Gallagher and Roger Lundin, *Literature Through the Eyes of Faith* (New York: HarperOne, 1989).

2   Arthur Holmes, *The Idea of a Christian College* (Grand Rapids: Eerdmans, 1987).

3   Brian J. Walsh and Richard Middleton, *The Transforming Vision: Shaping a Christian Worldview* (Downer's Grove, IL: InterVarsity, 1984).

4   In Fall of 2007, Waynesburg College became Waynesburg University. For continuity, I will use the current name even though some of the specifics mentioned took place before the official change.

5   Parker Palmer, *The Courage to Teach: Exploring the Inner Landscape of a Teacher's Life* (San Francisco: Jossey-Bass, 1997).

Reading *Jane Eyre* with Would-Be Janes:

Christian Identity and Gender Identification in British Romantic and Victorian Literature

Bruce Boeckel (Fresno Pacific University)

reader-response

In "Reading Jane Eyre *with Would-Be Janes," Bruce Boeckel discusses the theological and gender issues that arise among young, female Christian readers who strongly identity with Jane and read the novel as a Romance. In this course on British Romantic and Victorian Literature, he also challenges students to consider the theological-ideological presuppositions of Romantic poets such as William Wordsworth. He argues that discussion of such faith issues occurs best when the teacher honestly reveals his or her own theological commitments and fosters a hospitable environment for others to do so as well. Bruce is a member of Millbrook Presbyterian Church in Fresno, California. He currently teaches English and is chair of the Division of Humanities at Fresno Pacific University. He is completing a book entitled* The Enlightenment's Double-Bind: Utopia and Terror in the Mythic Speculations of the French *Philosophes.*

> I will throw all on the altar—heart, vitals, the entire victim. He will never love me, but he shall approve me.
>
> —Jane Eyre considering St. John's marriage proposal

This essay addresses theological and gender issues from a recent course on the British Romantics and Victorians. The essay gives particular attention to student responses to *Jane Eyre*, a novel that raises theological questions common to literature courses of many kinds. In addition, *Jane Eyre* raises complex issues of gender, issues that seem somehow even more tangled from the cultural distance of twenty-first-century California and a course in which one male student and the teacher are the only two men in the room.

Before we move on to *Jane Eyre*, however, I will discuss, in a more general way, two issues that I have tried to clarify in my own mind in order to become a more effective teacher. In particular, I believe that Christian higher education should provide training in and modelling of intellectual virtues. Among these are a balancing pair: open sensibility and critical thinking, both of which are crucial to understanding literature. As someone trying to model these intellectual virtues at a Christian college, I thus face two basic questions. First, how am I going to identify myself to students? In other words, what stance will I take? Second, how will I foster a hospitable environment for exchanges of ideas among students from various Christian backgrounds?

The Teacher's Identity: Three Options

Fostering intellectual virtue and honest exchange of ideas is not easy. Of course, in any undergraduate college classroom, there typically will be differences of age and education, perhaps also differences in culture and background, between teacher and students. These differences, as well as the differences among students themselves, can block or complicate honest communication. At most Christian colleges, in addition, there are different denominations and kinds of Christian backgrounds represented in any given course, and the teacher may be among the dominant group (if there is one) or may well stand alone. For this reason, Christian undergraduates sometimes are apprehensive when they encounter a new professor. They fear that, on the one hand, they might be subjected to heavy-handed indoctrination, or, on the other, that their youthful Christian convictions might be subject to antipathetic critique. In addition to the challenge of the generation gap, therefore, teaching at Christian colleges involves some form of cross-denominational understanding or misunderstanding—and the difference can be crucial both to a student's field-specific learning and to the broader formative role of a student's in-class experiences.

Cross-denominational understanding is difficult even in the best of circumstances, among those of goodwill and those who are informed about various streams of Christian tradition. Because every Christian is shaped by a particular and limited religious background, there is no ideal preparation for this task, and every participant has significant deficiencies. A Christian thinker who has been raised in and remains in a particular denomination, for example, will have a deep appreciation for that particular tradition—and this is a significant insight and advantage. But that same person may have only a thin and external sense of other Christian traditions and may be partly blind to his or her own denominational prejudices. Every Christian denomination that I have encountered includes some form of denominational bigotry, usually not as an element of official church teaching but as an implicit attitude toward Christians outside the denomination.

Those Christians who have had a broader experience of various churches and denominations have their own advantages and deficiencies. This is my own experience, and it is one that is increasingly typical of North-American Protestantism. At best, a Christian with this type of multi-denominational background may have an appreciation for more than one denominational tradition, but he or she may also lack sympathy for those with deep-seated denominational-theological habits and convictions.

Fortunately, both students and teachers will encounter others from a variety of denominational backgrounds on the typical Christian-college campus. However, even if we suppose that such exposure to various Christian traditions is an advantage for cross-denominational understanding, that in itself does not eliminate all vestiges of denominational bigotry, nor does it automatically engender honest dialogue.

Given the typical denominational landscape at most Christian colleges, there are three basic options for approaching students (and colleagues) from various faith traditions. The first option is to reveal one's own denominational loyalties at the outset and to discuss things always from that theological viewpoint. For those who comprehend the full richness of a particular theological stream and who recognize the typical prejudices of their own denomination, this can be a very fruitful approach. Both students and colleagues will benefit from getting to know such a person, a best-case exemplar of a particular Christian tradition.

An opposed option is to bracket off one's own denominational loyalties (if there are any) and to take up a position apart from all denominations. For those who are attracted to the ideal of values-neutral instruction, who want to encourage independent thinking in students, and who are opposed to any tendency toward indoctrination, this option has great appeal. In much of my own teaching, I have tended to take this second approach, bracketing off my own beliefs, often playing the devil's advocate toward whatever idea is under discussion, ventriloquizing what the philosopher Thomas Nagel calls "the view from nowhere."

More recently, however, I have come to see that this noncommittal stance can sometimes hinder honest dialogue on matters of faith. What I have found more useful is a third option: a stance that openly reveals my own denominational and theological loyalties—I am a Reformed Christian, a Calvinist—but one that also includes other and contrasting theological viewpoints. My goal is to model a critical exploration of the alternatives one faces in adopting and shaping a Christian worldview.

Framing the Exchange of Ideas:
Christian Theology, Romantic Ideology, and Their Internal Tensions

Having identified myself to my students in this way, the second issue I confront as a teacher is how I will lay out a framework for discussion of a given topic, so that students will develop their own Christian thinking and learn to consider various viewpoints. I often find that the initial challenge is to get students simply to *recognize* that a given literary text actually *has* a viewpoint—other than simply to entertain the reader—that it addresses moral and religious questions, for example, in a particular way and for a particular purpose.

Igniting the spark of recognition and then laying out a framework for discussion are difficult tasks that often must be custom-matched to a particular text, course, and set of students. I thus will give a specific example, one related to the interpretation of Romantic poetry in my course on the British Romantics and Victorians.

Early in the weeks on the British Romantics, I had students read poems by William Wordsworth (1770-1850) from the 1798 *Lyrical Ballads*. An initial challenge was to get students to see that, despite the simplicity of the language, Wordsworth's poems do not simply repeat commonplaces or appeal to common sense. Instead, they strategically reiterate particular ideological claims that are central to Wordsworth's Romantic worldview.

A typical case is found in the two conversation poems that Wordsworth chose to open the second edition of *Lyrical Ballads*. In "Expostulation and Reply," William's friend chides him for daydreaming and neglecting book-learning:

> "Why William, on that old grey stone,
>
> . . . .
>
> [Do you] dream your time away?

> "Where are your books? that light bequeath'd
> To beings else forlorn and blind!

> Up! Up! And drink the spirit breath'd
> From dead men to their kind."[1]

Despite his friend's plea, William rejects the preference for bookish wisdom; he insists, instead, that insight "of itself will come" among these "things for ever speaking."[2]

In the following poem, "The Tables Turned: An Evening Scene, on the Same Subject," William continues his argument, now making explicit much that he had implied earlier:

> Come forth into the light of things,
> Let Nature be your teacher.
>
> . . . .
>
> One impulse from a vernal wood
> May teach you more of man;
> Of moral evil and of good,
> Than all the sages can.[3]

William now explicitly announces that he takes "Nature" as his "teacher" and that what he learns from "impulse" goes far beyond mere facts of biology or picturesque vistas. Indeed, William learns "[o]f moral evil and of good"; he discovers the elusive secrets of the nature of Man.

William's appeal to "Nature" is paired with Wordsworth's characteristic anti-intellectualism. Likewise, William's condemnation of civilized corruption is paired with an implicit appeal to childhood innocence. Although "William" here is a young adult, he indulges in outdoor daydreaming and rejects adult achievements "of science and of art"[4] exactly as does the typical child figure throughout *Lyrical Ballads*. By pointing out these repeated gestures, I hoped to get students to recognize that *Lyrical Ballads* contains not merely pretty poems, that they make crucial, far-reaching ideological claims that bear directly on traditional Christian teaching about humanity's moral nature and accountability.

In order to encourage a critical exploration of these issues, I prepared a handout outlining elements of the "Romantic Worldview or Ideology" (see Appendix A). As I explained to my students, I am struck by the *prima facia* conflict between the Calvinist doctrine of "total depravity" and Romantic assertions of the natural goodness of Man. But my handout also points to the concept of the *imago Dei*, which can be considered as a counterbalance to the notion of total depravity. In other words, there is a tension, even within Calvinist theology itself, on this question. Other Christian traditions also embody this tension, in one way or another, a tension contained in the story of the Garden of Eden itself.

The *Lyrical Ballads* are far more than pretty poems because they take up precisely these same biblical themes and provide a kind of alternative myth of the glory of man and woman, of their fall into corruption, and of the way back to paradise. This kind of mythic speculation is something that the neo-Romantics of the 1960s understood very well and practiced in their own right. As Crosby, Stills, Nash, and Young sang back in 1969, in the song "Woodstock":

> Well I came upon a child of God;
> He was walking along the road,
> And I asked him, Tell where are you going?
> This he told me:
>
> Said I'm going down to Yasgur's farm,
> Gonna join in a rock and roll band,
> Got to get back to the land to set my soul free.
>
> We are stardust; we are golden.
> We are ten-billion-year-old carbon,
> And we've got to get ourselves back to the garden.[5]

Students of all denominations benefit from an exploration of these biblical themes and of the alternative religious myths found in works of art such as *Lyrical Ballads*. Students also benefit from recognizing and responding critically to the ideological claims implicit in the popular culture of their own era, in songs like "Woodstock" and its more recent permutations.

Despite my own Calvinist point against Romantic belief in human natural goodness, I also suggested to students that other Christian traditions have been more sympathetic to the Romantic viewpoint, an important feature in the reception of Romantic poetry. Many Victorian readers of Wordsworth, for example, treated his poetry as Christian devotional literature, praising God for the wonders of Nature and of Man that Wordsworth so marvelously portrays.

Yet this sympathetic and devotional reading of Wordsworth may be simplistic in its own way, ignoring the incongruities in *Lyrical Ballads*, the dissonant notes that clash with Wordsworth's ideological claims (see study questions in Appendix A). In other words, there are tensions within Wordsworth's poetry itself on the ideological points that Wordsworth asserts with such feigned confidence. Wordsworth's belief in the natural goodness of Man is thus a characteristic example, an ideology that *appears* to be a direct contradiction of *one* particular tenet of (Calvinist) theology. Yet the relationship of

Wordsworth's poetry to Christian teaching as a whole is, on closer analysis, quite troubled and ambivalent, leading to different responses from different kinds of Christians.

Whether or not my students accept the doctrine of total depravity, whether or not they embrace the Romantic vision of human goodness, I have tried to frame a discussion of *Lyrical Ballads* that is open to contributions from many perspectives. I hope that students of all kinds can enter the discussion, exchange ideas, try on alternative viewpoints, and come to an informed appreciation of the tensions and consequences involved in any answer to these complex questions. I want my students to be *thinking* Christians, to pursue intellectual virtue, no matter the denominational identity that they may claim.

Jane Eyre as Christian Romance Fiction

We turn now to *Jane Eyre*. Here is a brief synopsis of the novel. Jane is the first-person narrator of the story. She is an unhappy and mistreated orphan in her aunt's household until she is sent off to the Lowood Institution, a Christian charity and orphanage school for girls. The girls suffer under the Scrooge-like provisions imposed by Mr. Brocklehurst, the chairman of the board of trustees. An epidemic sweeps through Lowood and claims about half of these weak, ill-clad, and ill-fed girls. This incident, including the epidemic, is based on Charlotte Brontë's own experience at a similar charity school.

Jane later escapes Lowood by taking a job as a governess. She is in the household and in the employ of Mr. Rochester, the novel's hero: Mr. Tall, Dark, and Dangerous. There is a courtship of sorts and a marriage proposal, but Jane flees when she learns that Rochester has a living wife, a madwoman that he keeps locked up in the attic. Jane ends up finding refuge in the home of Mr. St. John and his sisters. St. John also proposes to Jane, but she refuses him and goes in search of Mr. Rochester. She finds Rochester maimed and blinded by a fire at the estate. Rochester's mad wife has died in the fire. The path is now clear for Jane to marry Mr. Rochester, and she now rejoices in the role of wife and nurse-maid.

Jane Eyre was included in the second half of the semester on British Romantic and Victorian literature, a typical upper-division literature course at my school. Enrolled in the course were fourteen undergraduates, thirteen women and one man. *Jane Eyre* is a strongly female-oriented novel, and many of my female students identified with the young heroine because of her intellect, her thirst for knowledge and experience, and her courage in standing up against injustice. Because Jane Eyre is also an overtly Christian figure, because she often is taken as a model of female Christian virtue, many female students also strongly identified with her in that regard.

Yet because Jane Eyre too easily sheds her bitter past, because she too easily dons a garment of winsome virtue, she strikes me as an inappropriate and dangerous role model for the twenty-something, Christian women in my course. I am reminded of the tragic character Pecola Breedlove in Toni Morrison's novel *The Bluest Eye*. This poor, little black girl has scraped together three cents to buy some "Mary Jane" candy. But Pecola is attracted by far more than the candy's sweetness; she longs for the suburban prosperity that Mary Jane symbolizes. She fantasizes about *being* Mary Jane, about having the fresh-smelling clothes, the easy smile, the shameless blue eyes.

> Each pale yellow wrapper has a picture on it. A picture of little Mary Jane, for whom the candy is named. Smiling white face. Blond hair in gentle array, blue eyes looking out of her world of clean comfort. The eyes are petulant, mischievous. To Pecola they are simply pretty. To eat the candy is somehow to eat the eyes, eat Mary Jane. Love Mary Jane. Be Mary Jane.[6]

In its own way, the figure of Jane Eyre—Sandra Gilbert calls her "plain Jane"[7]—can be a sticky-sweet temptation and a form of wish-fulfillment for young Christian women. Jane may be "plain," but because she is also virtuous and *self-sacrificing*, God rewards her with the man of her dreams in the end.

That, more or less, is the plotline of some Christian Romance fiction. This plotline is, I would argue, a pseudo-Christian ideology that merits critical analysis. As a male instructor at a Christian college, however, I had to be very careful about how I approached this issue. Some of my female students identified powerfully with Jane, as I soon learned, and challenging the ideology of Romance fiction too directly could make these students feel that their faith, their prayers and desires, were under attack. In addition, these students could well feel that a *male* instructor has little credibility on this issue; he has little understanding of the travails of the modern-day Jane in the urban jungle of today's dating scene. Finally, differing views about the proper role of Christian women often fall along denominational lines, so I had to be careful to maintain a framework for cross-denominational understanding on this topic also.

For all of these reasons, I had to tread lightly in reading *Jane Eyre* with my female Christian students, my American would-be Janes. As with my denominational identity, I signalled to students early on that I am troubled by the ideology of Romance fiction. But I did not go into detail on that point and stepped back to allow students to do their own exploration and exchange of ideas.

As a stimulus for class discussions, I had students write brief reading responses for each reading assignment. These gave students, even shy students, an opportunity to articulate their ideas and to get some one-on-one feedback from me. The following pages summarize these reading responses and my handwritten comments. As we shall see, the theological and gender dynamics of these exchanges were quite interesting. To the benefit of the course, students often shared their thinking in class, allowing the written exchanges with me to spill over into verbal discussion among students. Unless otherwise noted, all of the student views expressed are those of female students.

In the following pages I give a summary of that exploration as it evolved in written exchanges between teacher and students.

Jane Eyre and Abusive Christian Males

The early chapters of the novel, covering Jane's childhood, evoked much sympathy from my students. One student responded by taking notice of Jane's friend at Lowood, the quiet and bookish Helen Burns.[8] The student's comment: "I connect with the bright girl [Helen] who loves reading, falls to daydreaming easily, and holds strong religious convictions." My comment: "So do I, despite being a man!" I suspect that this student was a bookworm as a child, just as I was, so this fascination with Helen Burns seems to transcend gender. The student's comment continues: "The more I learned of this girl, the more I liked her and the more I became convinced she would have a significant role" in the novel. My comment now points to gender-specific dynamics at play here: "So is this a 'Romance novel,' aiming for the female reader to identify with the female protagonist?" What this student does not yet know is that sweet Helen Burns is one of the novel's early female victims. Helen dies in the epidemic at Lowood School. With Helen gone, the reader's concerned sympathy shifts back to Jane, and this close identification is typical of my student readers. It is a convention of the traditional Romance novel to underscore the vulnerability of the heroine. Jane Eyre is prone to mistreatment by bad men, and only a *good* man can save her.

The Lowood chapters feature Mr. Brocklehurst and other bad men on the Lowood board, who seem to take a special delight in imposing pious poverty on these girls. A student notes the scene in which Brocklehurst demonizes and humiliates Jane in front of all the other school girls. The student can hardly fathom such petty cruelty. She asks, "Could this be a completely factual account, or is it an example of a young girl exaggerating a humiliating experience? Would any real minister do this to a ten-year-old girl?"

21

Suspicion against Jane as narrator often signals discomfort over Jane's defiance. Such elements of Jane's character, which do not fit the Romance mold, are disturbing to some of my students. Early on, we had taken special note of Brontë's preface to the novel, in which she defends her portrait of Mr. Brocklehurst and other Christian hypocrites, insisting that such critique does not constitute disloyalty to Christ and his Church. But some of my students are ambivalent on this point. One student remarks that "[f]rom the very beginning, Jane hardly seems a child." Jane is thus an unnatural figure. Students note that defiant Jane suffers much but also shows coldness toward others; she shows "little capacity to love." One student suggests that Jane may reject not only Mr. Brocklehurst but also the Christian faith that he claims to represent: "Jane has a more innocent view of the Bible and religion prior to her stint at Lowood. She adapts her own view after Lowood."

All of this makes me wonder what negative experiences my Christian students may have had with male religious figures in their own lives. Some students seem willing to side with Jane against Mr. Brocklehurst. Others are incredulous about Jane's account and seem to blame her for being cold, unchildlike, or even unwomanly. I suspect that especially female readers often relate to Jane in a deeply personal way. Their attitude toward Jane's defiance may be linked to their own experiences of hurt or healing in a Christian setting.

At other points, my students are less worried about Jane's personal defiance and consider the novel's representation of the "woman question" in general. One student even paraphrases the classic Freudian question: "What do women want?" Her comment: "We learn that Jane is restless and her life too placid. But what is she looking for? Love? Adventure?" Another student types out a key passage of the novel, a full paragraph, in which Jane as narrator complains that women cannot be restricted to quiet needlework, "making puddings," and "playing on the piano."[9] No, "women feel just as men feel," writes Brontë; "they need exercise for their faculties and a field for their efforts as much as their brothers do; they suffer from too rigid a restraint, too absolute a stagnation, precisely as men would suffer."[10] The student comments: "For me this passage was so strongly written [that] it should be noticed and examined." Of course, this was a key passage of the novel that we discussed in class, in the context of larger social and gender issues in mid-nineteenth-century Britain.

I have sketched out here, even in these early chapters, the main trends of reader response among my students. Some students notice the more programmatic statements of the older narrative voice, observations and expressions of concern about women's social roles. Such students read Jane's situation as symptomatic of larger issues and forces. Other readers focus more on the personal and psychic level of Jane's story, the younger voice expressing Jane's torment as a child or young woman.

Jane Abused by Mr. Rochester

This second approach was the dominant one in my course, at least at first. In the middle and later chapters, most students tended to focus more on Jane's personal history, especially her relationship with the male love-interests of the novel. Some of my female students thus tended to express the conventional responses associated with popular Romance novels. Readers go weak in the knees when Jane encounters Rochester; they lament when she leaves him and rejoice when the two lovers are reunited. It is a well-worn formula.

Other students were more skeptical, both about Jane's attraction to Mr. Rochester and about Rochester's treatment of Jane. One student comments: "Does Jane even realize that she is unhappy? I think it's because she's not getting the love that she yearns for [from Mr. Rochester]." The same student remarks that Jane "has long dreamed of freedom; however, marriage will . . . enforce her submission to a man." Another student notes Jane's sharp subordination to Rochester even without being his wife. Rochester calls Jane "a lamb, my pet lamb."[11] "What do these statements mean?" the student asks. "[Rochester] seems to treasure [Jane]—maybe in an almost childlike way, but she is not a child." The student perhaps sees a hint here that, despite being the Romance hero, Rochester is not so different from Mr. Brocklehurst in his treatment of Jane. She is still a "child" abused by a reckless, domineering male.

For these students, I gently suggest that the encounter between Rochester and Jane is troubling, that Rochester is abusive and that Jane seems strangely willing to submit to such abuse. Some students resist this suggestion, as we have seen, because they identify with and approve of Jane's entanglement with Rochester. What do I do with such resistance? What do I do about the tendency to read *Jane Eyre* in an uncritical way, like a formulaic Romance novel?

Because of my training and experience in interpreting literature, I could launch a full-blown argument on this point and overpower student objections. That is the kind of aggressive argument that I was taught in graduate school; that is the ethos of literary studies and what gets attention in the field. But that kind of overpowering approach may not be helpful to students. Sometimes less is more.

As a Christian scholar, often dealing with non-Christian literature and theory, writing for a broad audience, I have come to the conclusion that I need not fight every battle on every front. Instead, I aim to extract one or two small

23

concessions that a fair-minded person would grant. One such strategic concession makes all the difference. At a later point in their reading, as we shall see, many students were willing to re-examine Jane's troubling entanglement with Mr. Rochester, even if I did not push so hard on that point during the Rochester chapters.

St. John's Pious Proposal

The penultimate turn of the novel's plot, before Jane returns to Rochester, involves another possible love option for Jane. St. John is a young bachelor who also asks Jane to marry him. But St. John is a foil to Rochester, and he presents a different temptation. He is an extremely pious man, a student of the Scriptures, whose burning ambition is to be a missionary in India. St. John proposes marriage to Jane not because he feels erotic desire for her but because he believes that Jane would make a suitable missionary's wife. It is God's sovereign will, St. John believes, for Jane to serve as his missionary wife and helpmeet.

Among my self-consciously Christian students, this episode provokes interesting responses. One student did an oral report—I call it a "mini-lesson"—on this segment of the novel, a lesson on what she called "missionary dating" in *Jane Eyre*. She pointed to Jane's earlier relation to Rochester, often figured in the novel, and by Rochester himself, as a matter of "salvation." Jane is supposed to be the savior and redeemer of the wicked and wickedly handsome Rochester. This, of course, is the "missionary dating" that Christian-college women gossip about in our own day. Jane's second love option, as my student suggested, is a reversal of this equation; St. John now places himself in the savior's role in relation to Jane. The St. John episode helps students see the presumptuousness of the whole "missionary dating" enterprise, also in relation to Mr. Rochester. As the student insisted in her mini-lesson, St. John uses "God's Will" as a form of coercion, emphasizing his "humility to show how gracious he is in letting [Jane] join him" in his glorious Christian vocation. But my student does not accept St. John's claims at face value. "Is [St. John] really humble?" she asks. "*Is* Jane denying God when she refuses to marry St. John?" Of course, I was very grateful for this student's perceptive mini-lesson, connecting Jane's dilemma to modern forms of "missionary dating."

The difficulty here is that St. John's offer has a powerful pietistic appeal, as seen in Jane's reaction and in those of some of my female students. (Mr. Rochester's plea that Jane be his "savior" may be even more tempting.) One student notes that St. John may believe what he is saying: "[St. John] sees himself as . . . doing what is noble and saving souls." Yet this student also admits that St. John is "manipulating" Jane and usurping the role of God. My comment affirms and extends this good point: "St. John is 'sincerely' wrong and 'sincerely' self-deceived. A passage like this shows a Victorian reaction against the Romantic notion of sincerity—i. e., if you are 'sincere' you can do no wrong." Romantic reverence for sincerity is, of course, a component of the ideology of human goodness that students had discussed earlier in the course. I could question the supposed infallibility of Jane's sincerity in this episode, but I see that students are already coming to such insights on their own. This student has already conceded that St. John is self-deceived.

The St. John chapters focus the interrelated gender and theological issues that I faced as a male teacher in this course. Many of my female students have a strong emotional link to Jane Eyre because they too are tempted by St. John and others like him. Some of my students are theologically naïve, and, as one finds in many Christian circles, they tend to gauge the truth of religious claims by the sincerity and earnestness of the speaker. Students seem to want me to play this game on their terms. They want me to create the warm, comforting "Christian bubble." I hesitate do so, however, because I want students to engage in critical thinking.

But my position is tenuous, especially as a male Christian professor in a room full of modern-day Jane Eyres. If I am stern, telling them to read hard and think hard, do I become Mr. Brocklehurst, the oppressive male religious authority? If I make emotional or doctrinaire religious appeals, do I become like St. John, offering a form of piety that is accepted without analysis? If I underscore the novel's religious critique, if I question religious sincerity, especially *Jane's* Christian sincerity, do I become an infidel? Do I become like the wicked Rochester, seducing young Jane away from her Christian faith?

If I were a woman, perhaps I could embody an older and wiser Christian mentor. There are such female mentors in the novel: Helen Burns (briefly) and Miss Temple. But such roles are beyond a man's reach; the novel's male figures are certainly *not* counselors to whom Jane can go for guidance. If we imagine Jane talking with a Christian mentor, say Miss Temple, what would she hear in Jane's story? How would she encourage Jane and advise her? I ask *myself* these questions sometimes, when I'm doing academic advising with female English majors.

The reader may be wondering what was going on with the one male student in the course during all of this. Poor fellow! Unsurprisingly, he was attracted to the one "boy book" of the semester, the story of Pip in Dickens's *Great Expectations*. Under the heading "Love is like a jail," this student focused on Pip's tormented attraction to the cold and beautiful Estella. "Love is a source of torment," he said, yet "love is a craving that we seek." All of this could have framed a good reading of Pip's dilemma, but, instead, my lone male student chose to talk about his own situation, expressing resentment against restrictions placed on him by his steady girlfriend. I saw students' jaws drop.

I should perhaps explain that this male student is a California Latino. His mini-lesson fits well with what I have read about Mexican *machismo*, which usually reigns outside the home, and with what I have read about the Latino home being a matriarchal realm. For these reasons, I hesitate to condemn this student. I wonder if his mini-lesson was a form of acting out, expressing his reaction to a female-dominated classroom.

But let us go back to St. John and his manipulation of poor Jane Eyre. We see here a pious, self-deceived male figure using an arrogant, masculinist model of marriage and Christian service as a form of theological coercion against a woman. Because St. John is drawn as a less attractive figure than Rochester—he is chillingly pious rather than wickedly handsome—and because Jane ultimately rejects his proposal, students more easily recognize St. John's manipulative schemes. One student quotes the frightening climax of St. John's offer:

> [I]f you reject [my proposal of marriage], it is not me you deny but God .... Refuse to be my wife, and you limit yourself for ever to a track of selfish ease and barren obscurity. Tremble lest in that case you should be numbered with those who have denied the faith.[12]

One student remarks: "St. John's way of getting to Jane is through guilt. Mr. Rochester gets to her [in] almost the same way." We should notice the reference back to Rochester's abuse of Jane. Another student suggests that Jane turns to St. John and his missionary calling as a form of escapism. She asks, "Is [Jane] just throwing herself into religion to forget about Mr. Rochester? To console her pain?" We should notice the concession that Jane herself may be self-deceived about both Rochester and St. John. Another student wonders why Jane should *almost* [fall] under [St. John's] power," since by this point Jane should be able to "[see] right through" such forms of manipulation by Rochester, St. John, and others.

Jane Eyre as a Model of Female Martyrdom

As these responses suggest, the St. John episode enables some readers to break out of Romance-novel conventions, to critique the offer that Jane be St. John's missionary wife, even to reconsider Rochester's proposal that Jane join him at the marriage altar, "at God's feet, equal."[13] As one student notes, even as

Rochester's fiancée, Jane insists on keeping her subordinate role of governess. Another student raises these questions: "Does [Jane] really see [herself and Mr. Rochester] as equal? Sometimes I feel that she sees herself below him, but [at] other times feel that she sees herself above [him]. I don't think [Jane] ever feels *equal*."

In addition to my concern for cross-denominational understanding, I am concerned that both women and men flourish in their studies and in their Christian thinking. For that reason, I am troubled by the tendency in some Christian circles to emphasize self-sacrifice and self-denial as proper for Christian *women*, while intellect, leadership, and ambition are presented as properly *male* virtues. Typical of Victorian Britain, Brontë's novel does not raise the issue of women's ordination to Christian ministry, and my students did not raise this issue themselves. Indeed, I sense that most of them would reject an explicit ban on female ordination as somehow unfair and unmodern. But the modern-day Janes in my literature courses are often less conscious of the implications of a Romance formula in which Jane can only consider being a missionary's *wife*, in which her talents and her happiness find their proper fulfillment only in service to a mortal man. Perhaps because we avoided the divisive denominational issue of women's ordination, students could instead consider the larger question of whether *Jane Eyre* is truly a story of female flourishing or of equality between men and women.

The student above makes a good point in observing that Jane "[n]ever feels *equal*." I would suggest further that true equality, a climate where both women and men can flourish together, is impossible within the terms of the novel *Jane Eyre* because the novel seems always to demand a victim. The novel brings Rochester down below Jane's level by blinding and mutilating him. The other love option, with St. John, would be a *psychic* mutilation of Jane. The same student I have just quoted, a perceptive young married woman, quotes this crucial passage from the St. John episode. Jane speaks as narrator: "I will throw all on the altar—heart, vitals, the entire victim. He will never love me, but he shall approve me."[14] The student notes, "Jane is speaking of St. John here and his journey to India, but her language is like she is speaking of God." Here is my comment: "And this is mostly *sacrifice*, very little *love*. How many Christians view their Christian life in this way, as a kind of martyrdom?" This tendency to martyrdom is, I believe, the reason why there can be no flourishing equality in the novel *Jane Eyre*.

The tendency to martyrdom is also strong in some Christian circles, and the martyr's role often is urged especially on Christian women. This trend often merges with a broader social tendency to idealize and worship victims.

As a Reformed Christian, however, and for the reasons suggested in these comments on *Jane Eyre*, I do not think we should worship victims, even though some Christians look at the cross and see Jesus primarily as a victim. I do not see Jesus as a victim *in the final sense*, however, because, in the language of detective fiction, the crucifixion was an "inside job." In fact, Jesus was "in on it"; he was in on the planning from the very beginning, even "from the foundation of the world" (Matt. 25:34; I Peter 1:20). Christ's death was an act of divine love, an act freely chosen. There is no greater love. It was not the act of a merely human victim, driven by a martyr's complex. It is this non-victimary understanding of love, of *God's* love, that creates a climate for Christian women and men to flourish together as equals.

Endnotes

1   William Wordsworth, "Expostulation & Reply," in *The Longman Anthology of British Literature: The Romantics and Their Contemporaries*, 3rd ed., vol. 2A, gen. eds. David Damrosch and Kevin J. H. Dettmar, eds. Susan Wolfson and Peter Manning (New York and London: Pearson Longman, 2006), lines 1, 4–8.

2   Ibid., 26–7.

3   William Wordsworth, "The Tables Turned: An Evening Scene, on the Same Subject," in *The Longman Anthology of British Literature*, lines 15–16, 21–24.

4   Ibid., 29.

5   Crosby, Stills, Nash, and Young, "Woodstock," in *Déjà vu*, composed by Joni Mitchell, published 1970 by Atlantic Records.

6   Toni Morrison, *The Bluest Eye* (New York & London: Vintage Press, 2007), 50.

7   Sandra Gilbert, "Plain Jane's Progress" in *Signs: Journal of Women in Culture and Society* 2 (Summer 1977).

8   Charlotte Bronte, *Jane Eyre*, ed. Richard J. Dunn (New York: W. W. Norton, 2000), 46.

9   Ibid., 96.

10 Ibid., 93.

11 Ibid., 184.

12 Ibid., 348.

13 Ibid., 216.

14 Ibid., 345.

From "The Legend of Sleepy Hollow" to *Empire Falls*:

Embroidering the Scarlet Thread through Modern American Literature

Lisa Brandom (John Brown University)

Lisa Brandom, professor emeritus of John Brown University, takes time to reflect in the tranquility of retirement on the "scarlet thread" of representation of Christianity in modern and postmodern American literature. Through an American Literature II course, she offers insight into how to trace that thread in even the darkest of works and how to encourage students to find their own threads of understanding. Lisa is the author of The Skagway Connection *and* Four Women, One Century. *Her creative nonfiction, fiction, and poetry have appeared in* Undercurrent, *an NPR-sponsored literary magazine of Haines, Alaska;* The Arkansas Literary Forum, *and* Poesia.

Since my retirement three months ago from a small Christian liberal arts university, I have begun to reflect upon the continuing challenges that lie before us as professors of English. These challenges center on the task of integrating faith and content into the literature we teach since it increasingly shows a secular influence and an absence of all things Christian. It appears to me that we have three choices before us: we can teach only the literature that falls into the category we call the "canon"; we can teach all modern literature, hoping somehow that our Christian presence with the students can counteract the writers' preponderant use of sex, language, and violence; or we can intentionally set the literature into a context that allows students to see a continuing search by the authors for a "scarlet thread," even in the most modern of pieces.

Before I discuss the three choices above, including my own personal choice as an English professor, I would like to share a few personal stories from my thirty-five years of teaching. These personal experiences have helped to mold my thinking into its current shape. My first four years of teaching were in public institutions, most notably a small university in the Mississippi Delta and a junior high school in a midsized town in Northwest Arkansas. Since these schools were both public institutions, and the times were the early 70s when American society was in an upheaval of social and political culture, I had no difficulty teaching the literature contained within the anthologies I used. Actually, I had to be more concerned about the possibility of bringing Christian ideas *into* the classroom. My principal instructed each teacher in orientation not to share Christian beliefs with the students during class time; he was simply carrying out the wishes of the local school board at that time.

My next position was to teach English (as well as Bible, geography, history, drama, and journalism) at a small, newly-formed Christian secondary school in the same little town in Northwest Arkansas. Since I *was* the English department until the school grew and expanded enough to hire a second teacher, I initially had full curricular freedom to choose the texts for my students to read. All went well until the third year I was there. I had attended an ACSI (Association of Christian Schools International) convention in Dallas and picked up some curricular guides to integrating faith and content into some American novels such as *The Scarlet Letter, Huckleberry Finn*, and *To Kill a Mockingbird*. I ended up choosing all the novels to teach in my class and immersed myself in the guides, which I felt would assist me in teaching the Christian lessons regarding morality, values, and ethics I desired. All went well with the first two choices. After all, by that time they were recognized American literary classics. Not so, however, with the third choice!

This 1960 novel and subsequent winner of the 1961 Pulitzer Prize—*To Kill a Mockingbird*—was anathema to several of the parents of my students. The most memorable meeting regarding the novel's content took place between a Southern Baptist pastor and his wife and me in the room where I taught. My argument for teaching the novel to the students was that it featured a Christ-like character, Atticus Finch, who taught his children that one must stand up for his or her beliefs regardless of negative personal consequences. I also tried my best to discuss with the parents the additional positive themes of justice, prejudice in our society, and the danger of blind conformity to others' beliefs. For their argument, the pastor and his wife would focus only on the expletives in the text used by Atticus' daughter, Scout. Finally, after an hour or so of discussion, I asked, "Have either of you read the novel?" Their reply astounded me, "No, we haven't; but we know it's been very controversial. We would never read it, and we don't want our son to read it. You yourself could not possibly be a Christian to teach such a book!" After conferencing with my principal about the discussion, we agreed that students or parents who objected to a text would be offered an alternative such as *Anne of Green Gables*. Later, I was gently directed by my principal to choose a literary text from the A Beka series published by Pensacola Christian College. I eventually found these heavily-edited alternatives unsatisfactory as a solution to the problem and resigned my position after eight years of struggling with the administrators about content.

In 1981, I began teaching English as an adjunct at John Brown University, where I would later would go on to the full-time position of professor and chair of the department. I remember my first official orientation to the university. It was held at a camp retreat center a few miles away from campus. We were all sitting at a table, and the academic dean asked me a question about integrating faith and learning, the topic of the hour. I was too gun-shy by that time to offer more than a very traditional response: "Well, I do everything I can to draw connections between the literature I teach and the students' lives every time that I am in the classroom." One of the music faculty at the time literally jumped out of his seat and began screaming, "We have to do everything we can to combat this type of provincialism; it's impossible for us to become a world-class university and get beyond being viewed as a Bible college unless we do!" By this time I was thoroughly confused as to what the expectations were regarding the integration of faith and learning. Should I avoid all possible controversial topics and readings, or should I incorporate them again somehow into my teaching? I was hopeful that the latter could indeed be true. After all, we were preparing students for graduate school in public universities for the most part, and I knew their texts would not be edited.

I was blessed, I am happy to say, with an existing English department that had already combated such problems as reported above with parents and students regarding the secular nature of the literature as they saw it. The department had in place a philosophy of teaching literature that answered many of the typical questions that very conservative students will typically bring to us. For example, when students complain about literary content, they almost invariably come armed with Philippians 4:8: "Finally, brethren, whatsoever things *are* true, whatsoever things *are* honest, whatsoever things *are* just, whatsoever things *are* pure, whatsoever things *are* lovely, whatsoever things *are* of good report, if there be any virtue and if there be any praise, think on these things" (KJV). Our university statement typically addresses these ideas by reminding students that not all things are just, pure, and lovely. The world, as well as the Bible, shows us the reality of the human condition. If we focus only on those things which *are* pure and lovely, would we not fail to minister to the world because of our inability to see its problems? The discussion today continues, but I am realistic enough to conclude that, as Christian professors, we *can* handle the challenge if we choose one of the three possibilities to integrate faith and learning while teaching modern literature. Some specific literary examples of each method follow. I confess that I have tried them all.

Since my specialty area is American Literature (my dissertation analyzed the role of female professors in American novels), these are the literary examples with which I am most familiar. The first choice for us as English professors is to stay with the tried and true pieces from the American canon of literature. Ironically, however, today's generation Y, products of fast-moving television and music, often finds these pieces the most boring. Nevertheless, they are part of the canon of early histories, sermons, essays, and poems that typically are taught in American Literature I classes throughout the country. Because of the Puritan heritage in Massachusetts, the early pieces pose no problem in integrating faith and content. We begin with the early poets of Edward Taylor and Anne Bradstreet. Even when Bradstreet has severe trials in her life such as in the poem, "Some Verses Upon the Burning of our House, July 10th, 1666," she acknowledges her immense faith in the providence of God in her concluding lines:

> A Prise so vast as is unknown,
> Yet, by his Gift, is made thine own.
> Ther's wealth enough, I need no more;
> Farewell my Pelf, farewell my Store.
> The world no longer let me Love,
> My hope and Treasure lyes Above.[1]

Likewise, Taylor in one of the most famous of his early poems, "Huswifery," acknowledges his very being to God:

> Make me, O Lord, thy spinning wheele compleat;
> Thy holy worde my distaff make for mee.
> Make mine affections thy swift flyers neate,[2]

Numerous other examples abound in early American literature until the early part of the nineteenth century, when the body of literature begins to make subtle changes. With the advent of the early Romantics like Washington

Irving, there begins to be an acknowledgement by writers that perhaps literature does not always have to have a moral, but it can simply delight. Indeed,
one of the earliest examples of Irving's work, "The Legend of Sleepy Hollow,"
proves that it can engross readers. In this story, we have the hero Ichabod
Crane who resides as the school teacher in a sleepy little town called Tarry
Town, where a "headless horseman" terrorizes him so pitifully that he leaves
one sad night never to be seen again. Gone are the overt moral lessons of the
piece for the new purpose of pure entertainment. Since Irving, other writers
have joined suit.

Certainly, two other American writers of this time period also fall into
this new genre of literature, in which the overt moral lessons have begun to
disappear. They are Nathaniel Hawthorne and Herman Melville. Hawthorne's
masterpiece *The Scarlet Letter* and Melville's *Moby Dick* begin to show a trend,
while not excluding references to the Puritan God, of questioning traditional
theology. Hawthorne's Hester, while continuing to wear the embroidered scarlet letter upon her breast throughout the course of the novel, never verbally
expresses regret for her sin of adultery with Arthur Dimmesdale. She seeks
only to do penance by doing good works for the Puritan community. Unlike
the heroines from the sentimental American novels of a century earlier, who
always had to die in childbirth for their sexual immorality, this heroine lives.

As we shift to a brief discussion of Melville's *Moby Dick*, we see again the
changing landscape of American literature with a subversive reversal of color
symbols. The gigantic whale of the ocean, which threatens disaster for the ship
and those upon it, is white, not the traditional black. Melville builds upon the
thematic ideas of Emerson who did not define the world in the Puritan terms
of black and white, good and evil, but saw evil only as the absence of good.
These examples from the canon not only illustrate the traditional theology of
the past but also plant the emerging seeds for a secular literature to be born
in the twentieth century, which scholars will define as modernism and postmodernism. For those Christian professors of twentieth-century literature
who struggle with the shift, do we now move into a "hope for the best" attitude
as we teach what we perceive as Godless literature complete with an abun-
dance of sex, language, and violence? Do we teach uncensored and unedited
literature, hoping that we can be as "mature" as our students profess to be and
simply ignore any search for morals and ethics on the part of the authors? I
suggest that there is a better plan.

One of the most well-known sermons of the twentieth century occurred
on December 31, 1961, by Dr. W. A. Criswell, pastor of the First Baptist Church
in Dallas, Texas. Its title was "The Scarlet Thread Through the Bible"; it lasted

four and one-half hours and literally went from Genesis to Revelation. I suggest that we English professors can also seek to embroider the scarlet thread—a search for Christ and Truth—into our classes in American Literature II as well as American Literature I. This choice is the one I have made: to handpick the selections in contemporary American literature to reflect the protagonists' struggles with faith and the meaning of life. Here are some ways that it might be done.

First of all, it is essential, in my opinion, to establish the context for our students for the disillusionment (and subsequent rise of so-called Godless literature) that many people were experiencing at the beginning of the twentieth century. As we know from our study of American history, the nineteenth century was a time of great optimism with the advent of modern science, most notably the theories of Karl Marx and Sigmund Freud. Concurrently, many experienced disillusionment with traditional theology because it seemed to be at complete odds with the new ideas from science and psychology. On the one hand, we Americans believed we could create a perfect utopia since it seemed we were now intelligent enough, but on the other hand, we were astonished in the first half of the twentieth century to see our nation, and even the world about us, crumbling. America was experiencing social upheavals surpassing even the worst of the nineteenth century, the war between the North and the South.

By 1914, America found herself embroiled in the war that was supposed to be the Great War, the war that would end all future wars. Ernest Hemingway, though only an ambulance driver himself in the war, wrote extensively about the faith vs. doubt theme in his work. Of course, one of the most notable of his heroes was Harold Krebs of "Soldier's Home" who had left the role of schoolboy at a Methodist college in the Midwest only to return from the war an embittered man who could not share the truth of the atrocities he had experienced even with his family. He is unable to pray with his mother and believe any longer in the grace and love of God. At the end of the story, he leaves home again on a search for answers to life's big philosophical questions.

Another social upheaval in the early part of the twentieth century was, of course, the Stock Market Crash of 1929 followed quickly by the depression of the 1930s. Again, many American writers were disenchanted by the failure of big business on Wall Street and the subsequent poverty throughout America. Perhaps this poverty was felt most strongly in the cities across America where the jobless and soup lines seemed interminable. Theodore Dreiser, a naturalist writer of the time period, expressed this hopelessness early in the century in his novels as well as his short story, "The Second Choice," published in 1918. In it, the heroine struggles with her inability to change her life in any notable

34

way. She falls in love with a man of the world, Arthur, who is free to travel and see the world as he pleases. After sending her a good-bye letter, she realizes she must accept the proposal of her second choice, Barton, whom she has grown up with:

> Now she had to face once more what she saw as the same dull neighborhood, with women making the same break-fast every morning, and the men sitting on porches in the evenings, reading the newspapers in the same, expected, dreary way.[3]

By the middle of the twentieth century, the world had experienced yet another war with even more writers disillusioned not only with war being a solution to all problems but with the threat of the atomic bomb and possible destruction of the world through nuclear holocaust. The literature in America now becomes cynical as in the novels of Joseph Heller, including *Catch-22*. The exploits of Heller's group of World War II soldiers in Italy is at once absurd and always interspersed with moments of gritty realism.

After a few days of discussion of the social and political events of the first half of the twentieth century, my class then moves into contemporary American literature, falling away from the literary canon, into writers of gender, racial, and religious diversity. Have these authors followed the mainstream of Anglo writers in their disillusionment, or do they offer some hope that a "scarlet thread" still exists in American literature? If so, who are those writers, and how can we use their work in our Christian colleges to discover a pattern of a search for Truth and values?

I submit that we can choose among any number of modern literary texts and find such a pattern. The pattern typically falls into three categories of writing: those who uphold and support a traditional view of Christianity, those who present bizarre and comic characters to present the ideas of Christianity in a new and thoughtful way, and those who satirize or simply ignore Christianity in their search for meaning, perhaps going to other religions and philosophies instead. Even if the choice of the authors is the latter, class discussion can center on how the organized church has failed to provide answers for a modern society. The text I choose to illustrate these three patterns in examining the scarlet thread through postmodern literature is *A Modern Southern Reader* published in 1986 and edited by Ben Forkner and Patrick Samway, S. J.

One might, of course, argue that Southern literature may not be a representative sample of American thought in general since this particular part of the country has always been known as "the Bible belt." And it is true that while Southerners have, as Forkner and Samway acknowledge, retained "a commitment to the incarnational theology of the Bible,"[4] they have also in recent years followed the rest of the country in a number of ways. Most notably, these ways include losing their towns' regional identity by having the same fast food chains along the highway into the area, connecting more to global business and international events through twenty-four-hour cable news channels, and meeting other religions as immigrants move into the area from around the world. (Robert Olen Butler's A *Good Scent from a Strange Mountain* is one of many books documenting this change.) Indeed, Forkner and Samway conclude that Southerners have indeed joined the mainstream of American life.[5]

Let us examine a few examples from *A Modern Southern Reader* that illustrate the three patterns. In the traditional theological mode of the Old South, Christian writer Reynolds Price presents the story of "Uncle Grant." This seemingly autobiographical story features an itinerant old African American man who did yard work for the Price family and who was, for many years, the closest friend and companion of Reynolds. When he is twenty-one, Reynolds returns home to northeast North Carolina to meet with his friend one more time. Uncle Grant is now ninety and obsesses over his failure to be baptized properly so that he can go to heaven. Reynolds assures him that the ritual is unnecessary, stating "No. You'll see everybody you want to see [in Heaven], I'm sure. Give them best wishes from me!"[6] Later Reynolds reflects upon the fact that Uncle Grant trusted him enough "to put his salvation in my hands that last day I saw him [. . .] and believed what I said—that in Heaven he would meet the new folks he missed—and claimed he would see me there."[7]

Another writer, poet Miller Williams, author of several anthologies including *Why God Permits Evil*, writes from a traditional theological perspective in his piece, "After the Revolution for Jesus the Associate Professor Prepares His Final Remarks." In this poem, the persona flirts with other religions as a panacea for both peace and war and expresses his cynicism for entering wars. He ultimately concludes his poem, however, with a belief in the traditional Christian God. He states, "The desert religions are founded on sandy ways / to set ourselves free from that endless tumbling downward" and later "We are sent to war for money, but we go for god." The persona's final lines are "I will be eaten by God. / There is nothing to fear. / To die, the singers believe, is to go home. / Where should I go, going home? Lord, I am here."[8]

As we continue to follow the scarlet thread through examples from modern Southern literature, we now turn to the second pattern found: the use of comically absurd or unusual characters to present traditional theology. The premier Southern writer in this category is, of course, Flannery O'Connor. Two of her best-known stories, "A Good Man is Hard to Find" and "Good Country

People," certainly illustrate this possibility. In both we find some of the most bizarre characters imaginable who subvert traditional ideas of Christianity to teach deep spiritual lessons. The Misfit, a serial murderer, is presented by O'Connor as a Christ figure who brings instant judgment to a grandmother who fails to see that she herself is a sinner, not unlike the murderer, by the story's conclusion. Hulga in the second story is an intellectual who, like the grandmother in the first story, is an unbeliever who wants only to corrupt a boy she believes to be a Bible salesman.

One of O'Connor's lesser known pieces is "The Life You Save Might Be Your Own." A tramp with only half an arm, Mr. Shiftlet, comes to the house of an old woman and her daughter. After some discussion together over the nature of man, the desire for an innocent woman, and the body and the spirit, Shiftlet takes the old woman's car and her daughter, Lucynell, to marry. Later, he abandons his new wife, picks up a hitchhiker, and goes on his trip asking God to "Break forth and wash the slime from this earth!"[9] obliviously unaware that he is the biggest slime of all.

Students are initially shocked by this presentation of Christian theology in this strange and bizarre way, yet they are challenged to discuss how O'Connor's aim, to present the reader face to face with Jesus in every story that she wrote, can indeed be true.Her short novel *Wise Blood*, though filled with profanity, sex, and violence, is a piece that initially offends and disgusts students, yet they come to the truth of O'Connor's themes by the end of the text: Christian hypocrisy, apathy in the modern world for our fellow citizens and neighbors, and the impossibility of physical punishment and penance to achieve salvation.

Another example from *A Modern Southern Reader* of those who struggle with traditional theology occurs in John Finlay's "Through a Glass Darkly," in which the persona relates the story of his drunken uncle who hated Catholics and Jews. His uncle had been a career Army man who could never get release from his violent nature and pain—though he searched endlessly through both drink and the Scripture for solace. The nephew relates in the poem that his uncle could not get release:

> He couldn't rest there till I read St. Paul
> Out loud beneath a harsh and shadeless bulb,
> As if the words alone could make him whole.
> "Read *that* again," he shouted from the bed.[10]

In his poem "Northhanger Ridge," poet Charles Wright also illustrates the struggle to find solace through traditional theology. Though he recognizes

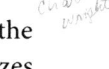

the influences of Southern Christianity upon the persona's life, he ultimately rejects Christ as being unable or unwilling to help those who struggle in a world of nothingness:

> Candleflame; vigil and waterflow:
> Lake dust in the night the prayers rise:
> From 6 to 6, under the sick Christ,
> The children talk to the nothingness, [11] (348)

In a postscript to the poem, Wright writes that the poem was written in Bible camp in the year 1949, when the poet would have been fourteen years old.

One of the questions that comes to mind as we read the second pattern of the scarlet thread in literature is, "What is our responsibility for talking through the disillusionment presented by the writers in relationship to their faith?" I have found that often the best times of integrating faith and learning in the classroom occur, not when reinforcing traditional and often clichéd views of theology, but when discussing the loss of faith in the modern world. Students amaze me with their insight into the problems of faith and often will relate, for example, their own personal experience of being in Bible camp and following the counselors' instructions to fast or to meditate on Christ's love for them when they felt very far away from a living, personable God. In other words, the best spiritual lessons and content lessons often can come from those moments when we move away somewhat from the text of the day.

The final pattern in modern American literature includes many stories, poems, plays, and novels that simply avoid any discussion of faith and God in their themes or that use satire to portray religion. How can one possibly introduce the idea of a scarlet thread when there is no evidence of one? For me the answer is two-fold. I introduce and review the sociological theory of Thorstein Veblen with his classical work, *The Theory of the Leisure Class*, in which Veblen discusses the concept of *anomie*. Basically, the word as it is defined "in contemporary English means a condition or malaise in individuals, characterized by an absence or diminution of standards or values." Individually, it is often accompanied "by an associated feeling of alienation and purposelessness."[12] In addition, I discuss my belief that, regardless of whether Christianity or God actually is referenced in the text, one often can find characters searching for meaning in their lives, and this quest may surface in addictive behaviors, various forms escapism, or finding solace in other religions of the world. Two examples will suffice for this pattern, and again both are taken from *A Modern Southern Reader*. The plays are Tennessee Williams's famous *The Glass Menagerie* and Carson McCullers's *The Member of the Wedding*.

In Williams's play, *The Glass Menagerie,* written in the 1940s, the characters of Amanda, Laura, Tom, and Jim live in St. Louis in an alley. Amanda, a
Southern belle from the past, lives only in her memories. In Amanda's world,
there were many gentleman beaus and callers. Her daughter Laura lives with
her collection of glass figurines, a childhood illness having left her crippled,
while Amanda's son Tom is a poet who works in a warehouse but who longs
to escape from his dead-end job in St. Louis and from his mother and sister.
Jim is a new gentleman caller, this time for Laura. By the play's final scene, we
see Tom's frustration grow with his family so much so that he smashes Laura's
glass figures. Tom leaves home, and in a final speech, the audience discovers
he has traveled around a great deal through the years but with many regrets:
"I would have stopped, but I was pursued by something. It always came upon
me unawares, taking me altogether by surprise."[13]

In McCuller's play, the heroine is a twelve-year-old gangly girl named
Frankie who has become obsessed with the upcoming wedding of her brother
Jarvis and his fiancée Janice. Frankie is living with her widowed father in a
small Southern town in the 1940s. In short, Frankie is bored (she is also a
hopeless romantic) in her small town and feels excluded. She states this to her
friend John Henry:

> The trouble with me is that for a long time I have been just an "I"
> person. All other people can say "we." When Berenice [the house-
> keeper] says "we" she means her lodge and church and colored people.
> Soldiers can say "we" and mean the army. All people belong to a "we"
> except me.[14]

By the conclusion of the play, Frankie is left alone in her little town with the
happily married couple on their honeymoon, her friends Honey and John
Henry dead (one from a suicide and the other from illness).

A recent Pulitzer-prize-winning piece by Richard Russo, *Empire Falls,* also
falls into category three. Here we have a protagonist, Miles, who runs a small-
town restaurant. He is recently divorced and the father of a fifteen-year-old
girl. Russo chooses satire to illustrate a belief in the hopelessness of religion to
solve the problems of the world. Two of the key characters in this small New
England town are priests. One struggles with homosexual tendencies, and the
other steals the church offering and heads for Key West. Later, the novel moves
inexorably toward unexpected violence and murder within a high school. The
conclusion offers resolution only within the realm of family, not God, though
the church is a visible presence on the New England landscape throughout
the novel.

The final examples of pattern three—pieces that show no overt references to traditional Christianity, or pieces that satirize traditional Christianity—are sadly perhaps the most honest portrayals of society today. The anomie and searches of the characters can provide ample discussion within the classroom of whether or not the scarlet thread has actually disappeared from literature or perhaps whether it is just presented in the form of a question. How can I, or how can my characters, find Truth and God in a postmodern world that seems increasingly moving toward European secularism? The dogmatic answers of the past are elusive for the students, but the search is worthwhile.

As I reflect upon the circular structure of this essay, and the questions I have raised about integrating faith and content in postmodern literature, I believe strongly in allowing students the freedom to express ideas that do not necessarily conform to traditional theology. Though it is true, as Paul states in the famous love chapter of I Corinthians 13, "we see in a mirror, dimly" (nasv) our limited vision should not preclude leading our students in American Literature II to seek the scarlet thread through the works they read. If it has indeed become invisible, replaced by the darker black pieces, they should be challenged to examine why and what, if anything, our culture and society can do to embroider it again.

Endnotes

1   Anne Bradstreet, "Some Verses Upon the Burning of our House, July 10th, 1666," in "Poems by Anne Bradstreet," *Poetry Archive*, http://www.poetry-archive. com/b/bradstreet_anne.html (accessed August 28, 2006).

2   Edward Taylor, "Huswifery," "The Poems of Edward Taylor," in *Fire and Ice: Puritan and Reformed Writings*, http://www.puritansermons.com/poetry/taylor. htm (accessed August 28, 2006).

3   Lynette Abel, *Aesthetic Realism & Life*, http://www.lynetteabel.org/L-ABEL-Sem-inar-Sure-B.html (accessed August 29, 2006).

4   Ben Forkner and Patrick Samway, S.J. eds., *A Modern Southern Reader* (Atlanta: Peachtree Publishers, 1986).

5   Ibid., 6.

6   Reynolds Price, "Uncle Grant," in *A Modern Southern Reader*, 153.

7   Ibid., 154.

8   Miller Williams, "After the Revolution for Jesus a Secular Man Prepares Final Remarks," *Why God Permits Evil* (Louisiana State University Press, 1978), 345–6.

9   Flannery O'Connor, "The Life You Save May Be Your Own," in *A Modern Southern Reader*, 356.

10 John Finlay, "Through a Glass Darkly," in *A Modern Southern Reader*, 356.

11 Charles Wright, "Northhanger Ridge," in *A Modern Southern Reader*, 348.

12 "Anomie," *Wikipedia*, http:///en.wikipedia.org/wiki/Anomie (accessed August 29, 2005).

13 Tennessee Williams, *The Glass Menagerie,* in *A Modern Southern Reader*, 455.

14 Carson McCullers, *The Member of the Wedding,* in *A Modern Southern Reader*, 376.

LET THERE BE LIGHT:

Faith Integration in the Literary Theory Course

CHRISTINE CHANEY (SEATTLE PACIFIC UNIVERSITY)

Dr. Christine Chaney tackles the important question of how to teach controversial theories and ideas within a Christian framework. Looking past the excesses of recent postmodern theory, Chris takes the students back to the intellectual history that shapes and informs our reading and interpretations. Chris is associate professor and chair of the department of English at Seattle Pacific University. She was founding Review Editor of the scholarly journal Pedagogy: Critical Approaches to Teaching Literature, Language, Composition, and Culture *(Duke University Press) and is the former assistant director of the PEW-funded "Preparing Future Faculty" project at the University of Washington Graduate School. She earned her B.A. primarily from the Los Angeles and Berkeley campuses of the University of California and her M.A. and Ph.D. from the University of Washington. While her ostensible teaching home is the world of Victorian literature, Chris's journal articles include "The Rhetorical Strategies of 'Turbulent Emotions': Wollstonecraft's Letters in Sweden" in* The Journal of Narrative Theory *(vol. 34, no. 3), Fall 2004, and "The Prophet-Poet's Book" in* SEL: Studies in English Literature 1500-1900 *(vol. 48, no. 4), Autumn 2008, guest-edited by U.C. Knoepflmacher of Princeton University. Her book chapters include "The Intimate Familiar: Essay as Autobiography in Romanticism" in* Romantic Autobiography in England, *edited by Eugene Stelzig of SUNY-Geneseo (Ashgate 2008).*

Why Teach Theory at a Christian College?

Perhaps no subject taught in Christian higher education today, with the possible exception of evolution, is more fraught with tensions and anxieties than the cluster of ideas called "literary theory" as taught in most university English departments. Therefore a fair question to ask at the beginning of an essay dedicated to faith integration in such a course is to ask, "why teach it at all?" or more frankly, "why should Christian college students be exposed to such dangerous relativism?" or some other version of this concern. I know that some Christian academics find the very term "literary theory" itself distressing since, to their mind, it stands for everything irreligious and aggressively opposed to meaning, truth, and beauty in culture and the arts. How can such a topic belong at institutions, they say, that claim the absolute centrality of God's sovereign and eternal Truth? I've even heard loud arguments against theory from the hallways of my very own department as the worst thing that ever happened to the study of literature, and have certainly seen deep hostility to theory's seeming 'hermeneutic of suspicion' at the highest levels of Christian academic leadership.

Usually, though, when such complaints have been voiced I've found that for these critics "theory" is a term standing in for the relatively recent and popularized excesses of post-structuralism, especially as it dominated the academy—and media—in the late 1980s and 1990s. And too often, I've noticed, the critic herself is unfamiliar with the writings of the theorists, preferring to disdain—often with good reason—the opacity and jargon of many thinkers in the field. But I beg those of my readers who may share these feelings to forestall a first impulse to reject this topic and let me try and reframe it instead for the simple reason that I believe it is vital to the teaching of English in our universities.

Specifically, in order to justify its importance in our undergraduate curriculum, I wish to reclaim the topic taught today as 'literary theory' back into the larger movement of ideas about truth and interpretation as a whole in Western culture for at least the past three hundred years, if not much longer. If we choose instead to see theory as one particular iteration in the centuries-old practice of textual hermeneutics then I believe we see it more clearly and more accurately—and also see its importance in the teaching of our discipline to our students. Lifted out of its momentary glare of publicity, what we call 'theory' can be seen as, in fact, part of the same canon of Western thought that includes such giants as Plato and Aristotle, Immanuel Kant, Samuel Taylor Coleridge, and Soren Kierkegaard.

For that reason, then, I argue for using a <u>historical framework</u> whenever teaching this topic to undergraduates at a Christian—or indeed any—university. When students can see that some of the more dizzying claims of Michel Foucault, Louis Althusser, or Jacques Derrida at the end of the twentieth century have their deep roots in Coleridge and Karl Marx in the nineteenth century (or even back to Plato and Aristotle and their precursors in ancient times), then they have something to hold on to when the intellectual air gets thin. And when students learn why the later thinkers' claims about 'gaps' and 'slippages' in meaning may not necessarily be evil incarnate but rather honest grappling with the implications of human language, then students are learning both about the history of Western interpretation and the humbling implications of being human in all our broken and limited understanding. And all of this learning is truth—God's truth—certainly a fit and important topic at a Christian university.

In addition, I believe it is also important for Christian students to be fully equipped to address the ideas of our time, too. Whether or not they intend to go on to graduate study, there is no reason to leave English majors at Christian universities with a less than full education. We are not afraid of the ideas of this world nor are we ashamed of the gospel, as Paul writes, feeling it somehow too fragile to withstand our inquiry or even doubts. The robust nature of Christian faith is indeed one of its best features. I believe it is important for faithful people to fully engage in the ideas of our cultural moment, and this includes the ideas implied by the broad term "literary theory."

And, finally, in the past decade or so theology itself as a discipline has begun to take up the questions inherent in the textual hermeneutics of theory as tools for understanding the sacred—uncovering, for example, the deeply Hebraic and rabbinical threads in Jacques Derrida's work as a tool for revisiting Old Testament scholarship. Professors like Jean-Luc Marion and John D. Caputo (whose book *The Prayers and Tears of Jacques Derrida* informs my example above) are leading voices in this conversation, among many others. And terms such as "postmodern theology," "Christian existentialism," "radical orthodoxy," and "non-dogmatic theology" are heard increasingly in the religion and theology departments of our own campuses as our colleagues also grapple with the exciting and unsettling changes in thought in our post-Enlightenment world. As I often say to students in theory classes, one doesn't get to pick one's own historical moment and, for better or worse, God has given us the transitional postmodern historical period in which to live, work, and have our being. It is up to us to enter into our time and place with fully informed hearts and minds.

One of the foundational pedagogical elements, then, of teaching literary theory at a Christian university is telling the students early and often that they will be challenged in ways they can't even yet imagine regarding truth and meaningfulness, something they've usually seen as self-evidently true and universal for all. And yet in the best scenarios they will emerge from this experience more fully equipped not just to deal with this fragmented world of ours but to be filled up with the wonder at the amazing gift of their own minds and the truly divine, mysterious, and transcendent nature of our God, who is in every age ever new and ever true.

As with any teaching we do, however, it is sometimes hard to know what effects will play out in the lives of our students, especially since it may be years before the students know themselves. But I would be remiss if I didn't state here clearly that some students really do struggle with the implications of theory for their own lives and faith both during and after their study of the course, usually because it asks them to examine what they believe and how they came to believe it. However, the words of one 2004 graduate of my course and our university (now pursuing her Ph.D. in English at the University of Illinois, Urbana-Champaign) is encouraging in light of all the potential pitfalls of teaching theory to students of faith (printed here with her permission): "I know that you are a bit paranoid about throwing your lit theory students into existential crises . . . but, for what it's worth, the class helped me salvage my own faith . . . If nothing else it gave me language to talk about things I hadn't been able to talk about before and made me realize I wasn't alone in asking the questions I was asking. And once I had the tools to talk about those things and a basic understanding of the conversation around me, I felt empowered to enter the conversation on my own terms and start coming up with answers to some of my own [faith] questions." So while many students will struggle not just with the difficulty of theory itself but also its deep implications for their lives, I remain convinced that its worth far outweighs its struggle and difficulties, *especially* in light of its potential to counter-intuitively strengthen and equip our students' faith in the end.

Students and Their Worries

In my experience, this course is more dependent than most on the make-up of students who enroll in it both because of the difficulty of its content but also for the way it deeply intertwines with issues related to values and truth-telling. The first time I taught literary theory as a new assistant professor things were deceptively easy. There were only a very small number of students who enrolled, almost all of whom were our brightest honors students. I quickly found that teaching the course as a proto-graduate seminar worked very well with this group, jumping right into the various theorists and schools directly and simply having the students read selections from the emerging theory canon in a good anthology. Of course, there was a lot of intellectual effort expended to simply understand the readings but, overall, I was quite pleased with how excited the students were to learn this material and how well they did at mastering it. However, the next time when I confidently went forward with a similar teaching plan, the course was much less successful. I found that three times as many students had enrolled and that this new group was much more mixed—there were "regular" English majors, creative writing students, a few from the philosophy and theology departments, as well as the more advanced honors students. Not only did my supposedly successful graduate seminar model work far less well but I also found myself spending huge amounts of time outside of class meeting one-on-one with students to help them understand the content and implications of the course material from all their varying backgrounds and educational/disciplinary frameworks. I might as well have been teaching the course thirty different times and in thirty different ways. There was soon so much fear and so little cohesion in the classroom community that in the middle of the term I had to switch gears drastically, resorting to a lecture model in order to at least provide some basic content to everyone all at once—which alternately bored and intimidated most students. In short, it was a teaching disaster.

Since that time, I've found a much better and more flexible model for teaching theory while integrating faith issues for a wide array of students—which is really the point, after all. The key to such a course is to first spend a significant amount of time helping the students gain an understanding of the whole notion of *interpretive frames* before ever even considering the theory schools themselves. Unless students can arrive safely at a place that will allow them to grant validity to differing forms of interpretation at a very basic level then the whole enterprise of this course is stillborn before it even begins. And we must admit frankly here that the students at our universities, who largely come from American Protestant or nondenominational church backgrounds, are often extremely resistant to the notion that there is more than one way to arrive at truth—or truths—in a text. Simply raising that topic explicitly in your course assignments will likely bring immediate alarms that such ideas seem to question the authority of Scripture, too, and related concerns regarding the bedrock tenets of their faith traditions. I recommend patience, love, and being very open personally about your own committed Christian beliefs as you enter into the several weeks that this topic will require in your course. You will be touching in class at this time on authority, meaning, representation, knowability, truth, words, images, trustworthiness, narrative, ideology, language, paradigms, and many other ideas that directly or indirectly brush up against students' deeply held but often underexamined (or unexamined) belief systems. Your classroom presence as a person of faith will be crucial to the success of these early moments of student fear and vulnerability. For the course to work at all they need to continue to see you, their instructor, as a trustworthy guide.

The point here, of course, is that you will need to keep working with your students to help them sort through the implications of interpretive frames for nearly all or part of the course, helping them to see that acknowledging many different ways of *human beings'* knowing in no way diminishes the unchanging and eternal truth of *Christ's* death and resurrection, which stands outside of our limited ability to try to know and love him. His truth is the straight "plumb line" that guides us humans—but we are often wobbling all over the place in trying to stay near and true to him. Indeed, in terms of faith, what this literary theory course does—perhaps more than anything else—is to help the students humbly learn that just because we humans see the same thing sometimes in fragmentary, and contradictory ways, that doesn't then mean that God is broken or fragmented or untrue. The point is that we *are* broken—otherwise Christ wouldn't have needed to redeem us. Indeed, the very notions of "the word made flesh" or "the virgin birth" are great examples of how Christians have always joyfully embraced mysterious and paradoxical but universally and eternally true things. The very delicate balancing act, I've found in my teaching of this course, is to help the students see that their particular faith backgrounds often are quite bound up with American and Enlightenment models of individualism and rationalism (and capitalism and materialism, too, to be quite blunt)—all of which are quite interestingly particular to our historic time and place and not necessarily "universal and Christian," as many of them seem to think. It is this contemporary American Christian worldview that frequently makes them so nervous in theory class. Looking deeply at the idea of interpretive frames—especially ones that invite multiple, non-hierarchical, non-linguistic, or communal modes of knowing, too, as at least *possibly* or *partially* meaningful—means they have to examine everything they believe or were raised to believe about being, knowing, and truth.

Taking on such deep and important topics is, I believe, the single hardest part of teaching literary theory at Christian universities today but also, as my previous student attested to above, a potentially very important and faith-strengthening experience for everyone, as well. So when this first "a-ha" moment of the course comes, as it inevitably does, when your students have a lot to say and argue about and then get deeply silent, thoughtful, and sometimes even troubled, you'll need to switch gears for a short time. When you give them some mental space to attend to the important work of sorting through that potentially huge sea of change in their own understanding (and it will take some time), I've found it helpful to talk to them for a while just then about how exciting it is to know how faithful God is to his people in so many different ways. I like to share a few stories about, for example, Celtic monks in Ireland during the "dark ages" and how they "saved Christianity" (as Thomas Cahill's book describes so well) by living in little cold stone huts and copying out the most visual and beautiful versions of the Bible ever seen. Or I might mention how, on our own campus, one of my favorite colleagues is a Greek Orthodox physics professor who deeply loves Jesus and also deeply embraces sacrament and mystery in his church tradition—just to show some easy examples of the broad range of faith even now. I have also sometimes invited faculty colleagues from our School of Theology to join us in these classroom conversations to gently help the students feel safe in accepting a broader understanding of Christian religious traditions—or interpretive frames around the reality of Christian faith. I try to keep these crucial, early teaching moments joyful and loving, as best I can, not judging or seeming to criticize current American churches. Rather I hope to help them see that Jesus is true whether we say so or not, and that coming to accept our own fragmented and partial human understanding in a literary theory course in no way jeopardizes our Lord's eternal truth and reality—rather it helps to better equip us for encountering the dizzying range of reality in the world and the historic moment we've been given. The first key, then, to overall faith integration in teaching the literary theory course is to explicitly address this concern about interpretive frames early and often throughout the term, and then again at every place where questions arise within the claims of the theory schools themselves.

Course Strategies and Frameworks

As we have seen, the course as a whole works by beginning with a vocabulary of terms and paradigms for interpretation itself, then coming to a gentle acceptance that seeing texts in multiple ways doesn't necessarily mean rejecting Jesus. From there, roughly a quarter of the way through the term, you can begin the work of reading and understanding the theoretical schools themselves, depending on how much time you want to devote to each one.

In a practical sense, teaching this course has been greatly aided by a number of excellent new texts designed for the purpose of helping undergraduates tackle literary theory in the past ten years. For explicitly Christian undergraduates, a somewhat dated but still very useful book is *Truth is Stranger Than It Used to Be: Biblical Faith in a Postmodern Age*, written by J. Richard Middleton and Brian J. Walsh in 1995, because it directly addresses the question of faith in the context of theory's claims. However, I usually just recommend that book on my syllabus, and refer students to it as needed during those stormy early weeks of wrestling with paradigms and interpretation. Instead, the text I've currently found most useful to teach directly during this important course period is Stephen Bonnycastle's *In Search of Authority: An Introductory Guide to Literary Theory* (3rd ed.), published in Canada by Broadview Press. That book used in conjunction with *Literary Theory: An Anthology* (2nd ed.), edited by Julia Rivkin and Michael Ryan (Blackwell's) for the theory schools themselves, and also accompanied by a dictionary of terms such as *The Columbia Dictionary of Modern Literary and Cultural Criticism*, edited by Joseph Childers and Gary Hentzi (Columbia UP), form the textual backbone of my current literary theory courses.

The Bonnycastle text does a fine job of gently guiding undergraduates toward a recognition of the interpretive frames that in fact already exist in their college studies and their worldviews, meeting them where they are, so to speak, and then moving them toward noticing the languages of interpretation that they already speak. He then does a good job of expanding that terminology into new ideas and less familiar terrain. The overall organization of the text is also quite a bit better than most books of its kind because he resists the temptation to be simply encyclopedic or historical in introducing the field to undergraduates. Rather he models a dialogic framework in the movement of his book's ideas that makes the text simultaneously easy to read while also clearly and concisely reiterating its topics. He also provides some excellent study/discussion questions at the end of each chapter for practical teaching use. And, finally, while Bonnycastle appears not to be a Christian himself, he is respectful in his language and discussion of religious faith and, in fact, provides a useful model of engagement for Christian students to see that embracing theory provides them the freedom and empowerment to take on intellectual debate with "real professors who write books" on their own terms, too.

Once you have successfully moved your students into an acceptance of interpretive frames and developed some shared vocabulary of terms, the hard work of actually working with the theory texts themselves then begins. It is at this moment that every professor teaching literary theory will face the next form of borderline student insurrection—and the second subsequent "a-ha" moment. Exactly why, the students often ask, did some idiot philosopher (most likely French) just make things up to muddle and mystify ideas that are really quite straightforward and simple? And also, what possible good could all this obfuscation ever have in the real world of just studying literary texts in college? This moment, by the way, isn't the same as the existential crisis over interpretive frames that comes early on in the course. Rather, this is later when the students have allowed for at least the possibility of different interpretations and are now trying to untangle the thorny knots of the theories and theorists themselves—most likely in the long middle part of your teaching term. It is here that I like to incorporate one of my two favorite metaphors in teaching theory—that theories themselves can be likened to something like the colored lenses or "gels" that theaters use on their spotlights to shade or direct the impact of their stage presentation. Coloring the lights blue darkens some things but brings out others—while also persuading the audience that it might be nighttime or a dream or a dark hiding place where the stage action is taking place. Similarly, red or yellow lenses will shape the presentation in other ways—daytime or a fiery furnace—and new understandings are gained in the story. Theory can be likened to these gels when applied to the study of literature—it is potentially a useful and interesting *tool* that brings out aspects of the works that might be hidden otherwise and which benefit our ability to bring many partially 'readings' of a work into a more full or holistic understanding. What underlies this discussion—and the second "aha" moment it often provokes in students—is that up until now they've been acting as if everything in the world is illuminated to them in a clear, white incandescent bulb that uncritically presents reality to them 'just as it really is—and has always been.'

Scholar Barbara Woolvord has usefully described how best to lead students to learn such complex new material at the university level and I find her terminology of "first encounter," "wrestling" and "mastery" quite compelling when creating the specifics of my syllabus and daily classroom plan during this period of the course. In the "first encounter" with a new theory school, students read on their own at home, usually only partially understanding the essay they've been asked to read, bringing to class two copies of the written study questions I've given them to sort out the basics. They will come to class full of questions and frustrations from having to "encounter" the theorist on their own—but now they are also really ready to learn more. "Wrestling" is what we do together in class. We hash out the thickets of the texts and its implications by working together to re-answer the study questions, opening the class up to discussion and shared thinking. I then go forward from there, generally guiding their learning by making sure they don't memorize wrong or misinformation as they work toward "mastery" over the topic. They also help each other learn in this three-part model by listening and modifying in writing—right then and there in class—the study question sheet they started with the night before, correcting, crossing things out, and adding new notes and information to this now "master" sheet. (I collect one copy of these study questions for myself, by the way, when they first come to class, just to keep track of what they are struggling with and how hard they're working, etc. These aren't graded study questions either, just participation check marks with a grade awarded simply for doing them every day.)

This pedagogical strategy has two purposes, to my mind. First, it makes students simply notice the important terms and ideas—and get them right by working through them together in class. But it also uses the questions themselves to mirror the movement of ideas in the reading selection, too, giving students a leg up in more quickly getting to the rhetorical and generic strategies being used by each author. By providing this "X-ray," if you will, of the theoretical reading, the students are given help but not spoon-fed in their own engagement with its ideas—and, in the best cases, students are empowered to critique the text, too.

Along the way, I also hand out short supplemental readings—sometimes from newspapers or popular culture outlets or sometimes from other Christian thinkers who look at a specific aspect of faith and theory—to show the students that theory is alive and well in our world. More than most other English classes I teach, the topics and questions that concern each section of a literary theory class are highly dependent both on the actual students who enroll but also on the world and cultural events that occur during our term of study. I've found this "to the minute" format to be quite successful in helping students gain a solid understanding of theory itself and its ongoing relevance while also allowing them to think deeply about their own identities and faith commitments.

That daily rhythm of reading, writing, and learning is the small structure that creates the overall framework of this literary theory course, designed to build knowledge and competency slowly. You can easily design your own relatively straightforward study questions for each reading, aiming for basic comprehension. I've also found that the teaching text created by M. Keith Booker to accompany the *Norton Anthology of Theory and Criticism* provides excellent example study questions for the theorists' themselves, as well. The next step in the structure of the course is to build on the taxonomy of learning by moving the students to do some writing of their own. After several days or weeks of a topic or theory, depending on how much time and terrain I want to cover, I then give the students prompts and ask them to write graduate-style, one-page response papers that emphasize synthesis and connection. This interesting method of writing was pioneered, as I understand it, at Brown University and my mentor Gary Handwerk, an excellent teacher himself, taught it to me in graduate school. In essence, the students have to write a short response paper, showing their understanding of a theory's basic tenets, in only the maximum space they can fit on one side of a single sheet of paper, using the smallest margins and single-space typing they can fit on their printer (fonts must be normal and readable, however). The students will end up with what would normally be a two- to two-and-a-half-page paper, of course, but the beauty of this unusual printing method is that the students are jolted out of their normal paper-writing ruts. In addition, their ability to notice the movement of their ideas and thinking goes up dramatically when it is all literally right in front of them on one sheet of paper. This method also serves to discipline them out of their normal tendency to just start exploding with words to try and explain the theory they are writing about and instead provides a stern and fairly rigid requirement to edit and truly synthesize. You may not wish to use this unusual essay writing method at length, but I urge you to try it at least once in such a course. You may find it surprisingly effective.

At the course's culmination, then, I ask the students to use their acquired theory competency to write a final essay in which they must apply at least two theoretical lenses to a canonical literary text of their choosing. The quality of these essays can vary wildly and you should expect to grade this work at least partly on the good faith efforts students exert in wrestling with such new and complex ideas. This class has likely been a life-changing one for them, and they will need a lot of conferencing and encouragement to be brave enough to really enter into a new, more hermeneutically rich and sophisticated way of writing about literature in this assignment.

Case Study: Teaching Nietzsche and Post-Structuralism

Now that we've looked at this course in its overall rationale and peda-gogical framework, I'd like to look briefly as a kind of "case study" at what the detailed specifics of this course look like when working with some of the most fraught thinkers and theoretical school—specifically Friedrich Nietzsche and the claims of post-structuralism. First, I have the students read two selec-tions in the Ryan and Rivkin anthology: "On Truth and Lying in an Extra-Moral Sense" and "The Will to Power." The study questions for that night's readings begin simply but are directive in that they show students the major distinctive—and influential—new claims of this thinker in each of those essay selections. For example, the first study question sheet looks like this:

> **Question 1:** In this reading, Nietzsche suggests that all language is ultimately metaphorical in nature, correct? To see how he gets to that notion, please write down the points he's making in each paragraph in your own words on a separate sheet of paper in a kind of list or outline—as you notice him shift from one idea to the next one in this argument. Don't worry that there's a correct list you are supposed to come up with, though. Just write down every shifting idea as YOU see fit so that you can better follow his line of reasoning here.

This exercise breaks down Nietzsche's sneakily persuasive rhetorical tricks for the students by getting them to do the work of noticing how the writer himself makes connections—and therefore builds his own seemingly convincing structure of ideas. Students are not often careful readers, especially of philosophically challenging material, and they are too often simply passive recipients of what they read. I find that the study questions are a good place to start training them to read more critically and become more attuned to rhetorical sleights of hand. This first study question also helps the students feel some mastery over the essay by reducing it to a sheet of notes instead that they can examine in a more detached way than a whole lot of text in an anthology.

The next study question asks them to articulate some initial reaction to the essay's implications, as well:

> **Question 2:** Now that you've completed that outline or list, stand back and ask yourself what do you think about Nietzsche's argument here and what it implies about the nature of words and language— that is, is EVERYTHING "literary" at some level, if all language is "metaphor"? What do you make of that idea? Is it true, in your opinion? And, if so, what does that say about science, for example? Is science some kind of "storytelling," too?

Going slowly through the implications of Nietzsche's argument here helps the students start to think about language and its implications for representation in this essay separately and as a rhetorical premise on its own, before the final study questions then get them to the really incendiary stuff:

> **Question 3:** Is Nietzsche's thesis about the "hardening" of metaphor into illusions that are then taken for truths seem convincing to you? Is that the only possible conclusion for suggesting that the world is framed by language and that language is always at some

level just a representation? Is it troubling to you? Does this idea suggest a crucial function for literature as describing the very ways that humans know anything, for example? And, finally, how does this big idea compare with other thinkers we've studied (such as the Russian Formalists) who've similarly discussed the relationship between metaphor and humans' ability to see truthfully?

These opening day questions for the week or two of studying post-structuralism ideally help students not just see that many literary thinkers discuss how metaphor itself is an anagram of human knowing but also help them recognize Nietzsche's *proto*-postmodern emphasis on language as the basis for truth in Western culture as an important precursor to the later thinkers such as Foucault and Derrida. This work also helps students (who are often both frightened and intrigued by Nietzsche) to see how his critiques are only persuasive if you take his rhetorical assumptions as a given. Having wrestled with these ideas at home by responding to the study questions, the students then come to class able to enter into a conversation about how Christian faith, too, is founded on "the word" yet doesn't harden into Nietzsche's "illusions" of truth—becoming incarnate truth in Christ instead, "the word made flesh." We see together how compelling Nietzsche's ideas have been in history, and yet by taking them seriously, we can see also how they can form a deeply suspicious framework of complete unknowability in the world, too, which comes perilously close to a kind of nihilism.

Nietzsche's embrace of the abyss, however, is nuanced by the other readings and theorists whose language-based critiques of truth and meaning take on other more affirmative models (such as Derrida's "silence which is not absence," and Deleuze & Guattari's model of the "rhizome" and "plateau"). After looking carefully at these four or five representative authors in the post-structuralist camp (Nietzsche, Derrida, Foucault, Deleuze, and Guattari), the response paper assignment asks the students to gather together what they've studied and begin to make connections and some evaluation. These are several recent examples of this prompt:

- What, in your view, are the most important strengths and weaknesses of post-structuralism as a theoretical framework for examining literature? Be sure to use at least three thinkers in your essay and examine the implications of this theory as thoroughly as you can in such a short paper.

- Discuss the relationship between structuralism and post-structuralism, paying particular attention to the ways in which the latter challenges key premises of the former, as best you can judge.

- Comment on Nietzsche as a forerunner to post-structuralism. In what ways do his ideas seem similar to and in what ways different from later thinkers? What accounts for these similarities and differences, in your opinion?

As I hope this case study example briefly illustrates, class time can be spent, in Woolvord's terms, wrestling together with the ideas and faith implications of each theorist, guided by the teacher's leadings and prompts along the way. Mistaken ideas or mystifications are hashed out in a psychologically supportive setting that, I hope, leads to the kind of "mastery" that is appropriate for the undergraduate setting—insight and a strengthened and enriched template for living a life of meaning and faith.

One word that describes the whole philosophy of this course, then, might be *conversation*. Every class session emphasizes student-to-student and student-to-teacher conversation, based on study questions prepared in conjunction with every night's homework reading. Every theorist in turn is introduced as being in conversation with the thinkers and ideas of his or her time period and earlier, by using a largely chronological approach to teaching the theoretical schools. And finally faith integration is woven deep into the fabric of the course by framing Christianity itself as also a kind of conversation—the "word made flesh" as literally divine language incarnate in the human realm to which we listen and respond. In addition, this metaphor allows that faith is an ongoing conversation in our own lives today, both with other people and other ideas, along with our unique privilege to be in conversation with God himself (the "I" and "Thou" of Martin Buber's—and Mikhail Bakhtin's—dialogic formulations). This framework has, I believe, served the course very well in integrating faith with literary theory course content. My conversation with the students often begins and ends in an attitude of shaping our class as a supportive community where we can help and even love each other through this material. Since "being," "knowing," and "the nature of truth" are on the table in a literary theory course, I believe it is deeply important to frame the class itself as a community in which it is possible to be both faithful and unafraid of the ideas of this world.

BIBLIOGRAPHY

Bonnycastle, Stephen. *In Search of Authority: An Introductory Guide to Literary Theory*. 3rd Edition. Peterborough, Ontario: Broadview Press, 2007.

Caputo, John D. *The Prayers and Tears of Jacques Derrida*. The Indiana Series in Philosophy and Religion. Bloomington: Indiana University Press, 1997.

Childers, Joseph, and Gary Hentzi. *The Columbia Dictionary of Modern Literary and Cultural Criticism*. New York: Columbia University Press, 1995.

Middleton, J.Richard, and Brian J. Walsh. *Truth is Stranger Than It Used to Be: Biblical Faith in a Postmodern World*. Downer's Grove, IL: Intervarsity Press, 1995.

Rivkin, Julia, and Michael Ryan. *Literary Theory: An Anthology*. Blackwell Anthologies. 2nd ed. Hoboken: Wiley-Blackwell, 2004.

Traversing the Wilderness and Roaming the Countryside:

A Negotiation of the Moral Landscapes between Colonialism and Romanticism

ANDREA K. FRANKWITZ (GORDON COLLEGE)

Andrea K. Frankwitz guides us on a panoramic journey through early American literature, exploring the dramatically distinct variants of spiritual terrain and offering practical pedagogical tools for probing this rich soil. Along the way, she observes how her young pioneers' foray into these territories might be fraught with the unexpected but will be sure to reap a bountiful harvest. Andrea currently serves as Chair and Associate Professor of English at Gordon College, an evangelical nondenominational school in Wenham, Massachusetts. Her current areas of research include nineteenth-century American slave narratives and Christological imagery in American poetry.

During my first year of full-time teaching after graduate school, the integration of faith in the classroom was, quite frankly, not really on my mind. Having graduated at the end of the summer, I stayed on as a lecturer at my alma mater, a secular university where discussions of faith would have to be surreptitious at best. The following year, though, as I began my first full-time tenure-track position at a Christian college, I found myself racking my brain trying to remember what the English professors at my own Christian undergraduate college had done to get the Word into the classroom. As an undergraduate and graduate student, I had been joyously absorbed in my literature and writing classes, trying to soak it all in, not thinking of pedagogical strategies.

Curious about what my new colleagues were doing to incorporate faith in their courses but initially embarrassed to broach the subject, I asked my students how they saw faculty members integrating faith. There were wide-ranging responses—everything from opening class with prayer to singing hymns in a different language. I have to admit I latched onto the prayer tack, just biding my time while I gave more thought to the organic relationship between faith and literature. Already in my teaching as a graduate student at a secular school, I had been put off by some distasteful manifestations of religious piety in the classroom. Once, when I taught the usually assigned composition class and used the portfolio system, I remember how one student, who had sensed I was a Christian, had written in her portfolio's introduction to her essays that part of her revision process entailed praying with her pastor about what changes to make in her drafts. In grading that work, I resisted the urge to say they should have prayed harder. That incident, though, certainly made an impression on me and has helped to shape some of my ideas on integration.

As a perpetual student of literature and as a Christian, I want there to be integrity in the process of integration in the classroom—justice done to both the literature and the Christian faith. Over time, I have found it helpful at the beginning of each semester to share my thoughts about integration with my students. In my Surveys of American Literature, I also typically explain the rationale behind my text selections—some of which may not address religious matters or may even challenge some Christian ideals—and talk about how these texts can give us a sense of the various voices in America and show us how literature has been used and has developed in certain time periods. In class discussions at evangelical Christian colleges, we clearly have more freedom to talk about faith matters related to texts than we would at secular schools, but I still want my students to use this freedom in a responsible way. Especially in the lower-division courses, it is important to talk about what are realistic expectations for authors and texts. To bring a little levity to the discussion, I sometimes hyperbolize a hypothetical situation in which we might be talking about a story by William Faulkner and rashly conclude, "He just needs to get saved." Of course, that elicits a few chuckles, but that opens the door, in a nonthreatening way, to encourage students to think critically about when it is appropriate to bring in matters of faith and when it seems forced or illogical, doing a disservice to the author, the text, and/or the Christian faith. When I initiate this conversation toward the beginning of the semester, it is so much less awkward than at a time later on when a wide-eyed student might have just offered a precious fallacy. This is not to say that I have not sometimes had to circle back to this discussion, but at least most of the class will be on the same page.

In an effort to be sensitive to matters adjacent to the Christian faith, I also give consideration to another potential influence in class discussions. At the start of each semester of teaching the Survey of American Literature I course at an evangelical Christian college, I remind myself of a few different external factors that may affect students' comfort level with some of the historical background of early American literature: students' denominational affiliations and their level of familiarity with the Old and New Testaments. Having now over the course of ten years taught in two evangelical nondenominational Christian colleges, I have grown accustomed to teaching students from a mixture of different Protestant denominations. Because certain denominations may privilege some doctrines and downplay others, I want to be especially sensitive to this as I provide historical background information and lead discussions about various belief systems as represented in colonial American literature. Over the years, I have also observed that what might be even more relevant in our class than any denominational affiliation is the students' own familiarity with the Bible or the number of biblical studies or theology classes they have taken. The first Christian university at which I taught required students to take 30 credits of biblical studies, whereas my present school requires eight credits. Perhaps it is no surprise, then, that students from the former school seemed a bit more comfortable and vocal in these discussions, though I have to acknowledge that there might be other factors at work too, such as West Coast/East Coast demographics, class dynamics, individual personalities, etc. As students' level of familiarity with the Bible becomes evident in class, I periodically make adjustments in context lectures.

Although from year to year I occasionally switch out various texts and bring in others to my Survey of American Literature I course, I design the syllabus to reflect the development of literature from, roughly, the seventeenth century to the mid/late nineteenth century. Within each of the three major literary periods traditionally covered by this course—the Age of Faith, the Age of Reason, and Romanticism—there are plenty of natural opportunities for faith integration. I also find it helpful to work with, formally or informally, some subcategories throughout the semester, such as religion, race, and gender, to address pertinent issues and developments in each literary period.

Whether or not I entitle a category on the reading list "Discovery," I usually jump-start the course with a few contrasting texts, such as selections from Christopher Columbus's Letter to Luis de Santangel Regarding the First Voyage and his Letter to Ferdinand and Isabella Regarding the Fourth Voyage, along with selections from "The Relation of Alvar Nunez Cabeza de Vaca," all three texts included in the *Norton Anthology of American Literature*. I have to confess that over the years I have wrestled with my choices for the initial course readings, sometimes in the past wholly leaving off these "Discovery" phase excerpts and just starting with some Puritan texts. Quite frankly, though, doing the latter feels like a cop-out. More often lately, I have included the texts and not put them under any heading. My concern, of course, is not really with the formatting of my Survey of American Literature I syllabus but with the kind of impression I might give with the selection of course readings. When I first began teaching colonial American literature, I glossed over some of the early readings, which I knew could be controversial, and hoped my students would not notice my discomfort. Gradually, I came to realize that openly sharing my own concerns regarding the representative works of this period (after some initial class discussions about the texts) could actually benefit students, especially if with any prior exposure they had only seen the texts in an uncritical light. My continual hope is that this conversation does not come across as heavy-handed or didactic.

Using the particular line-up of Columbus's letters and Cabeza de Vaca's "Relation" allows me to address literary, historical, cultural, and theological/spiritual matters from the outset of the semester, thus encouraging students to see early American literature as multidimensional. On the second day of class, when students have just finished these first readings, I ease into the discussion of these texts by having students spend ten minutes recollecting and writing about their first exposure to early American literature—what stories, events, and activities they recall, who the figures were, and what kinds of impressions stand out in their minds. After a number of volunteers eagerly share about making colorful hand-traced turkeys, learning of the first Thanksgiving celebration between the colonists and the Native Americans, or reenacting the Pocahontas story, I ask students to think about what has just been shared by classmates and to make some observations. What usually happens is that students will eventually note the pleasantness and commonality of these first impressions. Then I ask them to tell me about the time(s) when their initial pictures of early America might have altered and what accounted for that change. Discussion quickly becomes much more serious as students recount their feelings of surprise, confusion, shame, and sometimes even betrayal, when they found out that in the early period of this country things were not so rosy and that relations between the colonists and Native Americans were not so smooth as they had thought, and most shocking and disturbing of all, that Europeans were responsible for bringing devastation to many Native American populations.

Because my purpose for this discussion is not to heap guilt on students of European ancestry but to tease out a few of the historical complexities of this time period and to foster greater awareness and sensitivity to various cultures, I am careful not to belabor their time of disillusionment. In some classes, however, we have had fruitful conversations about why elementary school children may still be given these stories about America and about when students in general might be ready intellectually and psychologically to hear a more accurate and detailed account of what went on during this time in history.

The pairing of Columbus's letters and Cabeza de Vaca's "Relation" for our second day's reading provides a good balance of historical authenticity and accuracy. With Columbus, students see representative passages from the late fifteenth/early sixteenth century and their typical ethnocentric depictions of this country and its inhabitants; with Cabeza de Vaca's account, they have a more fair and balanced picture of the Native Americans. After the initial discussion about students' first-time exposures to early American literature, we move into in-depth examinations of these texts by way of looking at how these three texts reinforce or challenge our ideas, beliefs, and attitudes about the events and literature of these periods. Because there are so many layers to these texts and many different angles for approaching them, I can confidently rely on students to initiate some valuable observations that can take us further into these texts. Especially with early American literature, which to some students might not seem terribly exciting or relevant, I find it worthwhile to use students' own comments and impressions as launching points for discussion. In making room for this, I have noticed that students seem much more engaged because they can see, even more dramatically, that they have connections of various sorts to this literature.

Embedded in the historical and rhetorical dimensions of Columbus's letters and Cabeza de Vaca's "Relation," there are also opportunities for faith integration. In looking at the change in rhetorical postures between these two letters, we notice Columbus's apparent value system and how he strategically punctuates his letters with references to God, at the same time dismissing the Native Americans he comes upon in this land, as seen in his comment to the sponsoring merchant that some of his crew "found an infinity of small hamlets and people without number, but nothing of importance."[1] Cabeza de Vaca, on the other hand, though he too had been an explorer of sorts and had been taken prisoner, depicts the various tribes of Native Americans and their distinctive cultures with great detail and respect. His evident Christian faith comes across not only through his description of his experiences but also in how the natives respond to his Christianity in light of their previous encounters with other Europeans who have called themselves Christians. The Native Americans could not, then, understand how Cabeza de Vaca and his crew could also be considered Christians: "We had come from the sunrise, they from the sunset; we healed the sick, they killed the sound; we came naked and barefoot, they clothed, horsed, and lanced; we covet nothing but gave whatever we were given, while they robbed whomever they found and bestowed nothing on anyone."[2] As we focus on this poignant passage, I ask students to consider how, even now, others may understand (or misunderstand) the Christian faith because of how we interact with others and how we conduct our lives individually and collectively. Students then see that the literature of this time period implicitly raises some positive challenges for us in our faith and in how we live it out in the world, just as the Apostle Paul reminds us in II Corinthians 3:2 that we are epistles known and read by all.

In my early years of teaching American literature from the Age of Faith, I used to be surprised when my students appeared not to relish Puritan literature. I just could not understand why they were not clamoring for more. After thinking over some of their responses in class, sometimes muttered under their breath, I realized I needed to take action. It had become painfully obvious that my beloved Puritans were in serious need of some image management. I had thought it was incentive enough that the Puritans were also Christians; why shine the apple, I reasoned, when I knew my students would have to eat it anyway. What I found myself dealing with was the persistent cultural stereotype of the Puritans as a radical sect of stodgy people who did not enjoy life. To address these misunderstandings, I have found Harrison T. Meserole's *American Poetry of the Seventeenth-Century* and Sacvan Bercovtich's *The Puritan Origins of the American Self* immensely helpful. Now as I share with my students that the Puritans really *did* enjoy life—that they liked colorful clothing, beer and wine, and fine household furnishings—but that their aesthetics were attuned to matters of proportion/moderation and utility, they can more clearly understand that the Puritans did not govern their lives by arbitrary edicts but rather by sensible principles and by a desire to please God. This time in class provides a natural opportunity for us to reflect on and discuss what it means to live a principled life, what it might entail, and what it might cost (even in reputation, such as with the Puritans). When students see that they grapple with some of the same motivations and questions the Puritans did, they begin warming up to the Puritans.

In this section on the Age of Faith in American literature, the first primary text we look at is John Winthrop's lay sermon "A Model of Christian Charity," presumably delivered aboard the Arbella at the outset of a voyage to the New

World. Because Winthrop was so esteemed in his day and was soon to hold a position of prominence as governor of the Massachusetts Bay Colony, students, in reading his sermon, are able to get a sampling of some of the best and most influential thinking of the early seventeenth century. Beyond even its historical significance in capturing the tenor of this momentous occasion, the sermon lays out in a clear and systematic way a moral philosophy and plan for organizing the colony's new communal enterprise. Before even getting to the text, I ask students to think about the kinds of sermons they have heard and what has been emphasized, moving on then to talk about what components might make up an effective sermon. Of course, what should resonate with students are the numerous references to the Old and New Testaments. Rather than simply accepting the validity of Winthrop's ideas, though, I ask students to consider their merits and to analyze whether those ideas, which he infuses with biblical passages, are sound logically and well-grounded biblically. I have had some students who were taken aback with this "questioning" of a sermon, but overall students respond positively to this exercise and have expressed appreciation that we look at texts critically and treat the Christian faith seriously. Winthrop's "A Model of Christian Charity" has stood this "test" over the years and has even been a rallying point for various classes. After an in-depth examination of this foundational document, which proposes that the Company of Massachusetts Bay in New England set up their community according to the Gospel law of love because, in accordance with Matthew 5:14-15, they "shall be as a city upon a hill" (216), I ask students how far afield we are now from Winthrop's vision. After soliciting responses about what we can glean from Winthrop's sermon, I ask them to imagine a Winthrop addressing our present day congregations and what changes he might make to accomplish the same purposes.

Whether I put students in small groups or keep the large group format, I find it valuable to encourage students to spend more time with Winthrop's ideas. I ask them to address the implications and applications of "Christian charity" for various segments of society (with particular attention to those most relevant to them as Christian college students): Church, community, their own college classrooms, and their own residence halls. I ask them to address the following questions for each of these areas: What specific challenges might this particular segment of society need to overcome in order to practice "Christian charity"? What is required for that segment to be operating in "Christian charity"? How would this segment of society be different if "Christian charity" were in full operation? What proposal(s) would you like to make for this particular segment of society? I have found that referencing

Micah 6:6 and Psalm 15 might help students with organizing their thoughts for this activity. At a Christian college, which typically would require some biblical studies credits, it is fairly safe to assume that there might be at least a few students who have Bibles with them, though I usually try to bring in a few of my own for this class period.

If Winthrop's ideal of "Christian charity" may not be the excitement students are looking for in early American literature, they have it in wagonloads in *A Narrative of the Captivity and Restoration of Mrs. Mary Rowlandson.* With all of the murder, mayhem, and adventure in this text, it is no wonder that Puritan captivity narratives or Indian captivity narratives, as they were called, were bestsellers of their day. Before we get caught up in the gory details of this text, though, I find it useful to provide students with some background information regarding the Puritans. We look at, and hold up to Rowlandson's narrative, seven key points of Puritan theology: 1) God's absolute sovereignty, 2) Predestination, 3) Providence, 4) Natural/Innate Depravity, 5) Election, 6) Evil as inner, 7) God as revealed in the Bible. When students see, then, that the Puritans had compatible beliefs with some of their own Protestant denominations, and that, in particular, Calvinism, Presbyterianism (USA), Congregationalism, and the Reformed Church may be considered descendents of Puritanism, they tend to feel more kinship with them.

To further prepare students for understanding Rowlandson's narrative and other Puritan texts, I also spend time looking at the Puritans' propensity for producing histories and personal writings. In their histories, they want to show their communal place as the new Israelites in God's unfolding design for the world. Similarly with their personal writings, such as diaries, journals, personal narratives, and spiritual autobiographies, they want to chart what is happening for good or ill in their daily lives because they believe that God speaks to them individually through these things. Thus, generally if the Puritans were staying healthy, their crops were flourishing, and their businesses were prospering, they believed that God was smiling on them; conversely, if families were ailing, crops were dying, or businesses were failing, that God was displeased with them. After I explain this Puritan mindset to my literature students, I encourage critical thinking and integration by asking them about the implications of such an ideology, and where that belief stands in relation to Scripture. Students then see more clearly that such an ideology, though well intentioned, can lead people to become legalistic or judgmental and can also produce false conclusions. We look at the "gray" areas of this ideology, noting, for instance, that God sometimes disciplines or chastens us as Christians but that the unregenerate or unsaved sometimes also prosper.

After sharing with my students that the Puritan captivity narrative—the first distinctive American literary genre—derived from the spiritual autobiography, lay sermon, and the jeremiad, I ask them to look for these influences in Rowlandson's account. My hope is that students will see the spiritual complexities in this narrative, not simply the drama, and will gain an appreciation for how Rowlandson tried to make sense of her ordeal by reflecting on her experience and trying to discern why God allowed her to go through that captivity. This often opens up interesting class discussions about how God may use "wilderness" experiences in our lives to help us grow spiritually.

To help students understand why Rowlandson and other Puritan writers typically make references to Old Testament figures as they narrate their own experiences, I like to take at least part of a class period to talk about Puritan historiography, how the Puritans saw themselves as part of God's unfolding design for the world. I point out that to emphasize their collective and individual role in providential history, the Puritan writers employ typology, a hermeneutical tool for understanding the relationship between Old and New Testament figures and events, but further extend this beyond an intrascriptural reading to include themselves as the new Israelites and to depict the New World as their Promised Land. Beyond even the obvious theological dimensions of this philosophy by itself, we look at the historical ramifications for those around them. This provides a natural segue for us to examine Rowlandson's literary treatment of the Native Americans. Because she is so detailed in some of her descriptions, we gain a sense not only of Rowlandson's harrowing captivity but also of the Wampanoags' practices and rituals. We then look at how Rowlandson shores up her own and the collective identity of the Puritans as God's chosen people through sundry comparisons to Old Testament figures (such as Job, Daniel, and David) and to sheep, while at the same time rhetorically polarizing the Native Americans by likening them to Satan's hellhounds and all manner of wild beasts. Although students may initially think of Rowlandson's characterizations as peculiar, later in that class period (or in a journal response) I ask them to consider how our identities as children of God affect how we process our experiences and how we think of and interact with those who are not of the same race or faith. When students begin responding, sometimes we first hear what, ideally, we *should* hear, with biblically supported perspectives, but hearing that too soon has a way of either closing down discussion or at least momentarily silencing other responses. When I was fresh out of graduate school, I might have let the silence or apparent pious platitudes embarrass me into moving on or concluding class rapidly. Now, I work with the silence, whether created by students or myself. What tends to happen, after a few beats, is that some courageous students will share, from points of vulnerability, that they sometimes still struggle in responding to their own suffering, for instance, or to people they find morally repugnant or radically different from their own cultures. The point of this discussion, of course, is not to glorify fleshly or prejudiced responses but to encourage serious reflection on our growing understanding of the complexity of Christianity.

No section on the Age of Faith in American literature would be complete without attention to the seventeenth-century Puritan poets Anne Bradstreet and Edward Taylor. The juxtaposition of their work highlights their individual contributions. To aid students in their appreciation of Bradstreet and Taylor, I first provide a brief primer on the poetry of the period, looking at styles and common rhetorical devices, and then, with the help of Jeffrey Walker's essay "Anagrams and Acrostics; Puritan Poetic Wit," I highlight the playful and solemn sides of their craft:

> While Puritans did little to elicit belly laughs, they did relish exercising their poetic wit, especially in the anagram and the acrostic, two forms that required the poet to use the letters of a person's name to create words or epigrams that revealed aspects of that individual's character. Because many Puritans believed that nothing in their world was haphazard and that all indications of God's attitude toward them were highly important, some writers of anagrams and acrostics found great providential significance in the rearrangement of the letters in a subject's name.[3]

Wanting students to experience firsthand the air of play in Puritan poetry, I sometimes ask them to create acrostics and anagrams for their names. They really respond well to this and are eager to share what they have discovered, though with good humor I do have to interject that we will not take these as pronouncements from God.

Before immersing ourselves in the world of Anne Bradstreet, I find it necessary to talk with students about the role and expectation for women in the seventeenth century. As we then look at Bradstreet's "The Prologue," students have a greater appreciation for her courage in entering the field of poetry, traditionally the domain of males. This poem may be an unusual choice for suggesting faith integration opportunities because on the surface it does not even mention God, religion, or spiritual matters, yet it has a few embedded value systems that are relevant for understanding Bradstreet and Puritan culture. In using the persona of someone whose Muse is "foolish, broken, blemished,"

Bradstreet takes the culturally and, to Puritans, theologically requisite position for a woman—that of humility. As I walk my students through an in-depth analysis of the poem, they come to understand the necessary irony of her persona's claiming ineptness and lowliness all the while showing implicitly that she is well-read, witty, and highly skilled in writing poetry. We also consider how Bradstreet's use of irony, flattery, and logic allows her to make subtle inroads for female wits. So that students see a more complete picture of Bradstreet and do not precipitously conclude she was a radical feminist, we read more of her work, such as her poem "To My Dear and Loving Husband," in which she speaks of a love that is mutual, respectful, and passionate. Along with this, we read her letter "To My Dear Children," in which Bradstreet describes her own spiritual journey for the edification of her children. This epistle then provides a launching point, whether for a mini-class discussion or a journal response, to work with one of the bedrock principles in Bradstreet's letter: the ideas that in sharing our experiences or journeys we might help others gain some spiritual advantage or that in hearing the conversion experiences or trials of others, we may grow spiritually.

Although students typically find Edward Taylor's poetry a bit more difficult than Bradstreet's at first run, it offers a nice contrast in terms of focus and style. I point out to students, though, that differences in station and gender between these two Puritan poets may account for much of this contrast. In Taylor's "Prologue" to his *Preparatory Meditations*, we observe his background as a minister surfacing in his theologically nuanced lines. We consider the ways his "crumb of dust" persona and his requests to God "That Thou wilt guide its pen to write aright / To Prove Thou art the best / And show Thy Properties to shine most bright"[4] reveal a particular understanding of his relationship to God. After then explaining what is involved in a meditation (content, structure, and purpose) and looking closely at Taylor's "Meditation 8," I do the unthinkable and ask my students to write their own meditative poems. I wish I could say that students have produced dazzling poetry from this exercise, but that is not really my point anyway. The value, as voiced by many students over the years, is that the practice has given them a greater appreciation for the doctrinal intricacies of meditative poetry and pushed them, in an unexpected way, to use their minds, wills, and emotions to grapple with their own relationships to God.

While not as overtly religious as the Age of Faith, the literature of the Age of Reason provides bountiful opportunities for faith integration in the classroom. In particular, I find the work of Jonathan Edwards, Benjamin Franklin, and Phillis Wheatley useful for helping students understand some of the ideas and issues of the eighteenth century and also reflect on the Christian faith. During my first few years of teaching the Survey of American Literature, I used Jonathan Edwards's famous sermon "Sinners in the Hands of an Angry God" by itself, without any of his other writings. This text inevitably provokes lively, sometimes heated, discussions. Perhaps part of this reaction stems from my asking students to address the rhetorical merits and theological soundness of Edwards's methodology of using dramatic emotional appeals. Some students will say that if eternity is at stake, then he cannot be considered too heavy-handed in his tactics. Others, that conversions based on fear will not "stick." I probe further, asking them to consider whether it is possible to overemphasize God's wrath, and God's love. Interestingly enough, what students often initially miss in this sermon is Edwards's systematic approach. This, then, paves the way for a discussion of how Edwards serves as a transitional figure between the Age of Faith and the Age of Reason.

To help students see a more balanced picture of Edwards's faith, I now pair this sermon with his "Personal Narrative." As they read this spiritual autobiography and see Edwards wrestling with his faith, experiencing what some scholars term "auto-machia" or a "self civil war," students seem more willing to make allowances for the "Sinners" style of sermon. This increased tolerance appears to be based on the idea that he, too, has been in the same position as some members of his congregation, that of sitting away from God. Calling attention to how Jonathan Edwards's "Personal Narrative" may help contextualize "Sinners in the Hands of an Angry God," I ask my students to reflect on how our openness or vulnerability in sharing our personal faith with others may affect how receptive non-Christians will be to particular stances or ideological positions we might take.

Compared to the sober figure of Jonathan Edwards, his eighteenth-century contemporary Benjamin Franklin often seems worlds away to my students. Works of this Enlightenment man, such as the "Autobiography," capture the humanistic spirit of the age and, for us, implicitly present food, albeit of a different sort, for spiritual thought. I like to use the "Autobiography" in my Survey of American Literature I class because it epitomizes eighteenth-century American culture. To help students understand the background of Franklin's texts, I talk with them about how the decline of Puritanism, the rise of Deism, and new scientific advances (among other things) had so changed the religious climate by the mid-1700s that man, instead of God, was now commonly seen as the center of the universe.

As a starting point for discussing Franklin's "Autobiography," I sometimes put my students in small groups and ask them to pose collectively as a

Puritan who has just read this text and to write Franklin a letter, noting what they find admirable or useful in the text and what they have concerns about. This exercise has helped students think more deeply and critically about the "Autobiography" and has enabled us, in a fun and efficient fashion, to touch upon and probe further into many of his noteworthy experiences, some of which teeter between being commendable and questionable. One of the passages that naturally lends itself to faith integration is Franklin's "bold and arduous Project of arriving at moral Perfection"[5] by way of mastering thirteen virtues. Initially, students often dismiss this wholly, seeing it as an absurd and arrogant plan. I point out that, while as Christians we can generally agree that we will not on this side of eternity reach this "moral perfection" Franklin desires, we may not be giving his plan its due attention. I ask them questions such as the following: What appears to be Franklin's motivation for desiring moral perfection? What presuppositions does Franklin evidently hold regarding the nature of moral perfection and mankind? In our own strength, can we achieve moral perfection? Should we as Christians desire moral perfection? If so, what role (if any) are we to have in this process? What responsibilities, if any, do we have for mastering virtues or producing fruit? What might hinder our having fruitful lives? Beyond these questions, I also encourage students to consider this section of Franklin's text in relation to the "perfection" mentioned in Matthew 5:48, 19:21; Romans 12:2; and James 3:2. My aim in this discussion is not to reach a theological conclusion for the students but to tease out some of the complexities surrounding Franklin's idea.

Though she may not share Franklin's rags-to-riches story, Phillis Wheatley rose above her lowly and meager beginnings as a slave stolen from Africa to write compelling poetry that resonates beyond the eighteenth century. Because of her conversion experience noted in "On Being Brought from Africa to America," this poem works well for talking about the historical relationship between Christianity and enslavement. After a close reading of the poem, in which we look at Wheatley's ironic use of her audience's cultural and racial stereotypes, I engage students in a discussion of how we as Christians might still be enslaving people. From here, we move on to another poem, "To the University of Cambridge, in New England," in which Wheatley issues a challenge to the "sons of science" at Harvard to not, as they "scan the skies," and "traverse the ethereal space, / And mark the systems of revolving worlds," miss out on "The blissful news by messengers from Heav'n, / How Jesus's blood for your redemption flows."[6] Here again, Wheatley uses her poetry to address a significant cultural tension in the eighteenth century, that between science and religion. Through discussion of this poem, I prompt my students to think more deeply about the relationship between reason and faith and, more specifically, to consider what role reason has in a Christian's life. I think it worth noting with students that even in referencing these controversial topics, Phillis Wheatley broke through racial and gender barriers of her time.

To assist students in making the transition from the Enlightenment period to the Romantic period, I devote some time to explaining the historical background of early nineteenth-century America, part of which entails looking at some dramatically different belief systems. I find R. W. B. Lewis's *American Adam* particularly helpful in providing snapshot pictures of the two prominent strains of Romanticism, which he terms the "party of irony" (characterized by pessimism, the belief in innate depravity, and the idea that the past impinges on the present) and the "party of hope" (characterized by optimism, the belief in innate goodness, and forward thinking). Though I conscientiously explain that this is a bit reductionistic and certainly does not mean every Romantic writer can be categorized so neatly, Lewis's descriptors do give students a handle on some of the important distinctions. The work from both of these camps provides plenty of occasions for us as a class to reflect on our faith.

I find the imaginative stories of dark Romantic writers such as Nathaniel Hawthorne, Edgar Allan Poe, and Herman Melville particularly conducive for discussions of how a belief in innate depravity might affect authors' depictions and Christians' conceptions of human nature and human potential. In talking about this matter using Hawthorne's story "The Minister's Black Veil," for instance, I ask my students to consider not only the potential symbolism of the black veil and Reverend Hooper's possible motives for donning it, but also how the biblical directive to "be in the world but not of it" might take shape in our lives, how our beliefs as Christians may be misinterpreted by those around us, and how even biblically grounded beliefs (or secret sin repented of) may exact a price from us and those around us.

In teaching texts by Transcendentalists such as Ralph Waldo Emerson, Henry David Thoreau, and Margaret Fuller, I like to emphasize the tremendous cultural contributions of these writers. While a few students in the Survey of American Literature I class might show a ready liking for the Transcendentalists, more often I have found that a majority will need time to warm up to this group of Romantics. Because I have seen that some Christian college students may be inclined to disregard the Transcendentalists in their entirety on account of some apparently suspect spiritual beliefs, I find it important to mediate this reaction by looking at how they still may offer positive challenges for us as Christians. For example, when in discussions of Emerson's essay "Self-Reliance" students say that as Christians we should not be dependent on the self but rather on God, I ask them to consider whether it is possible to be too "reliant" on God and what this might look like. At first, students are startled by the question, but they start thinking about it more critically. As I clarify with my students, I am certainly an advocate for an increased dependence on God, as long as it is a "biblically sound" reliance. This then often leads to some interesting discussions addressing biblical descriptions of the "self" (that which is apart from God, and that which is in Christ) and the question of compatibility between our identity as God's children and the idea of self-reliance.

Lest I encourage my students to oversimplify Romanticism by thinking only in terms of the party of irony and the party of hope, I also include other writers, such as William Apess and Emily Dickinson, who cannot be classified so easily. Both Apess and Dickinson reflect, however subtly, the Romantic period's spirit of reform and belief in the value of the individual. Because Apess's "An Indian's Looking Glass for the White Man" and Dickinson's poems "I'm 'wife'—I've finished that—," "She rose to His Requirement—dropt," and "Title divine—is mine!" address cultural prejudices regarding race and gender respectively—biases that have long been tolerated by Christians—these texts seem especially ripe for conversations involving faith integration. Both writers graphically portray the result of these cultural biases: Apess shows Native Americans in all manner of ruin, and Dickinson shows married women as eclipsed, "dropt," "bridalled," and shrouded. Within class discussions about "An Indian's Looking-Glass for the White Man," I ask my students how Apess's background as a Christian, a white man, and a Native American man might make him an ideal candidate for addressing these matters of prejudice with his Christian audience. We then consider whether society now needs another "looking glass," and, if so, who would hold that up and what problems might be anticipated with that. Though it might be more comfortable in conversation to keep the matter of racism at bay by only asking about and responding to *society's* part in this, I think it necessary to bring it closer to home by asking students what roles Christians might have in racial reconciliation. I approach Dickinson's texts in a similar fashion, from specific to general. After doing close readings of these poems as a class, we look at the forms prejudice against women has taken and at the ramifications for women and the rest of society. Although it can be a bit risky, especially with students from specific Protestant denominations, I think it worth venturing the question of how some people might use religion, Christianity, or theology to justify thinking of or treating women as inferiors. Through these texts and conversations about race and gender, I want to encourage students to give more thought to the enduring question of how we as Christians can help promote understanding between different people groups.

I wish I could say that for my students and me this Survey of American Literature course is simply about reading and discussing literature and about growing in our faith and in our understanding of the human condition. Such is not the case, though. Because I know accountability and concentrated learning opportunities are good for students, I include five different assignment categories on the syllabus. Some of these course components, in particular, may have relevance for helping students think through issues related to faith. In addition to class discussions and assorted "journal" responses, the Blackboard engagements, group projects, and essays contribute toward this objective. The Blackboard engagements, which I describe in my syllabus, prompt students to choose a scene, issue, or character interchange in a given text and reflect on the theological implications or ideological assumptions embedded there. Students then describe how the ideas or values therein resonate with or challenge their own ideological framework. So that students are not simply writing these reflection paragraphs in isolation, I also ask students to write response paragraphs to other students' reflection paragraphs. This is a neat way of giving students a forum for commenting on something that stirred them but that we might not have time to talk about in class. As other students pick up these threads, the conversations can continue in meaningful ways beyond class. If students post claims that do not show keen thought or sound logic, others will call them on it. These strands can also make for interesting fodder for class discussions, so I occasionally print off a few pages to share with the rest of the class, who might not have responded to postings for that day.

I also require that students do one group project on a course text. For the group project, students will collaborate with a few other classmates to create some project that shows their understanding of the text and offers a thoughtful response to it, which in turn helps foster class discussion about it. Students generally get excited about this opportunity and do not think of it as intimidating because, regardless of their own creativity level, they have others to help them. This kind of assignment provides variety in course requirements and, more importantly, tends to provide the class with an unusual, if not surprising, way of understanding the text. Although I do not stipulate that this project be integrative in nature, sometimes students choose to highlight a spiritual dimension of a text.

Aside from a comprehensive midterm examination, the major assignments for this class are the two interpretive essays. During my first few years of teaching the Survey, I presented students with a list of prompts from which they would choose questions to respond to. After awhile, grading these essays just became tedious for me, as I had so many students writing on the same topics. Now I present students with a brief essay guideline sheet and require that they come up with their own theses. My philosophy now is that it is a valuable intellectual exercise for students to create their own arguments rather than to rely on questions and ideas from the professor. In this sophomore-level course, I usually have some students who are excited about the challenge of designing their own arguments. Some other students, though, initially appear panic-stricken. To help prepare students further, I generally spend at least half a class period explaining the essay assignment and giving some tips and cautions (in addition to reiterating my offer to provide feedback on theses and revised drafts). Although we may talk about matters of faith relatively freely in class discussions and Blackboard engagements, I require my students in writing their essays to direct and tailor their arguments to a general academic audience. As much as I want to encourage my students to explore their faith, I also believe it important for them to be able to engage texts on an intellectual level in the public sphere too. Because of this stipulated audience, then, I urge my students who are interested in writing about faith-related topics to be especially careful to make sure that they use sound reasoning and textual evidence to make their claims and develop a convincing argument.

Overall, my hope is that through the readings, discussion topics, and course assignments students will be engaged on a number of different levels. As we journey from Colonialism to Romanticism in the Survey of American Literature I course, we encounter bountiful opportunities to cultivate an appreciation for literature of this land, to grow in our understanding of the human condition, and to tend our spiritual gardens.

Bibliography

Bercovitch, Sacvan. *The Puritan Origins of the American Self.* New Haven: Yale UP, 1975.

Lewis, R. W. B. *The American Adam: Innocence, Tragedy, and Tradition in the Nineteenth Century* (Chicago: U of Chicago P, 1959).

Meserole, Harrison T Meserole, *American Poetry of the Seventeenth Century,* (University Park: Pennsylvania State UP, 1985).

Endnotes

1   Christopher Columbus, "Letters," in the *Norton Anthology of American Literature*, ed. Nina Baym, 6th ed. (New York: Norton, 2003), 35.

2   Cabeza de Vaca, "The Relation of Alvar Nunez Cabeza de Vaca," in the *Norton Anthology of American Literature*, 69.

3   Jeffrey Walker, "Anagrams and Acrostics; Puritan Poetic Wit," in *Seventeenth-Century American Poetry in Theory and Practice*, ed. Peter White, 247–57 (University Park: Pennsylvania State UP, 1985), 247.

4   Edward Taylor, "Prologue," in the *Norton Anthology of American Literature*, 26–28.

5   Benjamin Franklin, "The Autobiography of Benjamin Franklin," in the *Norton Anthology of American Literature*, 591.

6   Phillis Wheatley, "To the University of Cambridge, in New England," in the *Norton Anthology of American Literature*, 8–9, 11–12.

THE WHEEL OF FATE:

Using a Medieval Worldview to Bridge the Twenty-First-Century Gulf between Faith and Learning

JAMIE DESSART (WAYNESBURG UNIVERSITY)

Jamie Dessart, chair of English and fine arts at Waynesburg University, views herself a medievalist when it comes to the topic of faith and learning. In her article "The Wheel of Fate," she applies a medieval worldview that unreservedly integrates faith with knowledge to encourage her students to see that separation has not always been the case. Jamie is also the director of women's studies and has been involved in assessment and general education. She has published poetry and articles in women's studies journals and has presentations on Chaucer and J. R. R. Tolkien.

Loving medieval literature and teaching it to undergraduates can be a paradox. How can students, so inculcated in a twenty-first-century worldview, ever understand or appreciate the complete integration of religion and learning that represents the medieval world? There are times when I feel like giving up the effort to make many of them respect the depth and revelation that I so enjoy in authors like Margery Kempe, Geoffrey Chaucer, Julian of Norwich, and John Milton. It seems an anathema to a large percentage of my students, the way that God hovers in every statement and is present in every verse. And yet, purveyors of other genres and time periods often say that we medievalists must have it easy when it comes to integrating our faith with our discipline; after all, Augustine, Boethius, Aquinas, St. Jerome, and others were religious figures and church fathers. I believe that teaching medieval literature is the perfect place to confront students with their absolute, unquestioning acceptance of the ideal of enlightenment through science and separation of church and state. It's the perfect place—but it's not easy in the least.

A survey course in British Literature must begin with the earliest texts like *Beowulf* and spend a large amount of time on medieval authors, but I teach medieval authors whenever I can work them in throughout the course. It's become a running joke with students that I'll hit Capellanus's *Rules of Courtly Love* sometime during every semester. As an avid proponent of retaining older works in spite of student pressure to read only texts they deem easy, I insist that students not only meet a number of names they've never heard before but also take a dip into the history of our remarkable language. Ultimately, my insistence on including medieval works is not just an effort to force students to stop using the term "Dark Ages," but really to remind them that faith and learning have not always been separate, that they once were part and parcel of the same breath and thought. To understand the mileu in which this integration was the rule allows them an insight into why the two areas are apart now. To think like a medieval helps students realize what we've lost in years of separation.

On one of my soapboxes, I proclaim that we have allowed the medieval period to be cast as a dark time when there was no light, to use the terms I was taught in college. Yes, it was a chaotic, brutal time. No one can dispute that with evidence of plagues, wars, crusades, short life spans, and little knowledge of modern medicine. But we must be careful not to simply shutter the time as a backward period in the middle of two great eras, the Roman Empire and the Renaissance. Medievals ideals can still teach us today. They were more advanced in many areas than most people know, especially in the area of theology where great advances were made and many of the writers of the time still stand as classics. The very nature of their worldview can appeal to contemporary Christian scholars as we grapple with recovering the integration that medievals lived daily.

It is difficult, though, to get students to engage these texts. They often stumble over overt references to God in medieval literature. Sometimes, such references seem out of place in the plot, as in *Beowulf* when the reader moves from the glory of Heorot to the glory of God.

> Nor far was that day
> when father and son-in-law stood in feud
> for warfare and hatred that woke again.
> With envy and anger an evil spirit
> endured the dole in his dark abode,
> that he heard each day the din of revel
> high in the hall: there harps rang out,

clear song of the singer. He sang who knew
tales of the early time of man,
how the Almighty made the earth,
fairest fields enfolded by water,
set, triumphant, sun and moon
for a light to lighten the land-dwellers,
and braided bright the breast of earth
with limbs and leaves, made life for all
of mortal beings that breathe and move.[1]

To go from a bloody family feud, to evil spirit, to God as creator seems a great leap to the students; even when reading different editions, later amendments by scribes who were monks, and explanatory notations, students still don't understand how these passages could ever fit together. They pour over writers like Jerome, with his obvious misogyny and constant Biblical references, unsure what the connection is between a wicked, gossiping wife and St. Paul. Even in a more familiar work like Chaucer's *Canterbury Tales*, they struggle with Noah's flood juxtaposed against Alison's sexual escapades. What they are missing in the central ideal is that medievals lived with both intensely religious and celebratory sexual lives. Feuds, sex, evil, death—all could be answered by spiritual means and Alison and her lover can easily slip between their justified adultery and foretold Biblical devastation in a way a student in the early twenty-first century cannot.

In this essay, I will lay out a detailed plan of classroom strategies that I use to engage students with these texts and to illuminate their own worldviews with the light of the Medieval period. The lessons that follow deal with fostering an understanding of medieval culture, the importance of the Roman Catholic Church, the nature of books and learning, the medieval wheel of fate, and the juxtaposition of sex and death with salvation. Each lesson builds upon the last; as the students work their way through the three weeks allotted during the semester for these texts, they are also moving toward a different way to view the world. All the information presented, while often fun and interactive, leads us back to the twenty-first century and our own assumptions and ideas. Sometimes, I suggest at the end, we are the ones in the dark when it comes to the light of Christian learning.

Medieval Culture

To begin, the student needs to understand that the medieval period in Europe was dominated by the Catholic Church: religious institution, government, entertainment, and philosophy all rolled up in one. In a Brit lit survey, I always devote a series of discussions to exactly what a medieval person was like and what he or she believed. Designed to get the students to think as medievals, these exercises lead the class out of an American class system to a medieval structure. One of the first exercises I do is to divide the class into representatives of each major economic or social class of the time. I pick two students to be nobles and three to be their children; it always helps to have one of the noble children be a female and at least two male. Then I bunch four together as the Church, three as merchants, and tell the rest that they are peasants, usually half or more of the class. For the rest of the class period, I use the designated students when I talk about worldview of the time, explaining the societal structure of the time. The nobles, for example, always seem happy to realize that they have most of the money and land. They like to see themselves as the Knight who "loved chivalrie, / Trouthe and honour, fredom and curteisie."[2] The students as assigned to church roles don't care for the abstinence part of their lives, but they identify as fellow students with the clerk in Chaucer's party on the road to Canterbury who had "but litel gold in cofre; / But al that he myghte of his freendes hente, / On bookes and on lernynge he it spente."[3] The merchants like to know that they have money, but chafe under the notion that they have little power. The peasants, well, someone has to grow the food right? It always helps to know that some of the best intentioned of Chaucer's pilgrims are the poorest. And if the local lord cheats you at the mill when you bring your grain, some medieval plays are biting in their social critique of government and lords.

We then role-play for the rest of that specific class and I will return to these designations as we move through the next activities. Often, I will specifically disregard the peasants when discussing an issue, saying that only the nobles get to decide, and this upsets the students as they begin to understand that peasants had little to no say in the governance of their lives. Those playing noble sons do not like when faced with the choices of second sons—military or clergy—and all the young women are understandably defensive when they realize their fates are in the hands of their fathers. As one young woman said in class, "Why does it even matter that I'm noble? I don't get any choices in the matter!" Of course, the young women designated as peasants quickly noted that they had even harder lives, especially after we read Andreas Capellanus's *Art of Courtly Love* and they learn that the advice given to a noble man who desires a peasant woman is to simply take her, whether she is willing or not.[4]

What students gain from a hands-on activity like this is to begin to think outside of their contemporary worldview. My continued references to their designations makes them think in terms of a strict class system in which nobles are nobles by birth, and there is no "climbing the ladder of success" to be rich and powerful (more on that later). It also opens the door to talk about the role of the Church and how powerful and ever-present it was in medievals' lives. At Waynesburg, we have large numbers of criminal justice and forensic majors who are interested in the way justice worked during the medieval time. It stuns them to learn that the Church was a major dispenser of justice. By Chaucer's time, there were beginnings of secular lawyers and a legal system, but many a Pardoner and Summoner still worked their territories, summoning people to Church court for violations and selling pardons for sins. "Imagine," I say, "if the local Catholic Church knocked on your door and summoned you to appear before the court for engaging in premarital sex or blasphemy." "You can't legislate morality," some student inevitably cries. To think medievally, though, you have to accept that the Church was the ultimate arbitrator of right and wrong. Even kings could be called to the carpet by Church courts and officials—and many were, including Henry VIII, who petitioned the Church for a divorce from his first wife, Catherine of Aragon. All Episcopalians know where that led.

The Importance of the Roman Catholic Church

It is serious business for the students to acknowledge just how all-encompassing the Church was during the Medieval period. I walk the students through the pilgrims on the road to Canterbury, and they are amazed to see just how many are Church people: the Prioress, the Nun's Priest, the Second Nun, the Clerk, the Pardoner, the Summoner, the Parson, the Friar, and the Monk. Out of thirty-two mentioned pilgrims, almost one-third are from the Church. Students are also fascinated by the way in which Chaucer portrays these pilgrims: of the group, only the Parson and the Second Nun's tales are pious and religious. All the others have shadings from doubt to condemnation from Chaucer's narrator pilgrim. There are our bottom-of-the-barrel friends, the Summoner and Pardoner, and the Monk, who is supposed to live an austere and simple life. Of the last, Chaucer notes that he spend lots of money on hunting dogs and "He was a lord ful fat and in good point" ("Fat was this lord, he stood in goodly case").[5] Evident in the "General Prologue" is that the church in Chaucer's time was not only a large part of medieval life, but also that it suffered from corruption and decay just like any monopolizing institution. All of this helps the student come to terms with the ways in which religion was part of everyday life. It is important for students to understand that church people were involved in politics, culture, and entertainment, just as those of the secular world were involved in theology and spirituality. Chaucer's Prioress, the head of a convent, read romances just like many of Chaucer's listeners and was virulently anti-Semitic, an issue that was hotly debated during that time. To all medievals, regardless of their class or stature, religion was intertwined with all parts of life.

The State of Books and Learning

The next step I take is designed to build off this understanding of power, and corruption, to show just how dependent medievals were on the Church. I start with the established classes and talk about literacy and reading. "What, exactly, did nobles read? Did they read?" I will ask the students. They seem surprised at the numbers of the wealthy who were functionally illiterate, as well as the startling knowledge that the Church was where education happened. Yes, there were tutors and some nonreligious schools, but the Church was the central place for learning—the poor clerk of Chaucer is a great reminder. When I tell a group of nineteen-year-olds that, if they were living in 1300, they would probably be part of the clergy if they wanted to pursue an education, it is a notion that they really have to work to wrap their brains around; they are so used to the separation of church and state in contemporary K-12 education that they are almost programmed to resist the notion that knowledge resided with monks and clergy.[6] They may learn that Mendel was a monk, but they still see the science of genetics as in conflict with religious teaching. As Thomas Cahill said in his book, *How the Irish Saved Civilization*, it was the Church that collected and copied so much knowledge from the ancients and kept that knowledge alive after the fall of Rome.[7] With large repositories of books in monasteries and numbers of young monks willing to painstakingly make copies and illuminate new texts, education and learning naturally grow up around these libraries. "Here," I tell my students, "is the light in the Dark Ages, elaborately decorated, or illuminated, manuscripts of ancient books, the salvation of much of mankind's knowledge." Here is one way in which the Church, fountainhead of faith, preserved the learning and knowledge in many and all fields, for after the monks had copied religious texts, they also copied *Beowulf* and Chaucer and Langland and others, I remind the class.

To continue this discussion, I talk about the state of books and publication. Students buy and cast off cheap paperbacks without a backwards glance, and they need to be reminded that books were an expensive proposition to a medieval. The closest analogy I find that works well is to talk about textbook costs. It's not exactly the same, but the students understand the amount they spend on books for school, so they can transfer that understanding to all books. Add the illiteracy factor, and most students realize that books were a luxury only the very rich or the deep coffers of the Church could afford. What students are left with is a society where only a few held the knowledge and the ability to read and write. Everyone else is dependent upon those few to manage important tasks like legal documents, government records, and taxes. In an age when we are bombarded with information and encouraged to make up our own minds about everything from elections to celebrity hijinks, the medieval dependency on a few educated minds can seem either frighteningly silent or strangely peaceful. Students react both ways, and we open a discussion to a modern concept of Self, like those of Sigmund Freud and Jacques Lacan. Students understand the individualization of and postmodern questioning of any definition of the "I" much more than the sublimation of self to an abstraction like Fate.

At this point, students are beginning to see the light and I like to throw them a trick question: "What was the most popular book in the Medieval period?" Granted, I tell them, they didn't have a *New York Times* bestseller list, but we do know which books have the most extant copies today. By now, the students are feeling confident that they know the answer and someone will assert, "The Bible, of course." And, of course, they are wrong. Most don't know that the Bible of the medieval Catholic Church was only printed and read in Latin because they are so used to running to the store to buy one of the myriad English versions. Biblical translators, they discover, were burned at the stake for trying to bring vernacular versions of the Book to the people. They do not understand that reading and interpreting the Bible was a risky proposition then; it heightens the danger that was a part of the history of the Church. Students are fascinated to learn that medievals heard the Bible read and interpreted from the pulpit, and that people believed that only those trained (like clerks and priests) were able to address the Holy Word directly. This was more than simple illiteracy; medievals believed that education was necessary to interpret Scripture, an idea that has implications for the twenty-first-century student. Some denominations of the Christian church, like Presbyterians, still maintain that only someone with a seminary degree can be an ordained minister. Others, like Baptists, have come to believe that it is the call of God that is more important. Students learn about a fundamental difference between denominations and that the need for education to understand religious materials comes directly from the medieval time.

"So," they now want to know, "what was the book?" The answer is a book called *The Golden Legend* by Jacobus de Voragine,[8] a collection of day-to-day readings of Saint's lives. Just as our students enjoy watching television, medievals enjoyed hearing stories of all the saints who had been marytred in the cause of Christ. If they couldn't read for themselves, others could read the tales for a group. We usually read one or two of these hagiographies in class to get a flavor of what they are like. That's all it takes; the students gasp at the violent deaths, slit throats, boiling oil, rape, and other atrocities represented. Like poor St. Cecilia:

> For al the fyr, and eek the bathes heete,
> > For all the fire and all the bath's great heat,
>
> She sat al coold, and feelede no wo.
> > She sat there cool and calm and felt no woe,
>
> It made hire nat a drope for to sweete.
> > Nor did it make her any drop to sweat.
>
> But in that bath hir lyf she moste lete,
> > But in that bath her life should she lose yet;
>
> For he almachius, with ful wikke entente,
> > For he, Almachius, with bad intent,
>
> To sleen hire in the bath his sonde sente.
> > To slay her in the bath his headsman sent.
>
> Thre strokes in the nekke he smoot hire tho,
> > The executioner three times her smote
>
> The tormentour, but for no maner chaunce
> > Upon the neck, and could not strike again,
>
> He myghte noght smyte al hir nekke atwo;
> > Although he failed to cut in two her throat[9]

"Why," they ask, "would anyone want to read stories like this?" My answer is simple: "Why does anyone watch a cop show, or the evening news?" It is an easy connection to make. Those shows provide twenty-first-century watchers with scientific explanations of why we die, why bad things happen, and what's going on in the world. The world is a violent place, but works under an understandable set of rules. Saints provided medievals with an answer to death and destruction, the "why?" that all humans ask. We live, suffer, and die for Christ, to be tested in our faith. Students are comfortable with the emphasis on violence, that all life is about our faith is a challenge for them. Yet this is exactly where current ideals of faith and learning come into play. A Christian worldview should have Christ at the center of all things, although a twenty-first-century view will, by virtue of new knowledge and learning, be different from a medieval one. Now students are beginning to think about what a worldview with faith squarely at the center might look like. Granted, I tell them, I would not want to live during those times—I'm a fan of penicillin and quite happy with my administrative position—but we certainly have lost a spark in the evolution of our contemporary worldview.

The Wheel of Fate

Next, students must face one of the major tenets of a medieval worldview: the randomness of life. It helps, at this point, to play my favorite medieval game, the Wheel of Fate. A little Boethius goes a long way to pushing students more fully into a medieval mindset. I start by drawing two figures on the board:

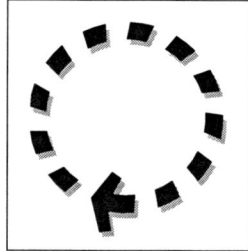

Figure 1

The first figure represents a medieval worldview based upon Boethius's ideal of the Wheel of Fate; I often use a medieval image of this concept to move them to a more complex view of this image of Fate, as seen in figure 3.

The second figure is a Modern worldview of inevitable progress and betterment. I always begin with the second figure because students' intuitively grasp the implications of the upward slope. Life, we believe today, is a journey from a beginning point (birth) to end (death). Throughout our lives, we are constantly moving "onward and upward," as C. S. Lewis puts it in *The Last Battle*.[10] Every event in our lives is one more step up the slope to

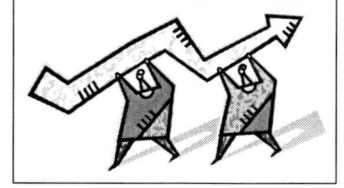

Figure 2

Figure 3

our successful end. Take human development as it's taught in most schools: babies need everything done for them, but by the time kids are two and three, they are walking and feeding themselves. Each step in an individual's evolution brings more skills and abilities that help to make the next step possible. Even the very term development houses the notion of progress. We are told by the media that each successive culture is more advanced than the last, and students' parents and grandparents are great examples of this ideal.

The Modern View of Progress

In our own lives, we use this ideal to talk about goals and where we are going. College advising is filled with questions of "what do you want to do with your life?" and "where do you see yourself in ten years?" Only slightly veiled is the idea that you will be better off in ten years; after all, that's what a college degree is for, according to so many of my students: to give them better lives, with better paying jobs, than their parents had—right? Those who don't follow the upward path are seen as failures by society at large, or eccentrics who "march to a different beat."

This focus on progress for progress's sake has a dark side that students know all too well. Many have been in my office, having chosen their major because it will get them a good job to make good money, crying and depressed because they really want to write poetry or join the Peace Corps. My general education literature courses are filled with students who are so focused on progress that they don't see any value in studying Oscar Wilde or Chaucer. I have to explain and cajole them to understand why they are here. I often share with students how, now that I have a career and family, my love of writing poetry has been shelved because it doesn't get me further along that path of progress. English majors get this since so many of them battled with well-meaning guidance counselors and parents over choosing writing and/or literature as a career.

All this focus on progress, my students tell me, leads to a very materialistic world that pressures them to succeed, be better, but they remember what they loved, memories now pressed between the pages of a high school yearbook. I walk them through the notion of control here—"Who is it that is in control of your life? Who determines if you are a success?"

"Me" is their first response. "I can be anything I want to be," they say, "and I determine what makes me happy." But then they hedge, as some suggest that society, family, government, country, and other institutions help to control their concept of who they are. They know Michel Foucault's ideal of governmentality[11] from the influences upon the formation of their world. Now, we are ready to discover Walsh and Middleton's questions of worldview: Who am I? Where am I? What's the problem?[12] By now they are coming to understand what their own worldview is; it's time to hit them with Boethius and the wheel.

I begin with a pop culture reference. "There's no Vanna White, but the Wheel of Fate is like the game show *Wheel of Fortune*. You can know the answer to the puzzle and hit lose a turn. You can have 5 Bs to buy and only get a $250 space. Bankrupt is a black sliver always lurking every time you chance the spin." I want them to see that this is what life was to a medieval;

everything that happened, every event was another spin on the Wheel of Fate where death, disease, fame, and fortune were mixed together. Unlike the popular game show, however, the medievals didn't get to spin for themselves; the Wheel spins on its own, at the whim of fate or God, and where a person ends up is completely out of his or her control. A corrupt Churchman charges you with a sin and demands payment for a pardon? The wheel has spun you downward. A Patron decides to pay you a retainer to write poetry? The wheel spins you upward. Imagine that every thing that happens to you is completely random, in the hands of God and beyond your control. How does that make you feel? Students hate to contemplate life this way. They are so sure that they are in control of their lives that it's uncomfortable to consider another way of thinking. They may not like the downside of the modern view of progress, but they dislike the medieval view of fate even more. But it is completely biblically based on the teachings of Christ. In Philippians 3:7–9, Paul says:

> But whatever was to my profit I now consider loss for the sake of Christ. What is more, I consider everything a loss compared to the surpassing greatness of knowing Christ Jesus my Lord, for whose sake I have lost all things. I consider them rubbish, that I may gain Christ and be found in him, not having a righteousness of my own that comes from the law, but that which is through faith in Christ— the righteousness that comes from God and is by faith.

Matthew tells us Jesus's admonition to his followers in 16:24–6:

> Then Jesus said to his disciples, "If anyone would come after me, he must deny himself and take up his cross and follow me. For whoever wants to save his life will lose it, but whoever loses his life for me will find it. What good will it be for a man if he gains the whole world, yet forfeits his soul? Or what can a man give in exchange for his soul?

The implications to students are clear—after explaining that they are in control of their lives, this passage speaks directly to them about loving the things of the world more than Jesus. If we are caught up in the upward race to gain more worldly goods, we have not taken up our crosses; we have not lost but are trying to gain our own lives. Progress is about gaining more of the World, and Christ is clear that this is the path to losing our very souls.

The Boethian mindset of fate is difficult, and we take the time to discuss further. Fatalism desensitizes medievals from reacting to corruption and evil in their midst; common theology of the time was that catastrophes and bad things happened because God willed it. Recent natural disasters are a good example of how some of this remains today. We've all heard someone saying that a natural disaster was God's retribution for some imagined sins, and even those who don't believe God causes disasters wonder why such tragedies happen to innocent people. Medievals accepted the corruption of the Church because it was the way things were fated to be. Without an ideal of betterment and progress, those born poor were fated always to be poor, just as nobles must be more spiritually valuable because they were born nobles. Later in the survey, I talk about the Divine Right of Kings and expound on the connections between the rise of literacy and the changing ideas about corruption and bad leadership. These exercises establish a basis that will continue throughout the whole course as we watch the changing worldview through works of literature.

By now, students pull me aside after class to say how interesting medieval literature is becoming to them. "I read 'The Miller's Tale' in high school," they confide, "but I didn't know it was so relevant to me." They are ready for the final part of their introduction to the medieval mind: the role of sex and sexuality. "How can people so steeped in faith, believing in the fated nature of their lives, and dependent upon the Church, enjoy ribald, dirty, sexual humor so much?" they ask. "Ah," I respond, "why shouldn't they? Why can't we have Noah's flood in the same story as a red hot poker and an adulterous love affair?" "Because," they sputter, "sex isn't something Christians should read, hear, or think about." To which I not too gently ask, "How many of you watch MTV, television, see movies, or read romance novels?" Just like the notion of separation of church and state in education, the separation of sex and religion came after the medieval period. We will see those changes when we encounter texts in the Renaissance, the English Civil War, and the Puritans, especially during discussions of the closing of the theatres during Cromwell's reign. Now, we look at texts like "The Wife of Bath's Tale" and "The Miller's Tale" and talk about sex and the church.

To a medieval, the earthy parts of life, including bodily humor, sex, adultery, and romance were part of who they were. To deny sexuality was to deny God's first directive to all humankind: "Be fruitful and increase in number" (Gen. 1:28). The Bible, after all, is filled with sexual escapades, despite what I learned in Sunday school as a child. "The Song of Solomon" extols the love of a man and a woman in explicit terms that many read only metaphorically. David slept with Bathsheba, Solomon had his wives, Dinah was raped, and Lot's daughters slept with their father. Sex can be fun for a medieval, and romances were very popular tales told in courts and small towns. Students read a few of these and quickly see that adulterers and old men who covet young wives are likely to end up humiliated and embarrassed. Like Saint's lives, fun fabliaux-type tales also reminded their audiences how quickly the wealthy and powerful can fall, and allowed listeners to laugh as protagonists brought themselves down through their own greed and corruption.

Though crude, "The Summoner's Tale," by Chaucer, is a biting commentary on the greediness of the Church. After the poor father who has lost his only son tricks the Friar in the tale by farting on his hand, the Church's worry is how to share the proceeds:

Who sholde make a demonstracion
Who should make a logical proof

That every man sholde have yliche his part
That every man should have equally his part

As of the soun or savour of a fart?
As of the sound or odor of a fart?

O nyce, proude cherl, I shrewe his face!
Oh ingenious, proud churl, I curse his face!13

Many students have read "The Miller's Tale" in high school, although I find that some had heavily censored versions that omitted the funniest passages and made the story disjointed and impossible to understand. Others simply didn't understand the tale because once we wend our way through barrels strung up in the attic and get to Nicholas's bare behind out the window, they are amazed. These are the same students who know every funny line from the latest bawdy comedy films, but they cannot picture a medieval noble laughing at bathroom humor. Joking about beards and branding? Throughout the tale, I point out how the antics of the main characters are directly related to their own sins and lack of faith. John, the old husband who marries a young wife, clearly has problems:

This carpenter hadde wedded newe a wyf,
This carpenter had recently wedded a wife,

Which that he lovede moore than his lyf;
Whom he loved more than his life;

Of eighteteene yeer she was of age.
She was eighteen years of age.

Jalous he was, and heeld hire narwe in cage,
Jealous he was, and held her narrowly in confinement,

For she was wylde and yong, and he was old
> For she was wild and young, and he was old

And demed hymself been lik a cokewold.
> And believed himself likely to be a cuckold.

He knew nat Catoun, for his wit was rude,
> He knew not Cato, for his wit was rude,

That bad man sholde wedde his simylitude.
> Who advised that man should wed his equal.

Men sholde wedden after hire estaat,
> Men should wed according to their status in life,

For youthe and elde is often at debaat.
> For youth and old age are often in conflict.

But sith that he was fallen in the snare,
> But since he was fallen in the snare,

He moste endure, as oother folk, his care.
> He must endure, like other folk, his troubles.[14]

That John "loved her more than his life" is funny precisely because many rich old noble men or men with money married young girls in the hopes of having sons. That the husbands might not be able to keep the "wild and young" wife in line is also true and funny. Even today when they see an old celebrity or tycoon married to a young girl, students admit to finding the situation funny, yet feeling uncomfortable at the same time. Mixed up in the sexual escapades of Nicholas, the boarder in John's house, and Alison, the young wife, is a serious warning about listening to false prophets. Nicholas convinces John that a second flood is imminent in order to get him tucked into a barrel in the attic while the two adulterous lovers share a night together, but the plan unravels when Alison's other suitor, an erstwhile courtly lover, comes calling at the window. What ensues is hilarious antics involving bare bottoms, windows, kisses, and a red hot poker. All the lies comes together when Nicholas, whose bare bottom was kissed by that same poker, lets out an anguished yell of "Help! Water! Water! Help, for Goddes herte!"[15] As John cuts the rope on his barrel, ready for the flood of water, the sins of all are revealed; the wheel spins, the fun night of sex comes to an end, and students enjoy the well-crafted, funny tale. Maybe, they think, medievals were not so different from the way we are today.

After our short time in with the medievals, students often come away with a deeper understanding of a very different worldview, one in which faith was an integral part of every day thought and knowledge. My goal is to prepare

90

them for the separation that comes next, with the rise of science and reason, and offer them a historical background for why faith and learning are separate today. It's not an easy task, as I must first make them aware of their own worldview in order to step outside of it, but it is a very hands-on way to bring them, however briefly, into a perspective that is alien to their thinking. These exercises allow them to be more critical in their ability to critique other worldviews that influence them today and allow them a glimpse into what complete integration of faith looked like in the past, so they might conceive of a way to bring the two back together in the twenty-first century. Next time they watch the latest crime scene procedural drama, I challenge them, try to think like a medieval and see the ways in which a worldview is at work informing the show. This is the greatest skill I can leave them with, the ability to stand outside of their own cultural values for a moment to truly be illuminated by another way of conceptualizing the world and, most importantly, themselves.

Endnotes

1   *Beowulf*, trans. Francis Grummere, lines I.31–46, available at http://etext.library. adelaide.edu.au/b/beowulf/b48g/chapter1.html (accessed June 14, 2005).

2   Geoffrey Chaucer, "General Prologue," *The Canterbury Tales*, in *The Riverside Chaucer*, 3rd ed., ed. Larry Benson (Boston: Houghton Mifflin, 1987), lines 45–6.

3   Ibid., lines 298–300.

4   Andreas Capellanus, *The Art of Courtly Love* (New York: Columbia Press, 1990).

5   Geoffrey Chaucer, line 200.

6   A colleague reading this section during a scholarship discussion group raised an interesting question about students from parochial schools. At Waynesburg University, our students are predominately from local school districts; our population of students from parochial or religious schools is growing, but they are a very small minority. Thus, I rarely have a response outside of the ones noted in the essay. I do have students who know their Bibles well and are themselves strongly faithful to their beliefs, but most are very compartmentalized from their educational experiences. I imagine that responses to these exercises would be different as schools with different student populations.

7   Thomas Cahill, *How the Irish Saved Civilization* (Anchor Books, 1996).

8   Jacobus de Voragine, *The Golden Legend*, trans. Granger Ryan and Helmut Ripperger (New York: Arno, 1969).

9   Jeffrey Chaucer, "The Second Nun's Tale," *The Canterbury Tales*, in *The Riverside Chaucer*, lines 520–8. Translation of this and all other Chaucer passages from *Elf*

Presents The Canterbury Tales, http://www.canterburytales.org/canterbury_tales. html (accessed on September 12, 2008).

10   C. S. Lewis, *The Last Battle* (New York: Collier Books, 1970).

11   Michel Foucault's idea of governmentality is spread throughout his works, beginning with his lecture entitled "Governmentality," delivered in 1978 at the College de France.

12   Brian J. Walsh and J. Richard Middleton, *The Transforming Vision: Shaping a Christian Worldview* (Downers Grove, IL: Intervarsity Press, 1984).

13   Jeffrey Chaucer, "The Summoner's Tale," *The Canterbury Tales,* in *The Riverside Chaucer,* lines 2224–7.

14   Jeffrey Chaucer, "The Miller's Tale," *The Canterbury Tales,* in *The Riverside Chaucer,* lines 3221–32.

15   Ibid., 3815.

FOSTERING FAITHFUL MINDS IN THE EARLY WORLD LITERATURE SURVEY

CHAD ENGBERS (CALVIN COLLEGE)

Chad Engbers earned his Ph.D. in early modern English literature from the Catholic University of America in 2003. He teaches early modern British literature, world litera-ture, and Russian literature at Calvin College. He believes that any college-level literature course should help students to develop faithful minds, minds ready to enter into dialogue with non-Christian voices, balancing respect for the autonomy of those other voices with a commitment to one's own position. He finds that Mikhail Bakhtin's concept of the poly-phonic novel serves as a useful model for this kind of balance. The early world literature survey helps to him to develop such minds because it includes a broad range of voices, often explicitly religious, that are far afield from students' ordinary experience. Students, Chad says, can be encouraged to enter this world of other voices as Christ entered the world of human beings: as an equal, but without sacrifice of spiritual identity. Studying the com-plexities of translation gives students an appreciation of otherness; studying the ideas of unfamiliar cultures can refresh students' understanding of their own commitments.

Faithful Minds

Like many people who take "the integration of faith and learning" seriously, I have reservations about that phrase itself. The word "integration" suggests that faith and learning are naturally separate domains that can be joined by cleverness or sheer force of will. I prefer to think of them as domains with con-siderable overlap in their natural state. As Ralph C. Wood observes elsewhere in this volume, "Christian tradition knows no sharp distinction between soul and mind" (212). Now, it is true that faith and learning can seem like separate enterprises. We can overlook our religious commitments in our scholarship and pedagogy, for instance, and we can attempt to put our academic habits aside when we pray or go to church. But such apparent separation of faith and learning is illusory. The worldview shaped by our faith is not easily put aside in the offices and the classroom, nor are the intellectual instincts shaped by teaching and scholarship easily abandoned when we are at worship or prayer.

We simply need to pay attention, to see the countless ways in which the challenges of higher education and the challenges of faith are the same, or at least similar. The task of Christian education is generally not the willful integration of faith and learning, but rather patient recognition of the common ground that faith and learning already share. As professors of literature, for instance, our task is not simply to give good notes on the readings, but to develop faithful minds. And a faithful mind, as I understand it, happens to share many habits and abilities that are valued by the academy at large, although Christians are likely to value them for slightly different reasons. In this essay, I will focus on two such qualities of the faithful mind, and I will describe some of the ways in which a survey of early world literature is uniquely suited to developing them.

Faithful minds exhibit what William G. Perry, Jr., has called "Commitment in Relativism," a phrase that includes both of the qualities I will be discussing: an understanding of many other viewpoints, complemented by a faithfulness to one's own viewpoint. A faithful Christian mind is committed to Christ, of course, but it also attempts to understand and interact with myriad non-Christian points of view. Such a mind is not only turned inward in contemplation of the soul, or upward in contemplation of God, but also outward in active engagement with God's world. Moreover, a faithful mind is likely to blur these inward, upward, and outward categories: we worship God, in part, by learning about and caring for his world and the creatures in it.

A useful literary model for the faithful mind is Mikhail Bakhtin's concept of the polyphonic novel. A polyphonic novel is one in which the author develops a position and voice of his or her own, but presents that position and voice as only one among many competing voices of relatively equal authority. It is important to remember that the author of a polyphonic novel does remain committed to his or her own ideas amid the noise of other voices. Authors naturally have advantages over the characters they create: they can employ omniscient narrators, cast some characters as foils or caricatures, and tweak the plot so that particular characters succeed or are punished. A polyphonic novelist employs none of these devices to privilege his or her own voice over those of the characters. He or she lets those characters develop and speak naturally and authoritatively. Such a novel is not essentially a thesis but an event.

A polyphonic novel enables dialogue by respecting the autonomy of other voices. This respect can be seen by comparing polyphony to dogmatism and relativism. A dogmatic novel ultimately contains only one true voice—that of the author. Disagreeing voices are occasionally allowed in a dogmatic novel, but they are always overruled. The author of a polyphonic novel respects other voices by allowing them to remain autonomous others, not puppets or caricatures. At the same time, these other voices do not drown out the author's own voice in a sea of relativism. Relativism is not dialogue, because it presents all viewpoints as arbitrary, allowing an individual to remain uncommitted to any view in particular. Dialogue, in Bakhtin's sense, requires a commitment to one's own voice. As Bakhtin himself writes, "the polyphonic approach has nothing in common with relativism (or with dogmatism).... [I]t should be noted that both relativism and dogmatism equally exclude ... all authentic dialogue, by making it either unnecessary (relativism) or impossible (dogmatism)."[1]

Bakhtin's ideal sounds wonderful, of course, but true polyphony is a tall order. A few years ago, a student who had just listened to my lecture on the polyphonic novel looked at me skeptically and asked, "Can a novel like that really be written by a single person?" I replied: "Not most people."[2] The concept of a polyphonic novel is useful as a pedagogical model not only because it serves as a caution against dogmatism and relativism—both of which pose real dangers in a world literature classroom—but because it can remind us as professors just how much we are asking of our students. A polyphonic stance, remaining committed in the midst of Relativism, is a cognitive ability that is beyond the reach of most students in a literature survey course.

But it is a worthy ambition, not only to further intellectual maturity, but because polyphony is a way to fulfill our Christian calling to understand and engage the world through our commitments to Christ. A polyphonic reader is *in* the world but not entirely *of* that world. Or, while we are juggling prepositions, we might say that a polyphonic reader is *with* the world, interacting with other voices on an equal basis, neither conquering them dogmatically nor surrendering to them relativistically.[3]

To get "with it" in this sense, students need to understand the literature they read not as abstractions in a book, but as actual voices in the world. Bakhtin describes the polyphonic novel as "not a system ... but a concrete event made up of organized human orientations and voices."[4] The Russian word Bakhtin uses for "event," here and elsewhere, is *sobytie*, which can literally be translated as "with-being." A polyphonic novel is an event, a with-being: the author's voice and all of the other voices are neither above nor below each other but *with* each other on the same plane. Christians have a model for this attitude in Christ himself: Emmanuel, God-with-us. We serve a savior who first served us, not counting equality with God a thing to be grasped but utterly entering the world of human bodies and ideas and words. He did not lose his kinship to the Father in moving among the world of Greeks, Romans, and Jews; in fact, it is that very kinship that made his time among earthly masses productive and meaningful.[5] We often speak of a Christian witness, but perhaps we ought also to speak of a Christian *withness*, because Christ himself performed his witnessing by moving among autonomous others as their equal.

The early world literature survey course offers two advantages for Christian students developing faithful minds in the polyphonic sense described above. First, it includes voices further removed from students' typical experience than those in many other literature courses; second, many of these voices are explicitly religious. Compare, for example, a course on the novels of Jane Austen. Christianity is an implicit part of Austen's England, but it is so much in the background that addressing it in any explicit and sustained way might feel arbitrary and forced. It is otherness that enables dialogue. Although Christianity is much more distant, in both time and space, from Akhenaten than it is from Austen, that pharaoh's hymn to the sun is at least of a genre that not only allows but demands religious inquiry.

The following essay is divided into two sections, corresponding to the two qualities of a faithful mind as described above. In the first, I suggest several ways for giving students a polyphonic understanding of the world by introducing them to other traditions without judging those traditions dogmatically. In the second, I suggest ways for students to develop a stronger sense of self from their encounters with other traditions, deepening and refreshing their own commitments rather than drowning in relativism. The sequence of this essay therefore roughly follows Perry's scheme, beginning with what he might label "Multiplicity" or "Relativism" and proceeding to what he would call "Commitment." My own syllabus is not everywhere structured this neatly; several of the examples I give in the second half of the essay are taken from the first few weeks of the course. I do, however, emphasize Commitment much more heavily later in the semester.

A World of Others

To develop a polyphonic sense of the world, students need to respect the otherness and autonomy of other voices, and they should understand how autonomous voices might relate to one another. Both of these phenomena—the otherness of other voices and the relationships that arise among those voices—can be made concrete by confronting issues of translation. One of the first problems faced by any teacher of world literature, in Christian and secular contexts alike, is the problem of teaching texts in a language other than the one in which those texts were originally written. It is no mystery that some meaning becomes lost or distorted in any translation, but these losses and distortions are particularly grievous in the case of literature, because the meaning in literary texts so often rests heavily on those very forms and nuances that are damaged in the move to a new language.

When my Russian Literature course arrives at Symbolist poetry—poems whose very soul is their sounds—I teach my students to read a few lines in Russian. I provide a strictly literal translation and also a phonetic translation, which we rehearse several times until the class can read them, if not fluently, at least fluidly. It might seem at first as if these materials would help students to cross the gulf separating English from Russian, bringing them much closer to the original text, and the activity does enable me to point out internal rhymes lost in the English translation they have read. But I suspect that in fact the exercise further distances them from the original, showing them just how deep and wide the linguistic gulf truly is. The sounds of Russian, especially those thick clumps of consonants, do not come easily to the American tongue, and my students struggle with words that a native Russian speaker would scarcely notice.

And even if I could somehow bring students across the linguistic gap, there would still be a cultural gap. The poems of Anna Akhmatova, for instance, are filled with direct references and indirect connotations lost on an audience with no real experience of the Soviets or their legacy. Several of Akhmatova's poems, moreover, are written in rhyming couplets that would sound antiquated to a Western reader, although much Russian poetry still follows such traditional forms. Akhmatova's translator D.M. Thomas has observed, "in Russian poetry one can still, so to speak, rhyme 'love' with 'dove.'"[6] Many translators of Akhmatova transfer her aesthetic into a modern Western context by rendering even her rhyming poems in free verse. In short, I can make my students read Russian, but I cannot make them Russians.

With early world literature, the linguistic and cultural gaps are greater still. Russian Symbolism, after all, is not terribly far removed from us. It developed in historical and literary contexts that are well documented and fairly well understood. For the earliest world literature, on the other hand, large portions of both text and context are missing altogether. We know comparatively little, for example, about the culture that produced *Gilgamesh*, and our text of that earliest epic poem consists of a scattering of twelve stone tablets, most of which have been damaged or broken into several pieces. Many of these pieces are missing, leaving actual gaps in the original text of this ancient epic. The *Longman Anthology of World Literature* offers ellipses in square brackets and footnotes to indicate where the text is incomplete. The *Norton Anthology of World Literature* ignores these gaps or silently fills them in, in either case giving the illusion of a complete text. At least a few students are scandalized by this revelation.

It is tempting for professors to follow the *Norton* in glossing over these losses and gaps, to treat the translations in the anthology as if they were the original texts. It is important to foreground issues of translation, however, for two reasons. First, it is only fair to admit one's inability to completely apprehend the original text. Such failure is no cause for shame—can we ever fully understand a text exactly as it was written?—but it is cause for honesty and humility. Second, translation troubles offer students a unique way to understand and respect the otherness of other voices.

My students write a comparative translation paper, in which they find two additional translations of some short passage from the anthology and compose their own translation of the passage, drawing freely from their various sources. More important than these derivative translations—which tend to be mediocre at best—are the essays that accompany them, in which students characterize each of the translations they have used and justify their own choices as translators.

If it is impossible to translate a few lines of poetry accurately, it is all the more important to acknowledge our limitations when it comes to understanding another religion. Before teaching the Five Pillars of Islam or the Four Noble Truths of Buddhism, I ask students to imagine that we must prepare a presentation on the essentials of Christianity for an audience who knows nothing about it. We get four or five bullet points, no more. I ask students to come up with the points while I take notes on the board. I am consistently impressed at students' ability to assemble and refine an impressive summary in about ten minutes, and I am always able to express honest admiration for their work. In all of the semesters I have done this exercise, however, no class has ever come up with a list that even distinguishes Catholic from Protestant. There is nothing in the list about the real presence, or infant baptism, or church attendance, or abortion. It is a good list, even an excellent one, but it does not tell anyone what it is really like to be a Christian. I then proceed to Islam with the humble admission that I have never been a Muslim or a Buddhist, so I do not know what it is really like to practice those faiths, and the lists I am about to give are inadequate to that task.

It is worthwhile to study other faiths, despite our inability to understand them perfectly, for the same reason that it is worthwhile to study the riddled text of *Gilgamesh*: the portions that we can understand give us insight into another culture and possibly help us to think about our own culture in fresh terms. But such study must proceed in humble recognition of its limitations. And it must proceed with due diligence, going beyond bulleted lists of beliefs to somehow demonstrate the complexity and vitality of another system of beliefs. It is not enough to acknowledge that a five-point list is reductive, and then to stop at a five-point list.

One way to respect the autonomy of an unfamiliar faith tradition is to search for conflicts within that tradition itself.[7] Sufism and mainstream Islam, for instance, offer useful critiques of one another, and the *Thousand and One Nights* offers yet a third view of Middle Eastern culture, one where Islam is more of a cultural backdrop than an explicit concern. It is wise to present a specific culture not as a single voice in the global dialogue, but as a polyphonic event in and of itself.[8]

Students quickly reach a point where they wonder—or should wonder—why we read world literature in the first place if the linguistic and cultural gaps are so great. In my own mind, I justify the study of world literature, in large part, because of the advantages it offers in developing a faithful mind: it helps students to develop an appreciation for the worlds of others, and it helps them to develop their own positions in those worlds. World literature can help any student to develop cognitively and ethically, but the ability to negotiate gaps and maintain integrity is particularly important for Christians who are finding their place in a largely non-Christian world.

To students, I justify our study of literature in translation by suggesting that reading world literature is in fact a deluxe version of the literary experience. The challenges we face in reading world literature are the same challenges faced by any reader; they are simply larger and more obvious in relation to world literature, making them easier to address explicitly. For example, Wolfgang Iser has described all literary reading as a matter of filling in gaps in the text.[9] Fiction writers know this truth instinctively: it would be pointless to describe every physical feature of a character. The writer chooses a handful of telling details, and the reader fills in the rest. This phenomenon can be illustrated quickly by asking students the color of Gilgamesh's hair. Although this information is given nowhere in the text, students probably have a specific idea—even if it is no more specific than "not blonde." This is a gap they have filled in, as they do in all literature. But in world literature, the gaps tend to be greater (and sometimes, as in the case of *Gilgamesh*, more literal).

More significant than the literal and conceptual gaps in early world literature, however, is the fact that readers are able to cross them. Despite the gaping holes in our knowledge of the historical *Gilgamesh*, modern readers traverse the distance between their world and his with surprising ease, returning to their own place and time with meaning that is imperfect and incomplete, but nonetheless real. What was meaningful for the ancient Akkadians is still meaningful when it is transferred across centuries and continents.

And transference is yet another basic quality of literature, where it often takes the shape of a metaphor. The words "metaphor" and "transfer" contain a common root: the Greek verb *pherein*, "to bear, to carry." *Pherein* is teasingly close to the Germanic word *fare*, the root of our word "ferry."[10] All literature ferries meaning from one thing to another, whether it is between "my love" and "a red, red rose," or whether it is a reader transferring the strength of friendship from Enkidu and Gilgamesh into more modern contexts for camaraderie.

Although there have of course been numerous theories of metaphor, one that works particularly well in the early world literature course is the cognitive linguistic model explained by George Lakoff and Mark Turner in *More Than Cool Reason: A Field Guide to Poetic Metaphor*.[11] Lakoff and Turner describe metaphor as "conceptual mapping" between two domains: a "source domain" is mapped onto a "target domain." When we say "my love is like a red, red rose," we are mapping the source domain of "red, red rose" onto the target domain of "my love."[12] We transfer one set of ideas onto a second, understanding one in terms of another.

Again, the early world literature course offers particularly dramatic examples of a phenomenon that is inherent to all literature (and, as the cognitive linguists would argue, to human thought itself). In this course, the ferries have traveled further, and are often quite literal: the stone tablets of *Gilgamesh* were physically shipped to England before they were known to the world, transported from the ruined library of an ancient king to the British Museum, where they were painstakingly restored by scholars seeking, among other things, corroboration for the flood story in Genesis.

The transfer of world literature from one culture to another does involve heavy losses, but it also presents the opportunity for substantial gains. In fact, David Damrosch has described world literature as "works that gain in translation."[13] World literature gains precisely because it is read in a culture other than its own, and this otherness enables dialogue. A case in point is the Egyptian love lyrics, written on papyrus by a eunuch working in the necropolis. Damrosch writes:

> It is a mistake to look in these poems for a direct transcription either of the scribe's experience or our own. Reading this poetry today, we triangulate between our world, the real world of Thebes three thousand years ago, and the erotic world that the poems project outward from the necropolis. . . .[14]

In other words, even a very short lyric poem becomes an event, a with-being involving multiple parties. The truth is that all literature creates such triangulations; a reader always maps his or her own experiences and expectations onto a text to some extent.[15] This mapping can be difficult to see when the real world of the author and the projected world of the text are close to the reader's own world, but with world literature the distances between these realms are greater and thus easier to recognize.

Two chapters from Damrosch's book *What is World Literature?* offer useful case studies in the ways ancient texts have been ferried into modern languages and cultures. The first chapter, "Gilgamesh's Quest," tells the story of the explorers who discovered the tablets of *Gilgamesh*, along with the mixed motivations for seeking the remaining tablets.[16] In the fourth chapter, "Love in the Necropolis," Damrosch returns to the original hieroglyphics of a handful of Egyptian lyrics and compares several modern translations of them, discussing the various gains and losses made by each. Both of these chapters help students to situate these texts in a world of others—not only the other culture that originally produced them, but the other cultures through which the texts have been translated and transmitted to us.

Another way to talk about the dynamics of transfer in world literature is to show the intertextual conversations and triangulations already happening among ancient texts themselves. Two of the pieces I use to demonstrate this kind of dialogue happen to come from the Bible. The first is Genesis 1:2, which we read immediately following the creation account from the *Enuma Elish*. When the opening lines of Genesis describe darkness on the face of the deep, the word the author has used for "deep" is *tehom*, derived from the same word as Tiamat, the slaughtered goddess whose carcass becomes the world in the *Enuma Elish*. The same word, when ferried into the Judaic tradition, takes on a much different meaning: the thing that *is* the created world in the Babylonian text is merely the precursor to the created world in Genesis.[17]

A second example is the Song of Songs, which we read immediately following the Egyptian love lyrics, whose echoes in the biblical book are quite easy to hear. Some students, eager to dismiss the erotic nature of Song of Songs, explain that the sexual love of the man for the woman is symbolic of the love of God for the Church. This interpretation is a clear case of metaphor, mapping the source domain of erotic love onto the target domain of divine love.[18]

To visually demonstrate this transfer, I show them a verse from the 1560 *Geneva Bible*: "My doove, that art in the holes of the rocke, in the secret places of the staires, shewe me thy sight, let me heare thy voice: for thy voyce is swete, and thy sight comelie."[19] I use the *Geneva Bible* because it contains substantial marginal glosses, neatly segregating source and target domains onto different parts of the page. The passage about the hiding dove is glossed as follows: "Thou that art ashamed of thy sins, come & shewe thy self unto me." Does the original verse clearly seem to be about repentance? And if it is not, is it wrong to map the concept of a sinner onto the dove? And if the original really is about repentance—as certain students will insist—then might we read some of the racier Egyptian love poems from the previous class in the same way? The world of others is a terribly messy place, especially when we begin mapping one concept onto another.

At this point, I usually think it wise to reassure students that I am not attempting to undermine holy Scripture by relating it to "secular" literature. On the contrary, I am attempting to portray the text of the Bible in a thoroughly Christian light. I plainly state my own belief in the divine inspiration of the Bible, but I observe that it should not surprise us to find God using human forms and metaphors through which to breathe his holy word. After all, if Christ himself—the Logos, the Word—assumed human form, surely the Bible might work in a similarly incarnational way, assuming human forms, a word-with-us.

In short, the world of others is a world of gaps and maps, a place where gulfs in language and understanding are constantly crossed by ferries connecting one culture to an other. It is a place of epiphanies and misunderstandings, a place where a single text is usually subjected to multiple interpretations, many of which contradict one another. It is this eventful world that Christ himself entered as Emmanuel, and it is this world in which his followers, too, are called to take a place.

A Sense of Self

Gaining a sense of self in a world of others, developing true Commitment while acknowledging Relativism, is a lifelong project for any person, and students who populate an early world literature course have frequently just begun that project. Patience is prudent. There are two ways to help students develop a sense of self in the early world literature classroom. The first is to work with the ideas that they already have—although they might not know they have them—by bringing those ideas into polyphonic conversation with voices from the world of others. The second way is for students to use such conversations to generate ideas that are new. It is important to recognize that for some students the first approach—acknowledging and questioning existing ideas—is very difficult, and the second is nearly impossible.

It is also important to acknowledge that both approaches are a matter of Christian perspective. Many students assume that "Christian perspective" on world literature is a more or less standard set of judgments that Christians would make about the rightness or wrongness of particular pieces of literature. Ordinarily, a professor can summarize these judgments, telling students what Christians think about Buddhism, Hinduism, and so forth. In my view, Christian perspective is ultimately something that should be fostered in students, not offered to them. Ideally, they will come to understand Christian perspective as something that shoots out of their own eyes. Whether they are looking at their existing ideas or spying out new positions to occupy, students should do so through the eyes of faith.

Christian professors are commonly asked how their classes differ from the same classes at a secular school. Whenever I face this question, I am tempted to turn it over to my students: "How do *you* approach this course differently from the way you would approach it in a secular school?" To place the onus for Christian perspective entirely on the students, however, would be unfair to students who are just learning how to be circumspect about their own paradigms, and it would not accurately reflect my own pedagogical methods. The truth is that I am a Christian, that it is largely my own questions about literature that shape the syllabus and daily class sessions, and that I try to be very explicit about the ways in which my faith informs the questions I ask. In other words, I attempt to model for students what it is like to have a sense of self in the world of others by being frank and forthright about how my own commitments have shaped the course.[20] Of course, many students too easily adopt the professor's voice as their own, so I spend most of the semester attempting to foster students' own autonomous voices, first by helping them to discern the voices they already have, and then by helping them to develop their voices on their own.

You are somewhere. This is the truth that I emphasize to students from the very first days of the semester. One of the first ways I make this point to students is by asking them to fill out a brief questionnaire—four questions, each with four or five numbered answers—about what they think is most important in literature: the author's opinion, the reader's reaction, whether the text is realistic, and so forth. I distribute the form at the end of one class as homework for the next (see Appendix B).

In the next session, I ignore the questionnaires at first and spend a great deal of time introducing the different aspects of a literary text that people might emphasize.[21] I use the four basic critical categories that M. H. Abrams identifies in the *Mirror and the Lamp*, and I use a particular poem that we have read—usually one of the Egyptian lyrics—to make the categories concrete. Abrams himself arranges the four categories into the familiar rhetorical triangle, with the "work" in the center and arrows pointing out in three directions to "universe," "artist," and "audience."[22] The diagram that I show to students, however, is re-configured as a Cartesian plane:

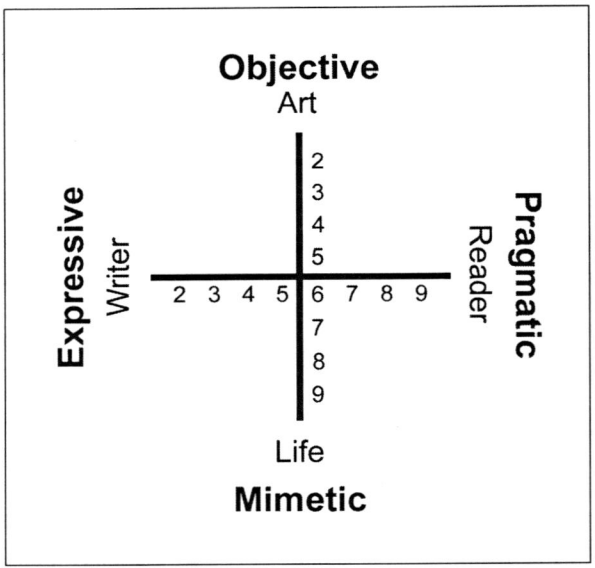

The advantage of arranging the material in this way is that the four concepts become compass points, and particular critical positions can be mapped. If we read an ancient Egyptian love lyric only to learn about the feelings of an ancient Egyptian, for instance, we are working in the southwest quadrant (between "Expressive" and "Mimetic"): we would be using the text to talk about the author's life. If we take up Wolfgang Iser's concern with textual gaps, on the other hand, we move into the northeast quadrant, because we have become concerned with the ways in which artistic structures influence a reader's experience.[23] Students generally listen patiently and attentively to this material, taking diligent notes. Up until this point in the class, the four-pointed map on

My range of texts... hundred, perhaps... styles... neuvian... [illegible handwritten note] ...whole... [illegible]

the screen is a world of others, an abstract representation of positions held by those strange creatures called literary critics.

"Where do you think *I* am?" I ask them, "and why?" After we have discussed my own critical orientation—and its influence on the syllabus, paper assignments, and lesson plans—I ask them the question of the hour: "Where are you?" Only then do I place the numbers along each axis of the diagram, and I ask students to get out their questionnaires. Adding their numbered answers to the first two questions will give them their position on the vertical axis; the sum of the second two questions places them horizontally. The numbers are contrived so that it is impossible to fall in the exact center of either axis.

"You are somewhere," I tell students. "You were on this map before you even knew there was a map. You have assumptions about what literature is and how to read it, and although you might move all over the critical map in the course of reading even a short lyric poem, there is probably one quadrant where you feel most at home. The same is true of the translators who have transmitted these ancient texts to us, of the editors who have gathered them into our anthology, and of the professor who assigns and teaches these texts. And knowing these positions can enrich the event that is a piece of world literature. But the main point is that you yourself are somewhere."

The questionnaire that students bring to class on this day is one example of a useful pedagogical strategy. It is easy for literature courses to fall into a two-part pattern: students read something and then react to it. Especially early in the semester, however, it can be very difficult for students to formulate their own reactions to a deluge of foreign material. Their own ideas drown in a sea of new ones. They are hesitant to speak in class—even when called upon—not because they are shy or reticent but because it is difficult to absorb strange new material and to formulate their own personal ideas at the same time. Even reaction papers demand this kind of cognitively demanding multitasking.

It is often helpful to employ a three-part pattern: students document their own ideas, then read the text, and then return to their original ideas through the ideas of the text. Students come to the critical compass class with their own place already mapped out by their answers to the questionnaire. It is often a good idea to assign *preaction* papers, papers in which students formulate their own ideas on a topic that will be addressed in a piece that they are about to read. Such papers tend to be more honest records of students' actual opinions, unaffected by their gut-level reactions to some strange new text.

Preaction discussions also work well in class. I frequently begin a session on the Bhagavad Gita, for instance, by asking students how they know what they should be doing with their lives. After an honest ten-minute discussion,

How does an assumption differ from a prejudice?

Ex. / The more/leum... the exercise (kind of conversation opener)—add one—but also (one) much out, such (ode) the instructor's foresight / and/d disposal...

institutional implications?

105

which I record in notes on the board, we consider the dialogue between Arjuna and Krishna, returning to the notes on the board in the last ten minutes of class to discuss ways in which *dharma* resembles and differs from the criteria they have described.

Whereas reaction papers tend to represent a student's last thought on a subject—and often they are impulsive and tentative thoughts—a preaction paper or discussion invites one to return to his or her thoughts with the new perspective offered by new material. The text becomes not a springboard for new ideas, but a lens through which to view old ideas in a new light. World literature is particularly useful in this regard, but like gaps and metaphors, the power of renewal has long been understood as a basic part of the literary experience. The Russian Formalist Viktor Shklovsky, for example, sees literature as a remedy for stale, habitual perceptions and ideas:

> Habitualization devours works, clothes, furniture, one's wife, and the fear of war. . . . And art exists that one may recover the sensation of life; it exists to make one feel things, to make the stone *stony*. The purpose of art is to impart the sensation of things as they are perceived and not as they are known. The technique of art is to make objects 'unfamiliar,' to make forms difficult, to increase the difficulty and length of perception because the process of perception is an aesthetic end in itself and must be prolonged.[24]

World literature is unfamiliar and often opaque, but for Shklovsky these are not only key ingredients in literariness, but they are precisely what makes literature refreshing and productive for a reader. The concept of *dharma* seems strange and confining to many American students, but when Arjuna's dilemma in the Bhagavad Gita is discussed as a matter of vocation, students not only find insight into the Hindu warrior, but they find fresh terms in which to consider their own familiar questions of career and calling. Opacity is a form of othernesss, after all, and literature's otherness enables dialogue. A similar point is made, in surprising similar terms, by J. R. R. Tolkien.[25] Although Tolkien is attempting to describe the particular powers of fairy stories, the power of "Recovery" that he identifies in such stories resonates with Shklovsky's claims for all literature:

> Recovery (which includes return and a renewal of health) is a regaining—regaining of a clear view. I do not say 'seeing things as they are' and involve myself with the philosophers, though I might venture to say 'seeing things as we are (or were) meant to see them'— as things apart from ourselves. We need, in any case, to clean our

windows; so that the things seen clearly may be freed from the drab blur of triteness or familiarity—from possessiveness. . . .[26]

In short, literature offers us the opportunity to see our own perceptions and commitments as other, as "things apart from ourselves."[27] My students, for example, are all too familiar with the language of "vocation" and "calling"; the Bhagavad Gita offers them a chance to think about their careers in the unfamiliar terms of *dharma*. Perhaps they envy the predictability of that ancient Hindu concept; perhaps they find it impersonal compared to a God who calls people by name. In either case, they have examined some of their own commitments from another point of view.

It is also possible to assign modest reaction papers that then become preaction papers. For example, the Hindu concept of *atman* can be taught by starting not with the Vedas or *Upanishads,* and not with any definitions or examples, but with the *Heidelberg Catechism.* Students are shown the first question of the catechism, and the first part of the answer to that question: "Q. What is your only comfort in life and in death? A. That I am not my own, but belong—body and soul, in life and in death—to my faithful savior Jesus Christ."[28] Most students at a Christian college or university should have little trouble writing a page or two reacting to this idea. In fact, it is prudent to ask specific questions to prevent mindless recitation of platitudes. Is this answer something students believe, or something they would like to believe? And if they do believe that they are not their own, is that belief actually comforting? What parts of real life make such a statement difficult?

At the beginning of the next class, students will be more ready to think polyphonically about certain Hindu concepts. Ancient Hindu texts teach that Brahman is all that exists. Variously described as a god, a set of gods, and a universal life essence, Brahman extends into everything and everyone. We are drops of salt water cast upward by a wave; eternal Brahman is the sea. It is in each of us, and it is the only part of us that truly exists. Everything else about us—our appearance, our opinions, everything that we might call our "selves"— is a transient illusion. *Atman* is the Hindu word for the part of a person that is truly Brahman; *atman*—often translated into English as "Self" with a capital "S." In the Katha Upanishad, one of the oldest religious texts in the world, a teacher (who happens to be Death) distinguishes my self from my Self:

There are two selves, the separate ego
And the indivisible *Atman.* When
One rises above *I* and *me* and *mine,*
The *Atman* is revealed as one's real Self.[29]

Wisdom, happiness, and what Christians would call "salvation" consist in recognizing this *atman*, and this recognition in turn requires us to distinguish temporary earthly things and commitments from our true Self.

Once this concept is introduced and explained, students are ready for a polyphonic dialogue that triangulates this passage from the Upanishads, the *Heidelberg Catechism*, and their own writing. Even students who are very familiar with the catechism—like the minister's son I once knew who could recite the first question and answer by age six—will find themselves thinking new thoughts, or at least thinking old thoughts in fresh terms.

Again, it is important to respect the otherness of other voices; the purpose of this exercise is not syncretism but dialogue. The differences between Christ and *atman* are tremendous and worth articulating. It is also useful to consider the rest of the answer to the first catechism question, for instance, where we are invited to confess, among other things, that "not a hair can fall from my head without the will of my father and heaven." This highly individualistic notion of providence is somewhat at odds with the selflessness (small "s") required to appreciate *atman*. Does the sixteenth-century *Heidelberg Catechism* actually endorse the kind of individualism that students have likely written about in their preaction papers? Comparison with the Katha Upanishad might easily make the catechism appear much closer to students than they initially would have thought.

In short, one way to develop a sense of self is to discover and refresh commitments one already holds. Nearly all literature can help students to accomplish this task, and world literature is particularly refreshing because it is so far removed from students' ordinary experience and vocabulary. To truly mature cognitively and ethically, however, students need the strength and courage to formulate new and original positions. These qualities are difficult to achieve in a fifty-minute session, of course, so this challenge typically involves thinking and writing out of class.

In my world literature course, students literally find a place for themselves in a world of others on days when a paper is due. I typically assign one or two thesis-driven essays on a particular topic, giving students a specific but open-ended thesis and asking them to support or attack it in an essay, modifying the thesis as they see fit. I require a refutation of differing viewpoints in these papers. On the due date, students bring their papers to class and meet in groups with about five other students. Each person presents his or her thesis and offers a two- or three-minute summary of the paper, after which the rest of the group is asked to discuss two things: further evidence or reasoning that would support the author's claims, and possible counterarguments or exceptions that the author has not considered. After the discussions, I ask each student to write on the back of his or her paper two or three ideas that were new or interesting, and two or three things he or she would do differently based on the conversation.

This exercise is useful for me because the items on the back of the paper often save me time writing feedback on the papers—a simple "yes" or "good idea" next to a student's own words is much easier than several sentences explaining a major oversight. For the students, however, the exercise makes writing real. They must literally hear other voices contradicting and confirming their own opinions, and they must literally use their own voices to respond. They must situate themselves within a small circle of others.

By the end of the semester, I ask students to do similar work on a larger scale, situating themselves not in a small circle of peers but in the world of literature that we have traversed. I have often used an exam question that asks students to identify particular pieces of literature from the syllabus that have challenged or contradicted their own religious commitments. The prompt asks students to clearly identify the elements of their own faith that have been challenged, the elements of the text that presented this challenge, and finally the ways in which the student has responded to the challenge: "Has your own spiritual understanding expanded to accommodate the new ideas? Is the work irreconcilable with your own beliefs, forcing you to keep it at arm's length? Or is the question still open as you sort through the issue?" Any stack of blue-books containing answers to this question will provide illustrations of nearly every stage of Perry's ethical and developmental schema. Even for very mature students, however, this question can be difficult to answer on the spot, so I have always provided it well in advance of the exam—usually, in fact, on the first day of the semester.

As Christians, we are called to be with the world. We are called to understand the voices of others, to respect their otherness, and to interact with them as equals without losing our own commitments. Literature—any literature—helps readers to develop this polyphonic sense of withness. To read literature is to triangulate, to participate in a living event. It is to transfer meaning across gaps between one's own world, the world of the author, and the world of the text. The early world literature survey offers a particularly rich set of such events, because these transfers are greater both in number—we must add the world of the translator to the list—and in distance. The otherness of the others is more pronounced.

A colleague of mine, when asked about the goals of the Christian college where he teaches, once famously replied that we try to make our students a little *less* fit to enter the larger world. What he meant of course, is that the claims of Christianity are often counter-cultural, and that we encourage our students to take those claims seriously. But less is more, and in some sense, the less our students conform to the accepted values of a "secular" society, the more they are fit to transform and renew that society. The ultimate goal, after all, is not to produce generations of misfits, but to prepare students to participate in God's transforming work in the world. To do that work, students will need to develop polyphonic stances, understanding not only other voices but their own otherness as well, and drawing from their own faithful commitments to participate meaningfully in the world of others.

Endnotes

1   Mikhail M. Bakhtin, *Problems of Dostoevsky's Poetics*, ed. and trans. Caryl Emerson (Minneapolis: University of Minnesota Press, 1984), 69. It should be noted that Bakhtin and Perry are using the term "relativism" in slightly different senses. Perry distinguishes between Relativism and Multiplicity. Relativism, for Perry, involves recognition that arguments depend on evidence and reasoning rather than mere opinion; that specific arguments might be better or worse relative to one another; and that on some issues reasonable people can and will disagree. Multiplicity is a lower developmental stage that most people, including Bakhtin, would likely describe as relativism. A student at this stage does not distinguish between argument and mere opinion, and because the student believes that everyone has a right to his or her own personal opinion, every argument is really as good as any other. Perry himself has observed that "Personalism" might be a reasonable label for this category. [See Perry's "Cognitive and Ethical Growth: The Making of Meaning" in *The Modern American College: Responding to the New Realities of Diverse Students and a Changing Society*, ed. Arthur W. Chickering, et al. (San Francisco: Jossey-Bass, 1981), 76-116.] When I refer to Relativism in Perry's particular sense, I have spelled it with a capital "R."

2   Paraphrasing Bakhtin, Gary Saul Morson and Caryl Emerson observe that "we might indeed conclude that polyphony was impossible if we did not have the example of Dostoevsky, who actually created it" [*Mikhail Bakhtin: Creation of a Prosaics* (Stanford: Stanford UP, 1990), 239].

3   In his chapter in this volume, Ralph C. Wood advocates a polyphonic stance toward non-Christian writers and critics: "we must take the anti-Christian and non-Christian naysayers ever so seriously, never setting them up as straw figures to be burned but rather honoring them as our worthy interlocuters," 213.

4   Mikhail Bahktin, *Problems*, 93.

5 Mikhail Bakhtin himself mentions two theological analogs for polyphony: Goethe's Prometheus, who "creates not voiceless slaves (as does Zeus), but *free* people, capable of standing *alongside* their creator" (*Problems*, 6, emphasis Bakhtin's); and the Judeo-Christian God, who enjoys with humanity "a relation allowing man to reveal himself" (285).

6 D.M. Thomas, "Introduction," in *Anna Akhmatova: Selected Poems*, ed. D. M. Thomas (London: Penguin, 1988), 11.

7 It is also useful to teach the conflicts within the Christian tradition, of course, especially with a room full of Christian students. For illustrations of this tactic, see Bruce Boeckel's chapter in this volume.

8 Carl W. Ernst, *Shambhala Guide to Sufism* (Boston: Shambhala, 1997) offers a useful overview of that mystical tradition within Islam. Ernst explains in his preface that the Muslims he talked to in writing the book reacted in a number of different ways to his course of study. Some "would sit back and observe in a dismissive way, 'Well, you should know that Sufism has nothing to do with Islam,'" while others "would lean forward enthusiastically and say something like, 'You're working on Sufism! Wonderful! Let me tell you, my grandfather was a *pir* [master], and I can take you to visit his tomb if you wish'" (xi). Contradictions such as these keep the course polyphonic by making it more difficult for students to reduce "Islam" to a monolithic list of abstractions.

9 As it turns out, Iser's development as a scholar roughly mirrors the trajectory I aim for in the early world literature survey, moving from a study of gaps in texts to "literary anthropology," that is, questions about what literature tells us about ourselves. A concise anthology of Iser's writing, including representative texts from each phase of his career, is *Prospecting: From Reader Response to Literary Anthropology* (Baltimore: Johns Hopkins University Press, 1989).

10 It would be splendid if there were some real etymological connection between the Greek *pherein* and the Germanic *fare*, thereby linking "metaphor" with "ferry." Alas, there seems to be no such connection. The *American Heritage Dictionary* traces the words to separate roots even in Indo-European (*pherein* to "bher-1" and *fare* to "per-2").

11 The notion of "conceptual mapping" described by Johnson and Turner [see Turner's *The Literary Mind* (Oxford: Oxford University Press, 1996)] has more recently been expanded and nuanced by Gilles Fauconnier and Mark Turner into a model they call "conceptual blending." See Fauconnier's and Turner's essay "Rethinking Metaphor" in *The Cambridge Handbook of Metaphor and Thought*, ed. Raymond Gibbs (Cambridge: Cambridge University Press, 2008). This more recent work will be of interest to any serious scholar of metaphor, and it undoubtedly better represents the intriguing nuances of human thought, but it is not as efficient to teach in a core literature course as the earlier, simpler version.

12 The first chapter of *More Than Cool Reason: A Field Guide to Poetic Metaphor* (Chicago: University of Chicago Press, 1989) makes an excellent supplement in any literature course. Teachers of early world literature might also want to consider the first chapter of Mark Turner's later book *The Literary Mind*, "Bedtime

with Shahrazad" (New York: Oxford University Press, 1996). Turner introduces his (and Lakoff and Johnson's) concept of metaphor by analyzing *The
Thousand and One Nights,* arguing that the kind of mapping or transfer that we
all do when we think and speak is particularly evident in the exchanges between
Shahrazad and her father. At the very least, the chapter offers the world literature professor insightful ways to discuss *The Thousand and One Nights* as being
a story *about* stories and how they work.

13 David Damrosch, "Preface," In the *Longman Anthology of World Literature,* ed.
David Damrosch, et al. (New York: Pearson Longman, 2004), xxii.

14 David Damrosch, *What is World Literature?* (Princeton: Princeton University
Press, 2003), 166.

15 Although Damrosch does not invoke cognitive linguistics to describe the process of reading world literature, he does approve of very similar terminology as
it is used by Andre Lefevere: "Lefevere argued, very cogently, that translations
never genuinely 'reflect' their original, whether faithfully or not; instead, they
refract their originals. Every translation is a negotiation between 'source' and
'target' cultures . . ." (*What is World Literature?* 167).

16 Damrosch's monograph *The Buried Book: The Loss and Rediscovery of the Great
Epic of Gilgamesh* (New York: Holt, 2007) studies the history of *Gilgamesh* at
much greater length, including an intriguing epilogue, "Saddam's Gilgamesh,"
which tracks the influence of the ancient epic in the little-known fictional works
of Saddam Hussein.

17 Pedagogically speaking, this observation should do two things for students.
First, it serves as an early example of the translatability of language, the suscep-
tibility of language to the other: even the same word, untranslated, can mean
something drastically different when appropriated by an other. Second, and no
less importantly, it affirms students' own insights. They generally do not have the
linguistic sophistication to know the origin of the Hebrew word for "deep," but
they should be gratified to find that what seems like highly specialized knowledge merely confirms their own insights about the differences between the various creation accounts.

18 The relationship between these two domains, erotic love and spiritual love,
can easily become a recurring theme in the course—it figures prominently in
Augustine's *Confessions,* Sufism, and the *Divine Comedy,* for instance, and naturally in the writings of Bernard of Clairvaux. This subject area is a real opportunity, because many Christian college students are themselves sorting out their
spiritual relationships to God, their physical relationships to other people, and
the ways in which these two domains relate to one another.

19 Song of Songs 2:14.

20 Bruce Boeckel articulates a similar pedagogical stance in the first chapter of this
volume.

21 In her chapter in this volume, Christine Chaney observes that facility with
"interpretive frames" is a prerequisite for students who study literary theory.
I developed this component of my world literature course to meet that need
among students, to demonstrate that "theory" is not particularly scary, and to

suggest that discussions of interpretive frames should not be confined to "the theory course."

22   M. H. Abrams, "Introduction: Orientation of Some Critical Theories," in *The Mirror and the Lamp: Romantic Theory and the Critical Tradition* (London: Oxford University Press, 1960), 6.

23   It is, of course, important to acknowledge that no reader is completely confined to a particular position. We might switch quadrants completely in the course of reading even a very short lyric poem.

24   Viktor Shklovsky, "Art as Technique," in *Russian Formalist Criticism: Four Essays,* trans. Lee T. Lemon and Marion J. Reis (Lincoln: University of Nebraska Press 1965), 12.

25   It is extremely doubtful that either author actually read the other. At the time Tolkien wrote "On Fairy-Stories," Shklovsky's essay had not yet been translated into English, and Russian was one of the few European languages with which Tolkien had no success.

26   J. R. R. Tolkien, "On Fairy-Stories," in *The Monsters and The Critics and Other Essays,* ed. Christopher Tolkien (London: Haper Collins, 1997), 108–161. Here quoting 146.

27   For another account of how old literature can help students to defamiliarize and recover assumptions they already have, see Jamie Dessart's chapter in this volume.

28   The *Heidelberg Catechism* is one of the foundational documents of the Reformed tradition, and in places it is rather inhospitable to certain other Christian denominations. The first question and answer, however, are quite ecumenical.

29   Katha Upanishad, II.2.13. This passage from the Upanishads is taken from the single-volume anthology edited and translated by Eknath Easwaran (Tomales, CA: Nilgiri Press, 1987). Easwaran is a Sanskrit scholar, a practicing Hindu, and a former professor of English literature. Like his edition of the Bhagavad Gita, his collection of excerpts from the Upanishads is clearly translated, judiciously annotated, and prefaced with a concise but useful introduction. Both books are useful resources to a professor who wishes to read beyond the excerpts and headnotes in a literature anthology, but who cannot sort through centuries of commentary on these ancient texts.

THE ENGLISH PROFESSOR AS TEACHER SCHOLAR:

Reflections on Faith and Learning Integration

DON W. KING (MONTREAT COLLEGE)

Don W. King, a long-time professor of English at Montreat College, offers his "reflections" on his thirty-year journey as a person of faith and as a professor of English in "The English Professor as Teacher Scholar: Reflections on Faith and Learning Integration." Using his Shakespeare course as a lens, Don introduces his reader to several key "integrative" questions. In his time as the editor of the Christian Scholars' Review, Don's editorial work has helped shape a genera-tion's understanding of faith integration in a variety of disciplines, including English. He is author of C. S. Lewis, Poet: The Legacy of His Poetic Impulse *(Kent State UP, 2001) and* Hunting the Unicorn: A Critical Biography of Ruth Pitter *(Kent State UP, 2008). In addition his book,* Out of My Bone: The Letters of Joy Davidman, *will appear in Spring 2009 (Eerdmans). He is also the author of numerous articles on C. S. Lewis and has served in several leadership posi-tions at Montreat College, including the vice president of academic affairs and interim president.*

Several years ago, I taught a junior-level middle English literature course with the primary focus on Chaucer's *Canterbury Tales*. One day, about a third of the way through the semester, I was discussing with my students an assigned book review and my expectations. After I completed my remarks, a bright young woman in the class raised her hand and asked: "Dr. King, are you trying to turn us into scholars?" Her inquiry caught me by surprise, not only because of its directness, but also because she had very deftly revealed a hidden agenda for all the classes I teach, though I had not realized it before her question. She helped me see that, yes, I was trying to turn my students into scholars. After recovering from my shock, I told them so. This incident is the catalyst for what follows, as I explore briefly several implications of what it means to be a Christian scholar and teacher within the discipline of literature (for the sake of brevity I will use the term Christian scholar to include both scholarship and teaching). While the first half of my remarks are descriptive of my musings on Christian scholarship, the second half are more personal and reflective.

Let me begin by briefly noting the "tools" necessary for Christian scholarship within the discipline of literature. First, persons interested in such scholarship will bring an informed, biblical perspective to their study of literature; indeed, knowledge of Scripture is critical for this enterprise. Avoiding the simplistic, such persons will grapple with the declaration that "all truth is God's truth" in light of the biblical record. Ideally, such persons will be guided by humility, civility, service, and honesty. I add by way of clarification that such persons will not use their faith to browbeat and coerce others into some prepackaged Christian mold. Second, Christian scholars of literature will harness their intellectual ability and rigor in order to explore all aspects of literary study. They will seek to discover truth—about themselves, others, the world, and God—no matter where the search leads. This means that while some discussions will remain open-ended, other will lead toward closure; that is, truth is not always elusive.

If the tools of Christian scholarship are biblical depth and academic expertise, what are the three most common perspectives on the subject? Some people believe these two ideas are mutually exclusive; that is, they argue that literary study can receive no insight from religious belief nor can faith be informed by academic inquiry. Such people would answer Tertullian's rhetorical question, "What hath Athens to do with Jerusalem?" by saying "Nothing!" The assumption here is that Athens (representing the high point of Greek rationalistic civilization) can learn nothing from Jerusalem (representing the pinnacle of Hebraic faith traditions). These people believe there is simply no point of contact between faith and literary study. Others believe each is fine in its own place; that is, literary study is worthy of sustained effort and so is a deeply felt relationship with Christ as long as the two run parallel with each other. These people would probably not be actively opposed to the idea that faith and literary study could inform each other, but they would not be particularly interested in nor motivated to discover how to bridge the two.

However, a third group, in which I include myself, believe faith and literary studies intersect in powerful ways. Indeed, I'd put it this way: faith and literary study are not mutually exclusive, they should inform each other, and Christian literature faculty members should seek proactive ways for such integration to occur. Faculty sympathetic to this view will approach literary studies from the perspective that a Christian worldview informs, supplements, enhances, exposes, comments upon, and enriches the truths they pursue in literature. Such people find this perspective cogently summarized by Dutch theologian Abraham Kuyper, who at one time also served as the prime minister of the Netherlands. Speaking at the inaugural convocation of the Free University of Amsterdam, he said: "There is not a square inch in the whole domain of our human existence over which Christ, who is sovereign over all, does not cry 'Mine!'"

For me to give you concrete applications of how Christian scholarship might work in literary studies, I begin with my own experience as a teacher of literature. However, two caveats. First, I believe that the enterprise of learning how to integrate faith and literary studies is a lifelong project. There aren't simple formulas to do this, so I hope no one will mistake my reflections as glib commentary or simplistic "how to" instructions. I have stumbled quite often along the way, missing golden opportunities in the classroom or working individually with students. At the same time, I believe I have learned a few things about integration that have made my teaching, writing, editing, and researching mesh effectively with my faith in Christ. Second, I doubt your own college or university is a wasteland with regard to Christian scholarship; indeed, I want to encourage you who are actively engaged in this enterprise and to collaborate with others on campus in considering how to go about this enterprise in a more intentional way.

With those caveats behind us, what difference has it made that I have been both a literature professor and a Christian? How has my own Christian scholarship developed? When I first began teaching in the mid 1970s, having earned my undergraduate and master's degree from large state universities, I had to decide if I should approach literature as many of my professors had in the late 1960s and early 1970s. They tended to treat literature as holy; literary studies for them verged on religious devotion. At the same time, my professors divorced literary study from any sense of divine truth and meaning. Literature may have been holy, but it had no direct connection to God. Then in the late 1970s when I began my doctoral studies, again at a large state university, and through much of the 1980s I had to decide if I should approach literary studies from any number of popular ideological perspectives. This approach associated literary studies with power/political agendas including Marxism, feminism, sexism, multiculturalism, and so on; often the ideology became the focus of such studies and those things that I most loved about literature—the power of language, the subtle nuances in discovering truth and meaning in life, the orderliness and beauty of literary forms (poetry, drama, fiction), the tender, poignant portrayal of the human condition, including the redemptive nature of human love as well as the destructive force of human selfishness, pride, and deception—all these things seemed subservient to the "cause," whatever it was. Still later, through the 1990s I had to decide if I should approach literature through the lens of postmodernism and deconstruction where the very meaning of the text is called into question. I reflect back not to disparage or attack (indeed, I have learned valuable things through this literary pilgrimage and the various "isms"), but instead I reflect in this way to throw into relief what I believe is one way (not the only way) a Christian literature professor can go about the task of integrating faith and learning.

For me this meant going back to the literal beginning. As I thought through the implications of integrating faith and learning in the study of literature, as I read what others had to say, I eventually realized that language, or more properly *logos*, is the primary way in which God has revealed himself, as both the beginning of Genesis and the Gospel of John reveal: "Then God said, 'Let there be light.'" (Gen. 1:3), and "In the beginning was the Word, and the Word was with God, and the Word was God" (John 1:1). In the Genesis passage we see God using *logos* or language to create the natural world. In a real sense God spoke into creation all that is. In the passage from John, a Christian sees an equally wonderful thing: that is, the Word, literally the *Logos*, Jesus Christ, is God's word to us.

These realizations had profound implications for me as I sought to integrate faith and learning. Among these was the fundamental truth that human language itself is a reflection of our divine connectedness, the *imago Deo*; put another way, that we have language and use language and enjoy language intimately and irrevocably links us to God. On the one hand, God used language or *logos* to create the natural world, and on the other hand he sent his *Logos*, his Word, his Son to us. One part of my task, then, is to explore and discover with my students how language and by extension literature participates in the revelation of God's natural creation as well as His revelation of his own character as portrayed in the life of Christ.

I have tried to consider the implications of this with my students when we read and study a novel; that is, in reading the novel we enter into not only the author's world but at least indirectly into God's. Although the piece may be fictional and not obviously focused upon God, the means the author uses to communicate, *logos*, is a gift of God and in itself connects us to the divine image. An author uses *logos* as the vehicle to portray his or her vision of life. For the Christian this means that no piece of literature is "beyond the pale," even if it is clearly antithetical to Christianity or God. The Christian finds in such a piece of writing the grand irony that an author uses *logos* to try to defy *Logos*, reminiscent of Isaiah 45:9: "Woe to the one who quarrels with his Maker—an earthenware vessel among the vessels of the earth! Will the clay say to the potter, 'What are you doing?'" At the same time, realizing this irony will quicken in the Christian not an attitude of self-righteousness but one of renewed commitment to exploring how language and literature link us to the idea of being created in the image of God.

Building on these reflections, how might the integration of faith and literary studies happen in the classroom? First, faculty members should to try to make connections between the literary texts being studied and relevant biblical motifs, themes, and ideas. While we can sometimes plan this out ahead of time, oftentimes such connections occur spontaneously during class discussion; yet we have to be sensitive and ever looking to make such connections—as scholars we have to be alert to draw quickly upon our own biblical knowledge in order to make links to the literary text. Often these serendipitous moments of integration will be more profound and influential than our deliberate efforts.

Second, we should develop a series of what I call integrative questions. The point of these integrative questions is not to answer questions; instead, they are designed to raise questions in our students' minds with regard to the course material and important biblical motifs, themes, and ideas. Over the years I have come to include these integrative questions in my syllabus and tell my students that while we may not ever directly address the questions in class, they undergird the kind of thinking in which I hope we will engage via course readings and discussions.

Here, for instance, are the integrative questions I include in EN 301, Shakespeare.[1] (As a caveat, I have never published an article on Shakespeare and don't consider myself a Shakespeare scholar.):

1. How does Shakespeare's portrayal of romantic love in the early comedies relate to a biblical view of romantic love? The mature comedies? What biblical texts comment upon the idea of romantic love?

2. In Shakespeare's "problem comedies," what is the relationship between law and grace? In what ways does his understanding of this relationship reflect a biblical one?

3. What appears to be Shakespeare's view of the nature of humankind in his histories and tragedies? Are we simply beasts or are we created "a little lower than the angels"? What difference does this make?

4. How does Shakespeare's knowledge of biblical passages, themes, motifs, ideas, and principles inform his plays? In what ways does he draw upon these rich resources as an artist?

5. What are the roles of confession, repentance, forgiveness, redemption, and reconciliation in his final plays, the romances? Is Shakespeare's understanding of these principles biblically informed and how so?

6. What appears to be Shakespeare's view of marriage? Do his plays reflect a static view of marriage or an evolving one? How so? What biblical insights about marriage inform our understanding of how Shakespeare portrays marriage?

On the first day of the course, I spend time going through the questions, even suggesting ahead of time how some of the questions invite significant biblical engagement. I believe it is important for students to see how deliberatively I am thinking about Shakespeare and these biblical ideas. I hope my example invites them to view their own study of Shakespeare through a considerably wider lens than they may have imagined when signing up for the course. For me, these questions set the context for my (not always systematic) attempts at integration throughout the semester.

Moreover, because scholars have effectively documented Shakespeare's almost-verbatim knowledge of large portions of Scripture—mostly likely via the Geneva Bible (1560)—a third avenue I pursue in regard to integration turns upon a brief study of the history of the English Bible, followed by a handout exploring the implications of this question: "If Shakespeare had a close knowledge of the English Bible and if his plays clearly reflect such, of what significance are these matters to our study of Shakespeare this semester?"[2] The discussion that follows often sets the context for our approach to studying the plays in terms of trying to make connections between the content of the literary texts and biblical ideas. In order to invite students to make such linkages I often suggest biblical passages that might inform their reading of the plays. Accordingly, when we study the early comedies, I assign parallel biblical readings assignments including the Song of Songs, Ephesians 5, and I Corinthians 13, and for the problem comedies, we read and discuss passages from Romans and Galatians. For the tragedies and romances, parallel biblical passages are almost ubiquitous, particularly from the New Testament.

At the same time, while I am intentional with regard to integration, I do not necessarily feel compelled to force the issue. For instance, as we begin studying *Measure for Measure*, I give students a handout that reproduces six biblical passages focusing upon judgment, forgiveness, mercy, and justice; then I invite a brief discussion of the biblical passages. After we have studied *Measure for Measure*, we then move into a study of the *Merchant of Venice*; together these are arguably Shakespeare's two most biblical informed plays. My students are not surprised when I give them the option of writing the following essay on the two plays that, by implication, invites them to consider the original six biblical passages (and others we have identified in the meantime): "Identify and discuss a common biblical theme found in both *Measure for Measure* and the *Merchant of Venice*. What biblical texts express best this theme and how do echoes of it appear in the plays? What is different about the way the two plays treat this theme, especially with regard to how the characters act upon the theme? Which play best expresses this biblical theme and why? Be specific by referring to the texts."[3] In response to this prompt, one student opened her essay this way:

> Throughout literature, biblical ideas and allusions have played a vital role developing an author's theme. From John Milton's *Paradise Lost* to the works of Flannery O'Connor, Christian themes are the foundation of varying literary periods and genres. Although not as obvious in his use of biblical passages as other authors, William Shakespeare draws a good deal from the Bible in many of his plays; in particular his biblical insights can be seen in the *Merchant of Venice* and *Measure for Measure*. Specifically, the interactions between Shylock and Antonio in the *Merchant of Venice* and Angelo, Claudio, and Isabella in *Measure for Measure* exemplify the biblical passage found in Matthew 7:1–2, "Do not judge lest you be judged yourselves. For in the way you judge, you will be judged; and by your standard of measure, it shall be measured to you." Based on my readings of the plays and this biblical text, I believe Shakespeare explores profoundly the question of mercy versus justice and comes close to articulating a definition of Christian forgiveness.

This student's thoughtful opening suggests how she plans to engage Shakespeare's texts as commenting upon, expanding, and supplementing biblical ideas related to justice and mercy; in addition, it hints at one of the many beauties of teaching Shakespeare: his multifaceted view of the human condition, one that is readily connected to the biblical narrative. While I could go on here, my point is simple: developing a series of integrative questions, regardless of the academic discipline, may be an effective way for faculty members to tackle proactively the enterprise of Christian scholarship.

After having been somewhat descriptive regarding Christian scholarship, I'd like now to be more personal and reflective. Beyond the classroom and teaching, the Christian scholar may have opportunities to engage in research. Christian scholars given such opportunities must be committed to critical learning that is deep, sustained, and biblically informed. They won't be satisfied with the facile, the simplistic, or the shallow; instead, they will go to extraordinary lengths to explore all aspects of a subject. This will include exhausting all avenues of research material as well as thoughtful dialogue with others, both peers and experts alike. A consequence of this will be the realization that while much is learned, much remains to be learned. Reading deeply on a subject and faltering attempts at putting into words what has been learned are the "bricks and mortar" of Christian scholarship. Moreover, meaningful scholarship of this sort is driven by a mind that is curious, not easily satisfied, thirsty for new knowledge, creative, able to integrate and synthesize, and given to playfulness.

Indeed, I think playfulness is a characteristic of many in the academy I see most absent today. Scholarship that is playful does not accept the status quo without question; it delights in challenging old assumptions and provoking the established paradigm, not for the sake of being an irritant, but because it sees a new way of dealing with an old issue. An interesting example of this may be seen in the life of J. R. R. Tolkien. Known by many today as the author of *The Hobbit* and the *Lord of the Rings* trilogy, Tolkien was a scholar of Anglo-Saxon literature and language. As a part of his studies in philology in the early part of this century, he became fascinated with a rather obscure piece of Anglo-Saxon literature about a larger-than-life being who had three separate fights with supernatural creatures of evil. Before Tolkien's work, this piece of writing was viewed at best as an archeological artifact of limited interest and at worst as a work of Anglo-Saxon history mutilated by the Christian priest who finally put it down in writing. Tolkien's playfulness as a scholar led him to argue in a seminal essay published in 1936 that the work was neither artifact nor Christian propaganda but instead a legitimate piece of literature deserving serious scholarly study. "Beowulf: The Monsters and the Critics" provoked a veritable tidal wave of scholarly reaction; so much so that today *Beowulf* is a standard text in English literary studies.

I think the example of Tolkien moves us toward perhaps the most personal thing I want to share about Christian scholarship: a Christian scholar should be in love with learning. If you don't love to learn new things and have your conventional wisdom challenged, you may never find peace as a Christian scholar. I was reminded of how important a love of learning is by a recent experience in one of the literature classes I taught in our adult program. At the conclusion of the course, Masterpieces of Literature (yes, this is a somewhat presumptuously named course!), I normally give a comprehensive essay exam. You know the type: "Write everything you know about topic X." Students usually leave such an exam with writer's cramp and a secret desire to throttle me. In this particular case the class had read and studied Sophocles' *Oedipus* cycle, Shakespeare's *Othello*, Dickens's *Great Expectations*, Emily Dickinson's poetry, and Alan Paton's moving novel about South Africa, *Cry, the Beloved Country*. One student, as I recall a man in his mid- to late-30s who worked for a major airline (he had a 160-mile round-trip drive to class once a week), wrote on the power of words in terms of several of the works I just mentioned. I wish I could quote his entire essay, but I'll limit myself to his conclusion:

> It is not by accident that these writers use their words to charge our emotions. Their task is to stir our innermost thoughts to provoke action on our part. As Paton wrote: "We believe that God endows men with diverse gifts, and that human life depends for its fullness on their employment and enjoyment, but we are afraid to explore this belief too deeply" (154). The [literary works] we have studied are examples of works by men and women that have used the God-given gifts Paton is referring to, and we continue to reap in the enjoyment and fulfillment of emotion they can offer. Like them we should not be afraid to explore our beliefs more deeply.

I was greatly moved by this man's essay, not only because he writes with grace, but even more so because his last sentence reminded me once again of what gives my life as a Christian scholar focus and purpose; his words, "like them we should not be afraid to explore our beliefs more deeply," ably illustrate a deep passion for learning, a passion I so profoundly share. And so it is that I turn to this matter of why I love to learn.

Why, in my fifty-seventh year, am I still in college? Shouldn't I have graduated and gotten on with life? Am I developmentally arrested? Am I hiding in college because I can't "hack it" out in the so-called real world? Do I enjoy the notoriously high salaries college professors command so much that I'm not willing to risk a life on the "outside"? Am I so hopelessly inept that I'm the epitome of the old "saw" that those who can, do, and those who can't, teach?

As I reflect on these and a host of related questions I can only give one answer: I truly love to learn. And I suspect many of my colleagues do as well.

For whatever reason, God has endowed us with this love, and it seems as if nothing can quite quench our thirst to know. For some of us this love is focused upon learning with a specific goal in mind; perhaps we want to do research that will lead to a medical discovery that will alleviate human suffering; for others, this love drives us to seek answers to age-old problems afflicting governments and economies; for still others, this love is bent upon solving specific social, religious, or environmental dilemmas. These are wonderful motives that drive love of learning. They are practical and applied.

But to be totally honest, my own love of learning is not so altruistic. I confess. I love learning simply for the sake of learning. I love to learn. Now don't get me wrong. I'm not saying I love to learn for selfish or egocentric reasons; indeed, one of the things learning shows me is how selfish and egocentric we human beings can be. Instead, I love to learn because I love to be challenged, stretched, and perplexed. I love the dissonance that inquiry into a subject throws at me. I love to be totally enmeshed in a reading or writing project, particularly if it involves a pet interest. Though in depth, detailed study of anything can become tedious, even if we like it, there is nothing like the sense of accomplishment, the rush, if you will, of diving deeply into a subject and coming back to the surface refreshed and renewed for further learning.

What's the value, though, someone might ask, beyond personal growth and renewal, of such fervor for learning? How can others, our culture and society for instance, benefit? Such a personal focus on learning can become so much indulgence if left to itself; navel-gazing in pursuit of learning, however idealized, is still navel-gazing. Perhaps even more formidable are the questions: "Of what value is learning for the Christian? After all, shouldn't our primary calling be to save souls? Why waste time on a life of learning?" These are hard queries to answer. Let me throw out three possible answers.

First, of what value is learning for the Christian scholar? Perhaps another way to put this is, does a life of scholarship or learning have the same kind of value for the Christian as that of being, say, a plumber, or an airline pilot? I suppose the best answer I can think of comes from 1 Cor. 10:31: "Whether, then, you eat or drink or whatever you do, do all for the glory of God"(nasb). Paul suggests here that the job function does not determine job value; instead, value proceeds from our ultimate focus. Can a plumber plumb to the glory of God? Can an airline pilot fly to the glory of God? Can a person learn to the glory of God? Yes. None of these positions is necessarily better than the others, for all can reflect a divine fulfillment of living life to the glory of God. After all, God is the one who gave us minds to plumb with, to fly with, to explore with, to enjoy with.

Second, shouldn't a Christian be primarily interested in saving souls? Now there is a sense in which this is true; after all, ultimately all of us are heading toward eternal union with or separation from God, and we should be keenly conscious of that as we interact with those we deal with day by day. But not all of life, whether we like it or not, is given over to purely spiritual things. Many ordinary human activities go on without a spiritual mandate: we take showers, cook meals, wash clothes, play sports, and so on. So it is that our lives are not entirely absorbed by spiritual things. And a life of learning can actually be an antidote to going the wrong direction with some of these ordinary human activities. As C. S. Lewis said, "If you don't read good books, you will read bad ones. If you don't go on thinking rationally, you will think irrationally. If you reject aesthetic satisfactions, you will fall into sensual satisfactions."[4] A love of learning is as valid an ordinary human activity as any of the others already mentioned and may even serve to redeem some of them. Learning, then, can lead to discovery of the beauty and truth God has created, even in ordinary human activities.

Third, is a life of learning a waste of time? Shouldn't we as Christian scholars be engaged more fully in practical things? Are we lovers of learning like the emperor Nero, fiddling while Rome burns? I'll answer this objection by asking questions in return. Is it a waste of time to discover truth? To find the answers to difficult questions? To solve problems? To reflect deeply, as Christians, on the human condition? To speak clearly and honestly on matters of values, ethics, and the moral life? To promote an attitude of stewardship toward the whole of creation? To encourage an appreciation for what is beautiful, true, and good in the arts and literature? To promote a genuine critical openness to the ideas and beliefs of others? To recognize the *imago Deo* in all human beings? To understand the past and its interconnectedness with the present and the future? To articulate boldly the implication of God's sovereignty over all creation and human knowledge? Are these endeavors a waste of time? I think not.

So, I love to learn for all these reasons. In learning I find the realization of my particular calling as a Christian scholar who is seeking to bring God glory. When I read a book, write a paper, teach a class, serve on a committee, meet personally with students, research in the bowels of some dusty library, or edit the *Christian Scholar's Review*, I'm so very privileged to live out this love. To all my fellow "learnophiles," I hope this love strikes a familiar chord; we are kindred spirits when it comes to this passion for learning. Together we learn the old truth that the more you learn, the less you know. Perhaps it is the realization that there is still so much to learn that drives us on toward more learning.

Though we may live seventy or eighty years, we realize all of our learning is just scratching the surface of all there is to learn about ourselves, others, the natural world, and God. But far from defeating us, this truth humbles us and pushes us ever on. As Tennyson's Ulysses puts it:

> Tho' much is taken, much abides; and tho'
> We are not now that strength which in old days
> Moved earth and heaven, that which we are, we are,—
> One equal temper of heroic hearts,
> Made weak by time and fate, but strong in will
> To strive, to seek, to find, and not to yield.

really?

I could go on and on, but let me bring this to a close. At most of your institutions, I have reason to believe, Christian scholarship is basic to your statement of purpose. Again, C. S. Lewis is helpful. First, in his essay, "Christianity and Literature," he considers, in part, the question of whether or not there is such a thing as a Christian novel or poem or play. Another way to put this is that he considers the question of how the faith of a writer should connect with his practice as a writer. He begins by saying:

> The rules for writing a good passion play or a good devotional lyric are simply the rules for writing tragedy or lyric in general: success in sacred literature depends on the same qualities of structure, suspense, variety, diction, and the like which secure success in secular literature . . . Literature written by Christians for Christians would have to avoid mendacity, cruelty, blasphemy, pornography, and the like, and it would aim at edification in so far as edification was proper to the kind of work in hand. But whatever it chose to do would have to be done by the means common to all literature; it could succeed or fail only by the same excellences and the same faults as all literature; and its literary success or failure would never be the same thing as its obedience or disobedience to Christian principles.[5]

To this he very wisely adds, however, that "the Christian [writer] knows from the outset that the salvation of a single soul is more important than the production or preservation of all the epics and tragedies in the world."[6] Second, in his essay, "Learning in War-time," written during England's darkest WWII days, Lewis affirms the legitimacy of faith and learning:

> If our parents have sent us to Oxford, if our country allows us to remain there, this is *prima facie* evidence that the life which we, at any rate, can best lead to the glory of God at present is the learned

life . . . I mean the pursuit of knowledge and beauty, in a sense, for their own sake, but in a sense which does not exclude their being for God's sake. An appetite for these things exists in the human mind, and God makes no appetite in vain. We can therefore pursue knowledge as such, and beauty, as such in the sure confidence that by so doing we are either advancing to the vision of God ourselves or indirectly helping other to do so . . . The intellectual life is not the only road to God, nor the safest, but we find it to be a road, and it may be the appointed road for us.[7]

Christian scholarship is a lifelong process, not a matter of simplistic biblical proof-texting, nor shallow, Sunday school moralisms. At the same time, faith in Christ should serve as a guide as we work through intellectual challenges, personal conflicts, and real-world decision-making. To neglect faith is to cut learning adrift on a sea of relativism; to neglect learning is to set sail on a faith journey buffeted by conflicting winds of pietism and legalism. We need faculty members and students who proactively combine their passion for learning with their passion for Christ.[8]

Endnotes

1   Course description: A study of the major plays of Shakespeare with special emphasis on the tragedies and comedies.

2   I suggest four distinct areas for exploration in regard to Shakespeare's biblical knowledge:

a)   What does Shakespeare's use of Scripture say about the nature of man/woman? Is he only another animal or is he "created a little lower than the angels"? Is he a creature with an eternal destiny or simply one bound to an earthly existence? Can he find meaning in life? Where? What is his essential character? Is he basically selfish or self-sacrificing?

b)   What does Shakespeare's use of Scripture say about the human potential for love? What are the roles of agape, eros, phileo, and storge? Is love a redemptive or destructive force? Is love the ultimate goal toward which man should strive? Is Shakespeare's concern with romantic love primarily pre- or post-nuptial? That is, is "romancing" more focused upon preliminary courtship than what happens after marriage? What is the role of sex?

c)   What does Shakespeare's use of Scripture say about moral responsibility/personal ethics? That is, does he suggest what is good and evil? Are humans ultimately responsible for their actions or are they simply predestined to do what they do? What is the source of morality? Are values based on personal, social, or absolute principles? What are the consequences of human behavior?

d) What does Shakespeare's use of Scripture say about God? Is He knowable? Is He trustworthy? Is He involved in human lives? Does He care about human behavior? Can we come to know Him better through reading Shakespeare's plays? Does Shakespeare's biblical knowledge and use qualify him as a Christian artist?

3 For the same assignment, I also offer students two essay options that are not deliberately intended to encourage integration between the text and biblical ideas:

a) Discuss Shakespeare's portrayals of Portia and Isabella. In your judgment, offer a brief character analysis of each, noting especially what makes them "tick"—that is, what motivates them, what inspires them, what calls forth their best, and what higher ends do they attempt to attain? In what specific ways are they different? Conclude by discussing which is your favorite and why. Refer to the texts to provide concrete examples.

b) In the Merchant of Venice and Measure for Measure, the role of a ruler is crucial. During the Renaissance, people sometimes suffered much at the hands of an abusive ruler because of their adherence to the idea of "the divine right of kings." In addition, rulers in their capacity as God's substitutes had four privileges: sanctity of person, absolute power, the right to enforce law and avenge evil, and the right to use extraordinary means to bring about justice and good fortune for the people. How do the rulers in these three plays illustrate or not illustrate the Renaissance model of a good ruler? Be specific by referring to the texts.

4 C. S. Lewis, "Learning in War-time," in *Fern-seed and Elephants and Other Essays on Christianity,* ed. Walter Hooper (Glasgow: Collins, 1975), 30.

5 C. S. Lewis, "Christianity and Literature," in *Christian Reflections,* ed. Walter Hooper (Grand Rapids: Eerdmans, 1989), 1–2.

6 Ibid., 10.

7 C. S. Lewis, "Learning," 33–4.

8 This note is a general acknowledgment to many writers and thinkers who have shaped my thinking regarding Christian scholarship over the last twenty years. I am indebted to many and have tried to give their ideas a fresh application in my own experience.

SEEING "THE CLEAREST GODS":

Teaching *King Lear* in China

Dr. Gregory Maillet (Atlantic Baptist University)

Greg Maillet received his Ph.D. in English from the University of Ottawa in 1996, then taught for one year at Peking University in Beijing, China, followed by eight years at the University of Regina. He moved to ABU in the summer of 2005, where he is also head coach of the men's basketball team. Greg's publications on William Shakespeare include "Desdemona and the Mariological Theology of the Will in Othello" in Marian Moments in Early Modern British Drama (Studies in Performance and Early Modern Drama) *(Ashgate, 2007) and numerous theatre reviews for the* Shakespeare Bulletin. *Greg believes that God is Him "in whom are hid all the treasures of wisdom and knowledge" (Colossians 2:3 KJV).*

Introduction

From 1996–97, my wife Jennifer and I taught English literature at China's largest and most prestigious university for the arts, Peking University, and there heard an interesting saying: those who visit China for a week write a book; those who stay a month write an article; those who stay a year don't write anything at all. Above all else, and in stark contradiction of Western stereotypes, nothing is more characteristic of China than complexity of culture and human personality. Nevertheless, perhaps because we stayed only ten months, I did publish one fairly general article on my experience teaching Shakespeare in China[1] and now, mindful of Horace's dictum that one's best ideas should be allowed to mature for a period of not less than nine years,[2] I feel ready to reflect more specifically upon my single best classroom experience in China: an intensive study of *King Lear*.[3] Though this play may be Shakespeare's most anguished study of evil and suffering, for me it offered a unique opportunity, within the academic and aesthetic study of literature, to at least indirectly teach the unconditional, self-sacrificial, redemptive love of Jesus Christ.

Some further context will help to make clear *King Lear*'s unique and unusual role in this common Christian aim. First, although Peking University has long been regarded as China's premier university for the liberal arts, and while many of its professors have a long history of support for democratic, free expression, in many ways unwise to detail, elements of the university remain under the control of an exclusively atheistic Communist party. Simply put, open public evangelism is not a prudent option for a visiting professor to pursue. Our Christian faith was not hidden or explicitly forbidden, and the university recognized and accepted that Christian ideas need to be discussed in order to understand and describe Western culture; however, evaluative commentary was avoided because the very real potential for human suffering to come from an openly political dispute caused common sense to dictate a careful dialogue rather than explicit conflict between cultures. Nevertheless— and such contradictions, again, are simply part of the reality of China—Peking University included many deeply faithful professors and students, the government sanctioned Protestant and Catholic churches in Beijing were overflowing and (according to foreign missionaries) taught accurate biblical theology, while private house churches also flourished.

Privately, many students questioned the ethics of communism, and in general there was an intense interest in spiritual questions. Our literature students, it should be noted, had studied English since their first days of school and were fully fluent in the language, yet also retained a deep interest in philology that is far less common among native speakers. Although initially quiet, these extremely bright students, elite achievers in rigorous language exams, were also very creative and even published their own journal called "One-Eighth," so titled in allusion to Hemingway's comment that the dignity of an iceberg is due to only one-eighth of it being above water.[4] Every seemingly reserved Chinese student, we learned, was far more intellectual and creative than we initially perceived. Always obvious, however, was their enthusiasm for linguistic study. Aided by the language quizzes and journals standard to my Shakespeare classes, many of these students showed a detective-like interest in tracking down every allusion, pun, or potential rhetorical figure of speech in Shakespeare's richly poetic language. Needless to say, teaching such students was a pleasure and a privilege, and several continued study in Western graduate programs and remain accomplished students of English literature. My debt to them, and sincere gratitude, is deeply heartfelt. Within the unique setting that was Peking University, our mutual study of *King Lear* offered me new insight not only into the play itself, but also how our Living Lord of Life, even when not explicitly acknowledged or invoked, can lead people to Himself.

In selecting *Lear*, however, my initial goal was simply to demonstrate the sublime complexity of Shakespeare's art, in particular its capacity to evoke what Keats calls "negative capability"—when we can accept "uncertainties, mysteries, doubts without any irritable reaching after fact & reason."[5] Keats was easily one of the Chinese students' favorite English poets, largely because his aesthetic tendencies so clearly contrasted the lingering utilitarianism of Marxist literary theory.[6] As a prelude to *Lear*, we therefore studied Keats's "On Sitting Down to Read King Lear Again,"[7] which allowed me to introduce, through a friendly and influential source, what I regard as the central theme of Shakespeare's great play: "the fierce dispute, / Betwixt damnation and impassion'd clay" (5-6). Having written an undergraduate honors thesis on, in part, *King Lear* and the *Book of Job*, I knew that *Lear* was, fundamentally, about the choice given us by God in Deuteronomy 30:15, between "life and good, and death and evil,"[8] a choice that always entails a "fierce [spiritual] dispute." Despite Keats's own agnosticism, I further felt that the conclusion of *Lear* had led Keats's poem on this play to conclude with a classical image that retains significant Christian relevance; looking ahead to his own death, the poet asks, or prays, to someone: "when I am consumed in the fire, / Give me new Phoenix wings to fly at my desire" (13-14). So while there is a "fierce dispute" amongst literary critics on "*King Lear* and the Gods" (as the influential atheist William Elton put it[9]), the poetic authority of Keats sowed two crucial questions in my students' mind: how, and why, is the concept of resurrection relevant to *King Lear*?

Performance, Philology, and the Pedagogy of *King Lear*

For the most part, however, I initially wanted to avoid thematic discussion that might lead to the accusation that ideas were being imposed upon rather than discovered within the text. Thematic discussion of literature should emerge gradually from a careful observation of plot, character, language, and, in the case of drama, the spectacle of performance. Few students in the class had ever witnessed a dramatized performance of Shakespeare, however, so another prelude to our study was the 1983 Olivier television version of the play.[10] Unlike his *Hamlet*, this production takes no obvious interpretive position, and at the time Olivier was himself elderly; thus the physical *pathos* of the role, combined with superb acting, made the film deeply moving. Further, seeing the entire play as a whole allowed a broader context and purpose to the study of individual scenes that we then began. With energy and vigor, the Chinese students dove into each scene, often beginning by asking questions related to the philology of individual words, phrases, or key speeches; after minimal encouragement and organization from me, soon they also reenacted key moments through dramatic readings, and from this simple perfomance pedagogy emerged the basis for a sound interpretation of Shakespeare that students then began using journals, to analyze and explore the broader significance of the play in their own lives.

The Chinese students' attention to language allowed them to notice what many miss in the opening lines of *Lear*: Gloucester joking, almost bragging about having conceived "a son for her cradle ere she had a husband for her bed" (1.1.114). The son is Edmond, but who is the mother? Nameless, used, forgotten—the Chinese female students especially mistrusted Gloucester and responded with sarcasm to his subsequent question, "Do you smell a fault?" (1.1.115). Though some were humored by Shakespeare's bawdiness, adultery was seen by all as a major fault, even without reference to the Mosaic law or the Christian concept of marriage; former Chinese leader Zhou Enlai, by contrast, was revered for having loved "only one woman" (Deng Yingchao). The socially destructive consequences of adultery were obvious to these students, and for them *Lear's* frequent subsequent references to this theme gave the play moral gravity and depth.

Similarly, the Chinese students also responded with natural empathy and understanding to the plight faced by Cordelia after her sisters, Goneril and Regan, flatter their father in an attempt to receive a larger portion as he divides the kingdom. In subsequent years, many of my Canadian students have faulted either Cordelia's intelligence or gratitude to her father, but in China the cultural reality of "face" gave a very different perspective. It is expected to be polite, say the right thing, and save "face" in all public settings, but that does not mean the concept is universally admired; on the contrary, the Chinese students tended to rebuke harshly the corrupt political machinations of the elder sisters, and to see wisdom and prudence in Cordelia's pledge to love Lear, "According to my bond; no more nor less." Despite the "one-child" policy in China, and the many ways in which the state usurps the role of the family, most of the Chinese students retained a deep reverence and respect for their natural parents, and correctly read Cordelia's "bond" for the absolute, heartfelt love that it proves to be.

By the opening scene's end, the Chinese students were very firmly on the side of those soon to be banished from the court, and saw in Lear's threat, "Come not between the dragon and his wrath" (1.1.122) a cross-cultural symbol of the abuse of political power. They stood with the loyally dissenting Kent, demanding, "See better, Lear" (1.1.156), and rebuking Lear's invocation of "Apollo" as an address, in Kent's words, to "gods in vain" (1.1.156-160). Within this context, they became open to some fairly direct biblical allusions that many modern Western readers entirely miss. For in response to Lear's rebuke of Cordelia's silent love, "nothing can come of nothing. Speak again . . .," the biblically literate reader recalls, on the contrary, that the creation of the entire universe comes *ex nihilo*, from God speaking the Word of his love. However foolish such a notion may appear, this same love later redeems the world through Christ being exiled from heaven and becoming a "nothing" on earth; in Paul's words, to be united with Christ is to be "as sorrowful, yet always rejoicing; as poor, yet making many rich; as having nothing, and yet possessing all things" (2 Cor. 6:10). Although Cordelia has foolishly lost her entire inheritance, the noble suitor France sees similar paradoxes in her: "Fairest Cordelia, that art most rich being poor / Most choice forsaken, and most loved despised, / Thee and thy virtues here I seize upon" (1.1.250–53). While it is important to explain that Cordelia is a "type" rather than direct allegory of Christ, and that typology is the more common religious lineage of Renaissance literary characters, the conception of Cordelia as Christ figure is developed later in the play. For now, France's odd exclamation just after this praise, "Gods, gods!" (1.1.255) shows the text itself suggesting the central theological questions that critics have subsequently debated: Is there a difference between upper and lower case gods? Are some gods real, others fictional? Is there, as monotheism claims, one living God who deeply cares about human evil and suffering? Is the Christian conception of God relevant to understanding *King Lear* which, though set in pre-Christian Britain, is written and produced within Renaissance Christendom?

The combination of moral evil and Christian wisdom found in the opening scene opened this latter possibility for the Chinese student, and Act Two of *King Lear* certainly continues to allow this interpretation. In the parallelism of the play's two major plots, in which wicked and good children are contrasted by the treatment of their elderly fathers, there is a very obvious and moving contrast that has important spiritual implications. Edmond proclaims "Nature" his "goddess" (1.2.1), and then deceives his father Gloucester and deprives his brother Edgar, much as Goneril and Regan had done to Cordelia, of his due family inheritance. Eventually the three wicked children form an adulterous, murderous tryst; what all three share is the practical belief that human nature is primarily the quest for material power and pleasure, and violence a natural way to achieve these ends. While I never drew this analogy, a significant number of students did classify their thinking as a form of the "power comes from the barrel of a gun" mentality still revered, in China and elsewhere, by some forms of political theory.

On the other hand, China also has a much older tradition of nonviolence, through the mixture of Taoist, Buddhist, and Confucian popular religion still common in China today[11]; combined with a reading of the ancient Christian hymn in Philippians 2:5–11, which sings of how Christ "made himself of no reputation, and took upon the form of a servant," students quickly saw spiritual significance in the numerous characters who echo Cordelia's initial "nothing" in reply to the general human desire for power. Hunted by his father and brother, Edgar pledges "I nothing am" (2.2.184), disguising himself as "Mad Tom" at war with a host of fiends. Lear's Fool recalls and mocks the King's failure to perceive Cordelia's true love by asking, "Can you make no use of nothing, nuncle?" (1.4.129). In the stocks after defending Lear's authority, Kent recognizes that it is from within the position of suffering servant that extraordinary change may yet be seen, for "nothing almost sees miracle / but misery" (2.2.156–57). Lear himself attempts to be the Jobean "pattern of all patience," pledging "I will say nothing" (3.2.37–38), but he keeps this pledge about as faithfully as his biblical predecessor. Miraculous changes in his own human nature are beginning to occur, however, as Lear learns to value the love of his friends and faithful daughter more than the comforts of power which he once enjoyed.

The main educator in this process is certainly the Fool, and for a number of reasons he became the students' favorite character not only in this play, but even the entire Shakespeare course. A large part of their attraction lay precisely in the area that takes considerable work to convey to most Western students: the linguistic jokes. Using humor that requires comprehension of concrete, literal references and then subtly transmutes to figurative puns or metaphors, the Fool also uses sarcasm to continue Kent's work and try to help Lear "see better." In the "egg" illustration, for example, the Fool says "Give me an egg, nuncle, and I'll give thee two crowns" (1.4.138); perhaps hoping for more royal power, Lear asks, "what two crowns shall they be?" but the Fool's real offer is much more literal:

> Why, after I have cut the egg i' the middle, and eat
> up the meat, the two crowns of the egg. When thou

> clovest thy crown i' the middle, and gavest away
> both parts, thou borest thy ass on thy back o'er
> the dirt: thou hadst little wit in thy bald crown,
> when thou gavest thy golden one away. (1.4.140–146)

The pun here teases with royal power, but then the literal meaning of the egg divides seamlessly into a double pun and metaphor which first demonstrates the fragility of the political dis-order that Lear has created by dividing his kingdom between Goneril and Regan, and then warns of the personal destruction of Lear's now naked human head.

Arguably, the Fool is also calling Lear an "ass," another common name for "fool," a point he elsewhere makes clear (1.4.159). Such critique was basic to the Renaissance rationale for the existence of fools, for those in power need soothsayers to counter the excessive flattery given by the masses. The historical lineage of the Fool fascinated the Chinese students, who saw him as a counterpart of the traditional "trickster figure," such as the monkey in the classic Chinese novel "Journey to the West."[12] The capacity of the weak, suffering servant to speak truth to power also has deep roots in Christianity, and here I introduced Erasmus's *Praise of Folly*[13] and Paul's preaching that "the foolishness of God is wiser than men" (1 Cor. 1:25). Shakespeare's figurative use of "nothing" again becomes clear when the Fool now numbers Lear himself as one of the exiles, one of the powerless: "now thou art an O without a figure: I am better than thou art now; I am a fool, thou art nothing" (1.4.174–75). Painfully aware and highly cynical of power politics, the Chinese students' journals highly praised the Fool's declaration that, no matter what, he would remain a loyal servant and true friend to his King:

> That sir which serves and seeks for gain,
> And follows but for form,
> Will pack when it begins to rain,
> And leave thee in the storm,
> But I will tarry; the fool will stay,
> And let the wise man fly. (2.2.251–56)

It is in the powerful performance storm scenes of Act 3 that the Fool's education begins to affect Lear, after the King has been sent out to die by his heartless daughters. In the existential nothingness in which man, in a material sense, seems no more than a "poor, bare, forked animal" (3.4.102), somehow Lear begins to care for the weak, the poor; here, certainly, some of the remaining Communist ideals taught to the Chinese students were openly expressed and affirmed. Yet they also could not fail to notice that the clearest expression

135

of these ideals, by Lear, are expressed in the form of a prayer; motioning for the Fool, "houseless poverty," to enter the hovel first, Lear then presents a formal but deeply heartfelt prayer:

> Poor naked wretches, whereso'er you are,
> That bide the pelting of this pitiless storm,
> How shall your houseless heads and unfed sides,
> Your loop'd and window'd raggedness, defend you
> From seasons such as these? O, I have ta'en
> Too little care of this! Take physic, pomp;
> Expose thyself to feel what wretches feel,
> That thou mayst shake the superflux to them,
> And show the heavens more just. (3.4.23–36)

As the physical, emotional, and spiritual heart of the play, this speech reopened the question of divinity; were the gods just? Can human compassion help us to show the true nature of God? Are we blinded from seeing God's nature by our own comfort in wealth or security in power?

Initially, it is easy to argue that *King Lear* makes a positive answer to these questions seem not only foolish, but mad. There are moments when Lear appears truly insane, such as when he adopts Mad Tom as his philosopher (3.4.144), or later when he runs screaming into the sea at Dover (4.6.199). More obviously, the play's subplot soon undercuts and almost seems to savagely mock its own positive metaphors of sight when Goneril and Regan, together with their husbands Albany and Cornwall, capture Gloucester and, dispensing with trial in charges of treason to Cordelia's invading forces from France, pluck out his eyes. Onstage violence in this grotesque form is rare in Shakespeare, and meant to be shocking; even today's Western students, though numbed by the far more excessive violence now common in film or television, will frequently object to watching this scene in class. While saddened by the horrific treatment of the elderly, the Chinese students initially reacted with resignation, with many citing the Fool's final lines in the play, "I'll go to bed at noon" (3.6.43), as the only wise response to the darkness of the mad, upside-down world. Yet many also offered extensive praise to the servant who stands up and fatally wounds Cornwall (3.7.70–80), citing him as evidence of human goodness even in the face of extreme evil. Most importantly, and quite unlike many Western critics, none accepted Gloucester's famous line on his fate—"As flies to wanton boys are we to th' gods; / They kill us for their sport" (4.1.37–38)—as the definitive comment on the play's divinity debate.

For whereas many see a "wheel of fortune" alternating hope and suffering within the play, and some see a darkly pessimistic movement ever further down into nihilism,[14] what surprised the Chinese students most was that neither Lear nor Gloucester simply dies upon meeting the full savagery of physical or human nature. Very attentive themselves to the structure of the play, the students instead marveled at how the suffering of both old fathers is quickly, almost miraculously treated, salved, cared for by the once rejected child. Through first Edgar and then Cordelia, the extraordinary scenes of Act 4 became the crucial moments in which these students, so long indoctrinated that they had become cynical about the dogmas of materialistic atheism, came to see the deep spiritual power of unselfish, self-sacrificing love. Moreover, while it is difficult to know the full ramifications of a radical social engineering program such as China's "one-child" policy, or to make definite claims about how these readers' familial experiences affect textual reception, there is no doubt in my mind that the Chinese students had an unusually intense form of identification with both Edgar and Cordelia, seeing in the endurance, courage, and absolute loyalty to their parents a familial bond that no external form of suffering could ever destroy.

Many sections of Act 4, perhaps the most extraordinary single act in all of drama, were read aloud in class and subsequently written about on papers and exams, but a favorite starting point was Edgar's working thesis on "the worst"; he begins with the very hopeful "the worst returns to laughter" (4.1.6), but then must face the sight of his blinded father, and eventually conclude that "the worst is not / So long as we can say 'This is the worst'" (4.1.28–29). Such realism resonated, as did the notion that suffering requires deeds more than words, but Edgar's conclusion here was read as hopeful defiance against the trials of fortune. After Edgar leads his father to the cliffs of Dover, the long speech that opens 4.5 was also particularly valued as a masterpiece of dramatic description; the opening five lines, for example, contain several words that the students' journals would carefully annotate:

> Come on, sir; here's the place: stand still. How fearful
> And dizzy 'tis, to cast one's eyes so low!
> The crows and choughs that wing the midway air
> Show scarce so gross as beetles: half way down
> Hangs one that gathers samphire, dreadful trade! (4.5.11–15)

This entire scene also became a favorite for dramatic reading; within the limited props available in our very traditional classrooms, the students were enraptured with how Edgar's words could create the cliffs of Dover within

Gloucester's mind, representing the landscape so vividly that the old man actually believes he is stepping to his death in walking off the cliff. Indeed, due perhaps to the general absence of Chinese societal prohibition against suicide, especially the suicide of a suffering, elderly blind man, many students had to be reminded that Edgar is not actually intending to lead his father to his death. What is Edgar's real intention? How, and why, does his plan succeed? These crucial questions provoked a superb classroom discussion.

Of course, Edgar's aside before Gloucester even "jumps" seems to give the answer away: "Why I do trifle thus with his despair / Is done to cure it" (4.5.33–34). But how does the "suicide" cure despair? Allowing, even encouraging, someone to commit suicide is certainly not a normal mental health practice, in either China or the West. Was Edgar expressing a kind of sadistic hatred for the father who had rejected him? After Gloucester "falls," Edgar's next aside suggests something more profound: "And yet I know not how conceit may rob / the treasury of life when life itself / yields to the theft" (4.5.43–44). Even after the Renaissance concept of "conceit" as extravagant metaphor is explained, this is not a line easily annotated. Edgar's conception is somewhat akin, perhaps, to the crucial Christian paradox that "he that loseth his life for my sake shall find it" (Matt. 10:39). For the Chinese students, the notion of voluntarily giving up one's life as a means of saving it was a concept that, outside of *King Lear*, few had any concrete way of expressing. Many were fascinated by the psychology of Gloucester believing that he actually had been mortally injured after his fall (4.6.50), but Edgar's resurrection question, "Alive or dead?" (4.5.45), is clearly the more fundamental point. While many students also found a kind of black humor in Edgar's subsequent wonder at how Gloucester *should* have "shivered like an egg" if he had "been aught but goss'mer, feathers, air, / So many fathom down precipitating" (4.5.49–50), all regained a sense of the comic sublime upon reaching Edgar's crucial conclusion: "Thy life's a miracle" (4.5.55).

Again, basic annotation of the meaning of "miracle" does not suffice; in a sense, there is nothing obviously supernatural about this moment, for of course Gloucester has not really stepped off the cliffs of Dover. Yet there is something miraculous, all of the students agreed, in having a terribly wounded person, so intent on suicide as to walk many miles and jump off a high cliff, then undergo the kind of radical interior change that suddenly makes Gloucester now want to outlive *any* affliction, and thus cry out: "Henceforth I'll bear / Affliction till it do cry out itself / 'Enough, enough,' and die" (4.5.75–76). How has this "miracle" happened? Again, Edgar himself has prefaced his father's declaration with a fairly direct, clear answer, but not one easily annotated; now taking a new disguise as casual servant, Edgar describes the "beggar" who had been leading Gloucester as a "fiend" or devil and attributes his father's salvation to divinity:

> It was some fiend; therefore, thou happy father,
> Think that the clearest gods, who make them honours
> Of men's impossibilities, have preserved thee. (4.5.72–74)

The paradox, of course, is that neither Edgar, nor his father, nor the audience, can say with any certainty who these "clearest gods" are, nor explain how they have preserved Gloucester's life. Yet he is alive, and in Edgar one has seen a very clear, deeply moving example of self-sacrificing love of the kind commended by Christianity; again one hears a fairly clear echo in Edgar's lines of Jesus's teaching that "the things which are impossible with men are possible with God" (Luke 18:27). If what once had seemed impossible—that the blinded Gloucester would again wish to live—now has become certain, was this possible only through the spirit of the Christian God, the spirit of self-sacrificial love, that is so clearly working through Edgar?

Seeing these "clearest gods" may not be possible solely through this scene, but the subsequent scenes with Cordelia, and the father who once rejected her, so clearly parallel the subplot of Edgar and Gloucester that it is very easy to draw a similar conclusion. Shakespeare seems to prepare his audience for this possibility through a fairly direct biblical allusion spoken, as often in Shakespeare's works, by a nameless "Gentleman," an undeveloped character whose words pertain to theme much more than plot. Lear, he says,

> hast one daughter,
> Who redeems nature from the general curse
> Which twain have brought her to. (4.5.201–03)

No Renaissance audience could hear this line without thinking of Adam, Eve, and the general curse of the human fall; at the same time, it is another good example of biblical allusion used as typology rather than allegory. No more than Goneril and Regan "are" Adam or Eve, does Cordelia in a simple sense represent Christ. Yet the allusion does establish a comparison in which Cordelia can be seen as Christ-like, a type of Christian who, like Edgar, mediates God's love to a man suffering from the curse of evil that begins with the human fall. Like Gloucester on the cliffs of Dover, Lear at the start of 4.6 perceives himself as spiritually dead, and does not recognize the child who has come to comfort him:

> You do me wrong to take me out o' the grave:
> Thou art a soul in bliss; but I am bound

Upon a wheel of fire, that mine own tears
Do scald like moulten lead. (4.6.38–41)

Even more than Gloucester, Lear experiences death as a kind of personal hell, and the Christ-like work done here by Cordelia thus bears a significant connection to the Christian concept known in Shakespeare's day as the "harrowing of hell," when Christ—between the crucifixion and resurrection—descends to the dead to lead out repentant sinners who happen to live before the coming of the Messiah.

The Chinese students were fascinated by this connection, once the distinction between typology and allegory, between likeness and identity, was grasped as a common technique of Renaissance art. Within this framework, one can argue for both biblical difference as well as similarity; for example, for Lear repentance is almost a moot point, since spiritually he already experiences the anguish of hell and certainly is not in "perfect mind" (4.6.55) during the meeting with his daughter. Yet when the key moment of recognition does occur, there is another case of figurative, allusive language that confirms both the concrete dramatic situation and Shakespeare's broader religious intentions. Though a King, Lear is first of all a human being, a father, and thus says, "as I am a man, I think this lady / to be my child Cordelia"; in turn, her response confirms her dramatic person, "And so I am, I am" (4.5.61–63), but also suggests the personal love of eternal Being, "I AM," expressed to Moses by the God of Exodus (3:14). Cordelia offers Lear the kind of unconditional love that Shakespeare's Sonnet 116 famously applies to marriage, but essential to Christian doctrine is that every human soul desires an eternal love, one that in the words of the sonnet "bears it out even to the edge of doom."[15] Cordelia humbly offers this to Lear, paradoxically asking him, "hold your hands in benediction o'er me" (4.6.51), and it is in these moments that the "great rage" (4.6.72) within Lear is extinguished. Perhaps alluding to his own famous sonnet, or to Paul's even more famous words on love in 1 Corinthians 13:7, in which charity "beareth all things," Lear closes the scene by commanding Cordelia, "you must bear with me," but also asking, "pray you now, forget and forgive," and humbling admitting his own human condition: "I am old and foolish" (4.6. 76–77).

As in Shakespeare's late tragi-comedies, the moment of recognition here is also one of reconciliation, and of resurrection. Cordelia's love lifts her father out of the grave, and even after her army loses the battle, Lear celebrates the joy of their new life together with a stunningly beautiful speech. Some regard this speech as a "song of innocence," but the Chinese students tended to read it as a gleeful rejection of the capacity of state power to prevent individual dissent or crack the bond of familial love, and this speech clearly became their single favorite moment in the entire play:

> Come, let's away to prison:
> We two alone will sing like birds i' the cage:
> When thou dost ask me blessing, I'll kneel down,
> And ask of thee forgiveness: so we'll live,
> And pray, and sing, and tell old tales, and laugh
> At gilded butterflies, and hear poor rogues
> Talk of court news; and we'll talk with them too,
> Who loses and who wins; who's in, who's out;
> And take upon's the mystery of things,
> As if we were God's spies: and we'll wear out,
> In a wall'd prison, packs and sects of great ones,
> That ebb and flow by the moon. (5.3.8–19)

As for all readers of perhaps Shakespeare's most painful tragedy, Lear's absolute hope here is challenged completely, horribly, by the subsequent murder of his "poor fool" (5.3.281). Yet as the history of *Lear* criticism clearly shows, how one reads the play's final moments depends to a large extent on whether one's vision has been altered, in the course of the play, from a purely materialistic outlook in which "the gods" (if there are any) either ignore or cause human suffering, to a foolishly religious perception of the reality, sanctity, and immortality of the human soul. The kind of spiritual communion just described by Lear, for example, is unaffected by human prisons or politics, and allows perception of the "mystery of things," the "negative capability" of Keats that here is specifically linked to service to God, service (as in Milton's later sonnet on blindness[16]) that consists most of all in standing against oppressive power and perceiving truth. Without confirming the identity of the divinity noted here, Lear has Judeo-Christian tradition on his side in adding that "upon such sacrifices . . . The gods themselves throw incense" (5.3.20–21); in the poetry of Psalms, the living God proclaims: "Gather my saints together unto me; those that have made a covenant with me by sacrifice" (50:5).

Given the obvious parallelism of the play's two main plots, it is not hard to argue, and very difficult to ignore, that what one ultimately perceives in Cordelia's and Lear's deaths should be affected by Edgar's account of Gloucester's passing; this moment is described rather than shown in the play, but our last glimpse of the two together is also relevant. Again depressed, Gloucester sits and says "no farther, sir; a man may rot even here" (5.2.8); his still-disguised son then seems to quote Hamlet[17] on readiness for death, similarly trusting in a "special providence" (5.2.165) that makes death the beginning rather than end of a journey. Edgar insists, "Men must endure / their going hence, even as their coming hither; / ripeness is all" (5.2.9–11), and despite his painful awareness of material mortality, Gloucester concedes the spiritual point: "And that's true too" (5.2.12). Tragically, this old father's journey into death begins just after his son reveals his true identity, but the emotion upon parting is complex. Edgar tells us that just before the battle in which he fatally wounds Edmond, he had asked his father's "blessing," and revealed his own identity:

> but his flaw'd heart,
> Alack, too weak the conflict to support!
> 'Twixt two extremes of passion, joy and grief,
> Burst smilingly. (5.3.188–91)

Gloucester dies, in other words, by the clash of emotions experienced in this moment, the grief in how his own sin led to this tragic moment, and the joy in recognizing that his son was truly alive; it is poetic perception, not simplistic optimism, to recognize that only the latter emotion actively endures, for after the sudden "burst" of the heart, joy somehow continues on, adverb modifying the subject's continued activity, "smilingly."

These suggestions of resurrection, with many parallels, are developed much further in the death of Cordelia. Certainly her death makes us first question the existence of any of the "gods" whom Albany calls to her defense once he finally realizes her danger and exclaims, "the gods defend her" (5.3.231), and also makes us doubt Edgar's judgment of divinity's role in punishing Gloucester's adultery through Edmond: "the gods are just, and of our pleasant vices / make instruments to plague us" (5.3.161–62). Albany, certainly, is like Job's misguided comforters in proclaiming simplistic justice: "All friends shall taste / the wages of their virtue, and all foes / the cup of their deservings.—O see, see" (5.3.278–80). Finally, there can be no doubt that Lear experiences the extreme limits of human grief when he enters carrying Cordelia's dead body: "Howl, howl, howl, howl … She's gone for ever" (5.3.232–34). Yet is it madness or complete foolishness for Lear to then propose a "resurrection test" and ask for "a looking-glass," so "if that her breath will mist or stain the stone, / why then she lives," for "if it be so, / It is a chance which does redeem all sorrows / that ever I have felt" (5.3.237–241). Yes, the test is incoherent and interrupted by more anguished questions—"why should a dog, a horse, a rat have life / and thou no breath at all" (5.3. 282–83)—but in the Folio version of the play Lear's final words do see and express a vision of Cordelia's lips moving: "Do you see this? Look on her! Look, her lips! / Look there, look there!" (5.3.286–87).

The question of whether or not the revision from Quarto to Folio reflects an authorial intention to stress spiritual vision fascinated the Chinese students, as it should every Shakespearean scholar; even the most ardent atheist among them did not seem to consider dismissing Lear's final words as madness. For one cannot ignore that the keen-eyed servant Kent, who had urged Lear in the play's opening scene to "see better," now himself sees Lear's passing as the start of a journey, and Lear's spirit as a person who retains respect:

> Vex not his ghost: O, let him pass! he hates him much
> That would upon the rack of this tough world
> Stretch him out longer. (5.3.289–91)

Given this spiritual perception, it is not at all foolish to conclude that Lear dies perceiving that the child who loved and served him is alive, resurrected in another world to which his heart, now bursting like Gloucester's, also joyfully travels. Kent, again, has absolutely no doubt about this, and perhaps mortally wounded or simply ready to die since his vocation as servant to Lear has ended, he leaves the play by rejecting Albany's offer of political power in favour of following his King to the afterlife: "I have a journey sir, shortly to go: / My master calls me; I must not say no" (5.3.297–98).

Conclusion

The fact that *King Lear*, unlike the tragi-comedies or romances that were to dominate the final part of Shakespeare's career, does not conclude with a clear affirmation of the joyful reality of resurrection from death nor a clear praise of Divinity does not make its spiritual message any less compelling. Like many other audiences of the play, the Chinese students deeply appreciated the interpretive freedom implicit in Edgar's final instructions to both the characters on stage and present audience: "Speak what we feel, not what we ought to say" (5.3.300). The play does produce extreme emotions of grief, and yet to echo Gloucester's final words it is "true too" that at play's end an extreme experience of joy is also possible. Very specifically, this is the kind of joy to which C. S. Lewis later applies the German term "sehnsucht,"[18] a longing for eternal rest, beauty, and peace that is bittersweet so long as we remain within the rack of this tough world.

Even the most logical atheist, however, must admit that this joy is possible only *if* there does exist not merely the humanly-projected "gods" who manipulate the human lust for power to violent ends, but also the "clearest gods" (4.5.73) of self-sacrificial compassion who would be served by Cordelia's and Lear's perception of truth in the prison of this world. It is these "gods," Lear promised his daughter, who "shall bring a brand from heaven / and fire us hence like foxes" upon any human attempt to "part us" (5.3.20–23). Like all audiences, my Chinese students were left with their own choice: whether finally to see Lear and Cordelia together in the grave, or kneeling and blessing each other, with Kent, in God's heavenly kingdom. That so many rejected materialism in favor of themselves becoming "God's spies" who see into "the mystery of things" (5.3.15–16) was a testament not only to the drab boredom and failed ethics of an atheistic education—an education sadly shared, of course, by many Western students—but moreover to the moving power of Shakespeare's spiritual, dramatic art, and the divine image of life that our loving Father writes upon every human heart.

Endnotes

1 Gregory Maillet, "On Teaching (and being taught) Shakespeare in China and Canada," in *Shakespeare and Higher Education—A Global Perspective, Shakespeare Yearbook* 12 (2001): 79–107.

2 Horace, "The Art of Poetry," in *The Critical Tradition: Classic Texts and Contemporary Trends*, ed. David H. Richter (Boston and New York: Bedford St. Martins, 1997, 82–94), 92.

3 William Shakespeare, *The Tragedy of King Lear: The Folio Text*, ed. Gary Taylor, in *William Shakespeare: The Complete Works*, gen. eds. Stanley Wells and Gary Taylor (Oxford: Clarendon, 1988), 945–974.

4 Ernest Hemingway, *Death in the Afternoon* (1932), reprint edition (London: Jonathan Cape, 1958), 183.

5 John Keats, "To George and Thomas Keats" (1817), in the *Norton Anthology of English Literature: The Major Authors*, 8th ed., gen. ed. Stephen Greenblatt (New York and London: Norton, 2006), 1871.

6 See, for example, Mao Tse-tung, "Talks at the Yenan Forum on Literature and Art" (1942), in *Mao Tse-Tung on Literature and Art* (Peking: Foreign Languages Press, 1967), 1–43.

7 John Keats, "On Sitting Down to Read *King Lear* Again" (1818), in the *Norton Anthology of English Literature*, 1829.

8 Biblical citations within this essay refer to the Authorized King James Version of 1611.

9 William R. Elton, *King Lear and the Gods* (San Marino, CA: Huntington, 1966).

10 *King Lear*, directed by Michael Elliot (Granada Television, 1983). Performers included Laurence Olivier, Anna Calder-Marshall, and John Hurt.

11 For a mainly Christian overview of this complex reality, see Hans Kung and Julia Ching, *Christianity and Chinese Religions* (New York: Doubleday, 1989).

12 Wu Chengen, *Journey to the West* (1590), trans. Anthony C.Yu. (Chicago: University of Chicago Press, 1983).

13 Erasmus, *Praise of Folly* (1515), trans. Betty Radice (Harmondsworth: Penguin, 1971)

14 James Black, "King Lear: Art Upside-Down," in *Shakespeare Survey* 33 (1980): 35–42.

15 William Shakespeare, "Sonnet 116," ed. Stanley Wells, in *William Shakespeare: The Complete Works*, 765.

16 John Milton, "Sonnet 16" (1645), in *John Milton: The Major Works*, eds. Stephen Orgel and Jonathan Goldberg (Oxford: Oxford University Press, 2003), 81.

17 William Shakespeare, *Hamlet*, ed. Gary Taylor, in *William Shakespeare: The Complete Works*, 655–688.

18 C. S. Lewis, *Surprised by Joy: The Shape of My Early Life* (1955), reprint edition (New York: Harcourt Brace, 1997), 7.

AT THE INTERSECTION OF FAITH IN FRESHMAN COMPOSITION:

A Conversation about Ethics with Donne, Lewis, Sayers, King, and Swift

MARY ALICE TRENT (ORAL ROBERTS UNIVERSITY)

In this essay, Mary Alice Trent chronicles the conversations on ethos she has had with and witnessed among freshman students. Students examine the epistemologies of faith in action, as they pose the following questions: "How do we come to know the ethics of God in light of our personal struggle with ethics?" "How do we represent (or present) the authenticity of Christ to the world?" "What does it really mean to be a Christian (or steward of social justice)?"

In the English department at the small Christian university where I teach, my freshman students and I can only imagine what a conversation would have been like if John Donne, C. S. Lewis, Dorothy Sayers, Martin Luther King, Jr., and Jonathan Swift frequented a local coffeehouse together; particularly since these brilliant thinkers and writers lived in different time spans and on different continents. It seems as though we can hear King, Sayers, and Lewis discussing theological matters associated with the Trinity and the aesthetics of God's workmanship. Then again, we can see Swift and King taking their eloquently philosophical messages of hope and social justice to parliament and to the streets, speaking to the status quo and the masses of people, advocating equality for all of God's children. The poet of our conscience, Donne would today remind us of all truth, pointing to God, as he'd bellow out verses in coffeehouses near and far.

Though we can only imagine what it would have been like had they all lived in the same era, the legacy of their works still inspires generations upon generations across the globe. In many ways, I see their works as simultaneously working together in my freshman composition courses, as we explicate their respective literature and discuss the discourse of faith and *ethos* with each other.

In *Rhetoric*, Aristotle defined ethos (the moral character or virtue of the speaker) in connection with *logos* or intellect, and *pathos* or emotions; for he believed that an effective rhetorician was one who mastered all three classical appeals in public discourse. Using Aristotle's groundwork as the backdrop, I engage students in conversations from a Christian worldview: considering *logos* as the Word of God; *pathos*, the compassion of Christ; and *ethos*, the ethics of God. Though times may change, resulting in changing trends, as even the English language has undergone a metamorphosis over centuries, the ethics of God has and will remain constant.

In order to personalize the concept of the constancy of God with the ethos of God, my students and I share personal accounts of how God has demonstrated this in our lives. In many cases, students and I have shared stories about how, time and time again, God has proven His word by revealing truth in the form of financial blessings and physical healings for us or family members and friends.

Before sharing my personal story, I begin by reading Proverbs 3:3–5 wherein Solomon tells us to trust God without ceasing and lean on His understanding (not our own), knowing that God will guide our way. Then I tell one experience that involved my not wanting to obey God due to unforgiveness that I was feeling toward another person who had offended me. Though the pain of the offense was legitimate, what God illustrated to me was that I took my eyes off of Him and succumbed to my sinful nature. When I surrendered to God, He showed me that His ways are sovereign and His wisdom is infinite and that my ability to comprehend what He knows is limited. As a result, I realized that forgiveness was not an option but a requirement for living the abundant life God has for me. My choice to forgive was as much a spiritual decision as an ethical one.

When students and I study "Holy Sonnet XIV" by John Donne, they trip over the language of the metaphysical poet and view his words as remote and archaic. But when we dissect the words more closely, students begin to see that Donne's poem is, in essence, about a persona whose sinful nature is struggling to surrender to God's will. The theme of the poem is essentially an all-out battle between good and evil, and that makes sense to this millennial generation of *Facebook—MySpace—text-messaging—iPhone* users.

148

Even though the persona desires to be with God, the battle between good and evil is denoted by phrasing like, "usurped town, to another is due."[1] To further complicate matters for the persona, he cannot comprehend the inability of his reason to defend him on toward truth. The apparent contradictions presented throughout the poem heighten the struggle between the persona's spirit and his flesh.

In order to further examine this poem, we reference the words of Paul in Romans 7:9–25, where he chronicles his struggle to do what is right in the presence of evil. He concedes that the only way to be a victor over sin is through the advocacy of Jesus Christ. In the end, the students realize that the poem is as much about the ethics of God as it is the persona's ethics.

Using Donne's poem as their inspiration, students are required to write an original poem on the theme of good versus evil and use a metaphor that illustrates this theme, as Donne has achieved in his poem. Students are encouraged to use as many sensory impressions as possible in their poems. Like Donne, they have to write the poem in first person. Central to their work is taking into account the ethics of the poem's persona.

While Donne's work illustrates the ethics of the individual along with God, C. S. Lewis poses the question, "What are we to make of Jesus Christ?" In his essay of the same title, Lewis explores the moral teachings of the man, Jesus, and the proclamations of Jesus's identifying Himself as God. In short, Lewis would seem to question the ethics of Jesus Christ. Upon closer examination, students realize that throughout his writing, Lewis refutes faulty claims against the divinity of Christ, e.g., legends conspiracy and "ghost-survival."[2]

Reading Lewis is a testament to young postmodern Christians who often struggle with how to present the Gospel to non-Christians without preaching and becoming dogmatic. We discuss how the Bible is logos and how this logos informs our pathos; not the other way around. Once Lewis has presented his arguments, he actually comes out in defense of the ethics of Christ, thereby ending the essay with reference to the words of Jesus: "I am the Truth, and the Way, and the Life . . . . I am Life. Eat Me, and drink Me, I am your food."[3] Given the smooth, clear syntactical style of Lewis, students conclude that his arguments are highly logical, that his ending exhibits emotional appeal, and that his claims support the ethics of Christ. In the end, students conclude what Lewis appears to have a dual purpose: He intends for his audience to understand that Christ was both moral teacher and part of the Godhead and that the real question is what Christ will eventually make of us (Lewis 47).

Like her Inklings counterpart, Dorothy Sayers was a premiere thinker of the faith during her time, and students discover this in analyzing "The Dogma Is the Drama." Students realize how effective satire can be at instructing and informing an otherwise uninformed audience, as Sayers does in this piece. Her work is an indictment of the ethics of misguided Christians who misinform non-Christians by presenting false statements about the Christian faith.

She postulates that Christians need not water down the Gospel or drape it with verbose ornamentation: The doctrine of the Christian faith is all the drama there is. She accuses misinformed Christians of presenting faulty claims about the Trinity, that all three are "incomprehensible" and that theologians fashioned the Trinity to complicate Christian life.

Sayers further argues that "original sin," as defined by the Church is "Anything we enjoy doing."[4] Sex is sinful unless the act is conducted in marriage and the couple experiences no enjoyment in doing it. Other sinful expressions include debauchery, drunkenness, murder, "not attending church," and "cruelty to dumb animals."[5] While the former three are sinful, the latter two are Sayers' satirical renditions of some Christians' misinterpretations of Scripture.

Students find her satire quite amusing, but they concede that her points are not uncommon responses that they hear among some twenty-first-century Christians. Students decipher the layers of meaning to get to the core of Sayers' message: Christians have an ethical responsibility to present the Gospel for what it authentically is; nothing more, nothing less. When we fail to do so, we misrepresent the ethics of God.

Using her essay as a springboard, I ask my students to think about how Internet access, along with other media, has made it easier to manipulate the message of the Gospel, as well as other written texts and oral texts. For example, students share how easy it is to upload sections of sermons that misrepresent the original message or how pseudo-images and voices can be used to underscore the ethos of any speaker. Still other students contend that the information highway has brought the Gospel to those in remote areas of the world who would have not heard it and who may not have access to Bibles. Some students argue that for this latter reason it is paramount that Christians not water down the message, as Sayers argues in her essay.

The writing activity that I assign to students after reading and discussing Lewis and Sayers is one that challenges students to think about their role in sharing the Gospel without compromising the message. Lewis and Sayers examine the ethos of Christ by refuting false claims against the divinity of Jesus. Sayers extends her claims to include the character of God and the Holy Spirit. To this end, I require students to think about conversations they have had with others who have argued against the Gospel. After presenting their arguments, they must offer rebuttals, using scriptures and theological claims, citing biblical scholars and theologians.

In "Letter from Birmingham Jail," Dr. Martin Luther King, Jr., challenged the ethics of his audience, fellow clergymen, to be extremists for love, as Christ modeled during His thirty-three years on earth. Articulating the urgency for social justice and an end to segregation between Negroes and Caucasians in America, King built an ensemble of cohorts of all races and religions, both males and females.

As we study this selection, I observe students struggling to fully understand the concepts of "white only" and "colored only," since all of the traditional students in the classroom were born over twenty years after the Civil Rights Movement had reached its pinnacle. Nonetheless, some students of color can relate to racial profiling and understand inadequacies in the current justice system, which they attribute to institutional racism. Some whites are uncomfortable talking about race relations, since they don't want to offend anyone, yet others can see it for what it is: an opportunity to dialogue in a safe classroom environment on a topic that's still taboo.

Like King, part of my challenge is to appeal to all of my students from a Christ-centered mentality. Fundamentally, it's a conversation about ethics. King defends his nonviolent campaign with logical appeals from the Bible, as well as historical and philosophical rhetoric. Appealing to the moral conscience of his audience, King defines two types of laws: just laws and unjust laws; he argues that just laws are in accordance with God's law but that unjust laws are out of order with God's law.

King ends his letter with a plea to the Church; some might even call it a warning. He contends that the God's judgment is upon the Church. King further argues that the Church will lose her relevancy if she does not "recapture the sacrificial spirit of the early church"[6] or if she fails to maintain her "authenticity" (339). In so doing, the Church would be nothing more than "an irrelevant social club with no meaning for the twentieth century."[7] For a generation of twenty-first-century churchgoers, my students can relate to King's closing statements. Church for them is one that has no walls and no doors because the church is the world; the mission field is the world. Anything short of that, they argue, dilutes the sanctity of Christ's calling in their lives.

Students and I discuss ways in which the Church can be relevant in a postmodern culture that defines relevancy as changeable based upon individual human circumstances. In a society that shuns absolute truth, students use King's letter to help them further shape their own epistemology. There's no doubt that King believed in the absolute authority of Jesus Christ and that King's ethics were governed by his Christian precepts.

Like King, the next writer, Jonathan Swift, challenges the moral fiber of his readership to end the suffering and social injustice that was occurring in Ireland during his day. There is absolutely nothing "modest" about Swift's proposal, but students and I discuss the impact of his title in light of satire. Since the Irish were being treated poorly by the Englishmen, Swift writes a tract that would heighten the cruelty of the injustice by seemingly exploiting the poor recipients of this inhumane treatment. He preys upon the most vulnerable: the babies of the poor.

Examining the proposal in more details, we notice that after the writer has given substantial reasons for implementing his plan, he concludes that he and his wife are exempted from participating since she is beyond childbearing age (Swift 219). I discuss the ethics of the writer with the students and the role that satire plays in the closing paragraph. In satirically advocating Swift stewing, baking and roasting babies, and making gloves for ladies and boots for men out of baby's skin (217), Swift was in fact, of course, trying to get the attention of those in positions of power who could make the necessary social changes to better the lives of the poor in Ireland.[8]

Many millennial thinkers in my freshman composition class relate Swift's measures to the verse in James, chapter 2: "Faith without action is dead."[9] Stewardship extends beyond the sanctuary: It is the ethics of everyday life. The students and I discuss what it means to live an ethical life. In doing so, we refer to the logos of God as it is mentioned in Isaiah: "The Spirit of the Lord God is upon me; because the Lord hath anointed me to preach good tidings unto the meek; he hath sent me to bind up the brokenhearted, to proclaim liberty to the captives, and the opening of the prison to them that are bound."[10]

The assignment that I give students here is inspired by King's letter and Swift's proposal. They are required to choose a topic that poses a dilemma in society. They must take an ethical stand and argue for or against the issue, as King and Swift did. Students bring in logos, pathos and ethos. For each point of logos, they should offer a pro, con, and rebuttal. Each use of pathos, which should correspond to a specific logical appeal, should be in the form of anecdotes, stories and testimonies.

After grappling with the ethics of God in light of our personal struggle with ethics, representing (or presenting) the authenticity of Christ to others, and understanding what it really means to be a Christian (or steward of social justice), my students conclude that apart from God we are sinful and incapable of being good, since God is our sole source of goodness. At best, our ethics should mirror the character of God's heart.

In his research, Dr. Kevin Ryan posits that educators play an instrumental role in influencing the values of their students. He alludes to six E's of character education: "example, explanation, exhortation, ethos (ethical environment), experience and expectations of excellence."[11] Leading by example is like living a sermon without preaching it. Educators have a great deal of influence in their classrooms, and they have ample opportunities to mentor students. Explanation refers to their ability to engage students in moral discussions so that students can examine what they know and how they come to know it. Exhortation motivates students to do their best, urging them and directing and redirecting behavior toward an ethical end. Ethos refers to establishing a classroom environment that is respectful and conducive to wholesome learning. Experience moves students out of the classroom into social networking in the field, e.g., service learning projects, where they learn to serve others, resulting in less focus on self-gratification.

As educators, we have a moral obligation to assist students in shaping their epistemologies so that they will be better informed Christian citizens in a global network, which can translate into servant leadership and discipleship.

Endnotes

1   John Donne, "Holy Sonnet XIV," in *Strategies for Reading and Writing*, eds. William R. Epperson, Linda C. Gray, and Mark R. Hall (Dubuque: Kendall/Hunt, 1999), 11.

2   C. S. Lewis, "What Are We to Make of Jesus Christ?" in *Strategies*, 47.

3   Ibid., 48.

4   Dorothy Sayers, "The Drama is the Drama," in *Strategies*, 56.

5   Ibid., 57.

6   Martin Luther King, Jr., "Letter from Birmingham Jail," in *Strategies*, 339.

7   Ibid., 339.

8   Jonathan Swift, "A Modest Proposal," *Project Gutenberg*, http://www.gutenberg.org/etext/1080 (accessed March 6, 2009).

9   James 2:26.

10   Isaiah 61:1.

11   Kevin Ryan, "The Six E's of Character Education," *Center for the Advancement of Ethics and Character*, http://www.bu.edu/sed/caec/index.html (accessed September 23, 2008), qtd. in Ann Lathrop and Kathleen Foss, "Integrity, Ethics, and Character Education," in Mary Alice Trent, *Ethics in the 21st Century* (New York: Longman, 2005), 212–221.

SHAPING LIFE INTO WORD:

Faith Integration in Autobiography/Biography

MELANIE SPRINGER MOCK (GEORGE FOX UNIVERSITY)

Melanie Springer Mock shares the joys and challenges of teaching autobiography/biography to evangelical students who, while sharing a common story, rarely know how to move beyond the platitudes of life as a Christian. Using Anne Lamott's Traveling Mercies: Some Thoughts On Faith *as a model for the course, Melanie walks us through her "decentralized" approach to a semester-long course in autobiography/biography in which her students are challenged to "more fully recognize the complexity, perhaps even the paradox, of human nature: that our goodness is compromised by our fallenness, and that each of us, no matter our life stories, are in need of God's mysterious grace and love." Raised as a Mennonite, Melanie, Associate Professor of English, currently serves as Chair of the English Department at George Fox University, a Quaker school in Newberg, Oregon. She is the author of* Writing Peace: The Unheard Voices of Great War Mennonite Objectors *(Cascadia Press, 2003).*

Each year, I begin my life writing course with a story.

When I arrived at a Christian college as a student in the mid-1980s, I had never encountered the Evangelical tradition of giving testimony: of publicly narrating my own sinful degradation, my gripping conversion moment, my new life free of sin. Raised in a Mennonite home, I had no great sins to confess, beyond stealing from my mom's purse or hitting my sister; and no miraculous conversion, having become a Christian almost by birthright, and without once uttering the Jesus prayer. At college, though, my own faith story suddenly seemed paltry, especially compared to that of my peers, whose

155

testimonies revealed they had spent high school perpetually stoned and petting in their parents' cars—until they found Jesus, of course. I decided my narrative, a lifetime of Sunday evening youth events and just saying no, would never pass muster with this Evangelical crowd. Bereft of the Damascus Road experience others might envy, Evangelical peer pressure compelled me to spin a good conversion story. And so, at the first opportunity to publicly testify, I embellished a narrative of degradation and sin, of drinking and drugs, of an Augustine-like transformation set at a local schoolyard.

My life writing students seem to like this tale of a Christian lying about her own conversion to the faith, recognizing the ironic transgression of "thou shalt not lie" in the testifying ritual most Evangelicals hold sacrosanct. Still, I imagine for many students, my college narrative sits closely to their own reality. A majority of the students are Evangelicals; raised in conservative Christian homes, they believe they have few experiences that make for gripping redemption stories. Although I did not emerge from a church tradition that placed value in public testimony, many of my students did, and they understand the significant place storytelling has in a Christian community. Years of hearing tearful redemption stories around church campfires have affirmed for my students a sort of artificially-constructed narrative hierarchy. Presumably, the best stories, like my counterfeit tale, convincingly trace God's grace at work in a sinner's life; the worst, like my real life (and entirely-too-tame) story, do little to persuade others of God's redeeming power.

On the first day of my Autobiography/Biography class, then, before even cracking the syllabus, taking the requisite roll, or telling my sham conversion tale, I ask my students to write for ten minutes about why their own life stories have value. The prompt immediately sets them to writing, often long and passionate manifestos unfettered by usual first-day inhibitions. Yet later, when I read this work in my office, I am often surprised by what my students say—though I probably should not be. These young writers affirm that, in a *general* sense, life stories matter. Their belief in a creator God, and a familiarity with the rhetoric of their Christian community, shapes what they produce in this initial activity. Students acknowledge that their stories are valuable: because each person is "fearfully and wonderfully made"; because God knit each person together in her mother's womb and cares deeply for each person created; because Jesus Christ died to save even one. For example, a student wrote "at first glance, my life doesn't seem particularly special or to be anything out of the ordinary … [yet] My life story is important because it was written by my Creator who put every detail into place and I know that I should live it out for people around me to see, or maybe even read about."

This affirmation of life stories, vaguely constructed and frequently cloaked in religious platitudes, often fails to consider the ways in which the students' own stories matter. Indeed, later in the first day's class, when I ask students to write about the single most significant event in their lives, most begin the activity with a disclaimer: "Nothing much has happened to me, but I would have to say the most significant event is . . ." Thus in the same class, even on the same sheet of paper, students provide contrary notions: *a priori*, every person's life story matters because every person is created by a loving and caring God; still, the student's personal life story does not matter, because it lacks any experience others might recognize as significant or worthy of consideration.

In the six years I have taught Autobiography/Biography, the course continues to morph into its present form, and will probably transform itself again and again, into perpetuity (or retirement, whichever comes first). Its current construction is based on the consideration of these two competing ideas: students feel they have nothing significant to write about their own lives, even as life has meaning because God created it. Therefore, my semester's work requires that I affirm one notion (that each life is special), while somehow disaffirming the other (that each student writer's life holds no special meaning). More broadly, my personal philosophy of faith integration compels me to assume this focus, to establish the value of each student's life story, and to help students find that value for themselves through writing. As a faculty member at a Quaker institution, I feel drawn to the Quaker calling of "finding that of God in everyone." Although Autobiography/Biography seems uniquely situated as a course where this can happen, I believe this mission drives each course I teach: that through writing, through finding meaning in our lives and shaping that meaning into stories, essays, poems, we are documenting God's living, breathing presence in our selves and in each other. The texts I use, the essays I assign, even the student-centered pedagogy I employ reflect (I hope) this fundamental belief.

Sharing my own bogus conversion story is a good starting point for Autobiography/Biography, as I am in a sense echoing what the students affirm—consciously or not—to be true, showing that I too believed my own story had little merit as it was (and showing as well that I was willing to recreate a story for audience effect). My own narrative also provides space for an important discussion about the value of life stories in Evangelical church traditions, and the ways giving testimony affirms for Christians the central role storytelling has in their lives and in their faith. We consider the ways testifying has shaped many Christians' understanding of the spiritual journey, and I suggest as well that the testifying tradition privileges a linear narrative which takes a believer through various stages of faith, from a pre-conversion self mired in the degradation of sin (and the darker the sin, the better); to a startling conversion moment, when the sinner meets Christ face-to-face; to a post-conversion self, unfettered by her former evil and living in the light of grace and love. Such a narrative structure, I argue, compels us to understand faith journeys in a particular way, and those who come by their faith another way often either feel their own stories diminished, or choose to construct a new self befitting the testifying pattern honored by their religious communities.

My intent with this discussion is not to undermine the significant role the ritual of giving testimony has in students' faith lives; I really am not a rabble-rouser, after all. Instead, I hope our initial discussion about testifying-as-life-writing provides new perspective about both the tradition itself as well as about the students' own life stories. I ask students to explore the ways this decidedly Evangelical tradition has informed their perceptions of self and helped to shape the ways they talk about their faith journeys. I also want students to understand the contemporary custom of giving testimony within the historical context of spiritual autobiography, and so we spend some time exploring the place of the conversion narrative, however marginal, in American literature. Because this is predominantly a writing course, the exploration is brief, though by tracing the conventions of spiritual autobiography through history, students can see how their own faith stories might be similar to that of the Puritans or of the early Quakers, who also patterned their conversion narratives in the linear fashion Evangelicals continue to privilege.[1]

Additionally, I spend a class period examining the ways conversion narratives themselves mirror the structure of dramatic progression used in fiction. We map the traditionally understood device of plot line in fiction: how a writer moves from exposition through a series of conflicts; that these conflicts, at their most intense moments, create turning points in the stories; and that the resolution of these conflicts leads to a story's denouement. Conversion narratives (as well as most good autobiographies) hew closely to this same structure, reaffirming the sense that the stories we tell about our faith and about our lives are shaped as much by rhetorical convention as by actual experience: a concept we return to often throughout the semester.

After talking some about structure, we turn to the "prelude" of Anne Lamott's *Traveling Mercies: Some Thoughts on Faith*. I have consistently chosen Lamott's memoir as a core text in the course for several reasons, most notably because students seem to connect with Lamott's style, her honesty and humor, and her struggle with faith and doubt. While I perennially worry that students will be offended by Lamott's language and her R-rated life experiences, this has never occurred; indeed, when Lamott spoke at a bookstore one hour away from our campus, I was pleasantly surprised by the number of my students who showed up early to get a good seat. And extra credit for hearing Lamott read was not even part of the deal!

My choice of *Traveling Mercies* is based on more than my students' positive response, though, as Lamott's text perfectly addresses some of the course's main concerns, about spiritual autobiography, about having a "good" conversion story, and about the significance of one's life stories. For while Lamott's oft-times irreverence and frequent use of the F-word make her book stand apart from most other conversion stories, a close investigation reveals that Lamott's spiritual autobiography follows the same narrative pattern of most testimonies, and that her approach to faith, or at least to faith stories, is as orthodox as most Evangelicals.

Lamott uses the preface, or "overture," of *Traveling Mercies* to describe her spiritual journey: a series of leaps, she says, from lily pad to lily pad "across the swamp of doubt and fear."[2] Certainly the lily pad metaphor, echoing Kierkegaard's own faithful jump across the abyss, suggests indirection, the lack of a determined trajectory that traditionally shapes spiritual autobiography. However, the narrative structure Lamott uses in her "overture" to describe the lily pad leaps reflects Lamott's decision to frame her journey within the conventional form of spiritual autobiography: one in which the self wallows in the degradation of a pre-conversion life absent God; moves toward and through the point of conversion; and arrives at a life made new by the saving grace of Christ.

So the class looks closely at the opening to *Traveling Mercies* and at the teleological narrative pattern that betrays this sense of tradition, even of orthodoxy. There, Lamott describes her early life with unbelieving parents; the attraction felt to homes founded on some sort of belief in God or love or religion; and the various experiences that affirmed for her the reality of God, if not of God's presence. Lamott's childhood, which seems relatively normal in the book's beginning, shows its fissures, and these fissures become cracks and then chasms with the deterioration of Lamott's nuclear family and the death of her father, both of which accompany Lamott's descent into darkness: a kind of darkness Lamott attempts to mollify with drugs, alcohol, illicit sex, and a continued groping toward truth. That search takes her on long walks with a local priest and to the back pew of a small church aside a flea market, where Lamott sings about Jesus but leaves before the sermon.

Though the small Marin county church could make everything "stiff and rotting" in Lamott "feel soft and tender,"[3] her quest for truth seems initially fruitless, for she remains unwilling or unable to embrace God. And so, as in many spiritual autobiographies, Lamott meets God—or rather, God meets

Lamott—when she is nearing the end of her slide toward spiritual and physical death. Bleeding, hung over, desperate, needing God: Lamott's narrative and surely, Lamott's life, hangs on this moment. Her story's climax, turning point, and then denouement follow. Having been saved, Lamott renounces her old life for the new and lives forever after in the light of Christ.

Studying the structure of Lamott's seeming unorthodox tale reaffirms for students the prevalence of a conventional shaping device in spiritual auto-biographies, including their own testimonies, and reflects again the ways dramatic progression forms the stories Christians tell about their transformations, Lamott included. We recognize as well the power of such a structure: how God's saving grace appears more powerful, more magnanimous, when extended to someone in the throes of big sin. I acknowledge that few of us will be in a place of darkness similar to that about which Lamott writes, and that few of us will have experiences with drugs, alcohol, and illicit sex in the ways Lamott has. Still, I argue, this should not diminish our own encounters with God or our stories about those encounters, however mild they may seem when compared to Lamott's, to a minister's in the pulpit, to a friend's down the hall.

This message is reinforced when we turn to the rest of Lamott's *Traveling Mercies*, to the short essays Lamott writes about her "thoughts on faith." If the opening chapter to Lamott's text apparently suggests students indeed need Big Events to tell significant stories about God's redemption, the remainder of *Traveling Mercies* impresses a different message: that our seemingly insignificant experiences—our chance encounters with friends, family, a store clerk, a hairy man on the beach—just as powerfully convey God's presence among us, and that our own lives' stories reflect the special imprint God makes in each of us. Given this perspective, even the most apparently mundane experiences might well be imbued with meaning.

Therefore, as the class studies the first essay in *Traveling Mercies*, they begin to reform their sense of what makes a "significant event" in autobiography. I ask students what actually happens in this essay, "Knocking on Heaven's Door." What is the grandiose experience about which Lamott writes? The answer, of course, is deceptively simple. Lamott faces delays on an airplane trip home. She bounces through some turbulence. She interacts with odd seatmates, including a born-again man reading eschatological fiction. She thinks about a conflict in her church, between a man dying of AIDS and an African-American woman. In other words, nothing we would deem unusually significant happens to Lamott in "Knocking on Heaven's Door," yet by the narrative's resolution, readers have a real sense that God's grace has moved through Lamott and the story's other characters.

I hope that in examining this essay, my students have experienced their first real awakening in autobiography: that good life writing does not have to be built on events outside the realm of their own experiences, and that even the seemingly ordinary events still reflect the power of God working through us. The rest of the essays in *Traveling Mercies* reinforce this idea, as they focus on the flotsam of Lamott's life, her narratives turning on events that might happen to any one of us: her car dies in the middle of traffic; she contends with an aging and imperfect mother; she loathes and then loves her big thighs; she learns to forgive a near-perfect acquaintance.

As a class, we discuss why these stories are so compelling, especially as Lamott details events that are, for the most part, unremarkable. After reading a few essays, students begin to sense the draw to Lamott's work—and, indeed, a secret to good autobiographical writing. Lamott's essays allow readers to step in to her individual experience, to see themselves in her own everyday struggle with grief, doubt, joy, forgiveness, love. Each essay becomes an act of exploration: as Lamott works toward a clearer personal understanding of God's mystery and wonder, she artfully draws the readers along on her journey. So that by each essay's end, both Lamott and the reader recognize a new facet of God's character, of God's grace and love, of God's special imprint on their own lives. In lending value to her life's stories, by shaping her life into meaningful word, Lamott suggests—by extension—that others can likewise find significance in their stories, however commonplace those stories might be.

With this affirmation from Lamott in place, students are ready to consider again their own assertion that "nothing much has happened to me." We turn, then, to the heart of the course, to the students' own writing. For their first major writing assignment, students are required to craft three autobiographical sketches, each at least four to five pages long (see assignment sheet at Appendix A). The assignment demands that students narrate moments in their lives, conveying to readers through their narration the special importance of each moment in defining the self. Ideally, our discussions about Lamott have, to this point, reminded students that they need not write about the "big events" in their lives: a hazard with the personal narrative that often produces, in first-year writing courses, a bevy of essays about grandmas dying, cars wrecking, and lives ruined by drunkenness and debauchery. And usually, despite our focus on Lamott's essays, the first autobiographical sketch produces a handful of epics from students who feel compelled to write about what they see as their lives' major turning points. But this is okay, too: sometimes these stories also need to be written, and sometimes students need to confront the challenge of writing the big stories before being able to contend with the seemingly small.

As my students begin crafting their autobiographical sketches, they do exercises similar to that which might occur in other writing classes. We spend time on invention, working through a number of prompts to distill potential essay topics and foci. Students share pieces of essays-in-progress with classmates, both soliciting and offering reader feedback. We explore different rhetorical devices used in autobiography, like scene and summary, flashbacks and flash forwards, segmentation and transitional space; and I challenge students to experiment with these methods during in class writing sessions.

Class time remains interactive, much like the other courses I teach, and this student-centeredness is informed as well by my sense of faith integration. Because I want to see that of God in all my students, I believe I must embrace a certain pedagogy that places value on the students' own thoughts and experiences, rather than creating a classroom atmosphere that positions my thoughts and experiences at center. If I really wish to see the full potential and worth of my students, something to which I believe God calls me, I must act in class as if every student has potential and worth. Somehow, privileging an approach wherein I hold and disseminate knowledge feels counterintuitive to this belief, and so I attempt to construct courses wherein power and knowledge is shared, rather than assumed by me alone.

To further support my convictions about the significance of a decentralized classroom, I allow students in Autobiography/Biography to establish part of the curriculum. Early in the course, students form reading groups of about four to six people who meet together four times during the semester, and as a group, the students choose three autobiographies/memoirs and one biography to read and discuss. From about the fifth week on, then, I do not hold classes once a week (usually on Mondays); instead, I meet with one of the groups to discuss the text they have chosen. Conversations may be guided by a set of questions I give students (see Appendix B), but often are not, as students grow comfortable in their ability to critique the first-person narratives they are reading. Sometimes, discussions about texts wander into storytelling about our own lives, as often happens when we read autobiographies with which we especially identify—or from which our life experiences significantly diverge. While I often reign in such discussions in literature classes—where students may too easily be distracted by seeing their selves in the work they read—I allow these conversations to flourish here, as valuing storytelling reflects again the course's central focus.

These groups have become my favorite feature of the course, the part of my teaching year I most anticipate. The reading load has at times been onerous for me, as I try to keep up with what each group is studying. Still, I have read some fascinating books I might not otherwise, thanks to my students' curricular decisions, including *A Prisoner's Wife*, by asha bandele; *Blue Like Jazz*, by Donald Miller; and the now-infamous *A Million Little Pieces*, by James Frey. The small groups also allow me to engage with students and their ideas in ways not afforded by class discussions, and my relationships with many students are enriched by our interaction. But perhaps most significantly, I note a camaraderie develop among students in specific groups as the semester progresses, and important and lasting relationships have at times been formed through the study of the autobiographies students are reading, and through conversations about their own life stories.[4]

By the semester's tenth week, students have completed three autobiographical essays. For each essay, I provide constructive criticism, as well as the necessary evil of a letter grade. Evaluating the students' writing for this course provides both pleasure and pain, a paradox I cannot readily resolve. I enjoy reading and responding to the students' stories; appreciate the depth and breadth of students' life experiences; and find most in the course are capable, and in some cases enviable, writers. However, placing letter-grade values on students' personal experiences has always been difficult for me, especially as doing so may seem to undermine my intent to affirm the stories they tell. I worry students might believe letter grades reflect my judgment of the experience, rather than of the way it is rhetorically constructed, despite my attempts to insist otherwise. Early in the semester, I try to deconstruct their insecurity with gallows humor, suggesting that students who write about a grandma's or dog's death will receive an A, but essays about cats dying will receive an F, as I don't care for cats. The joke doesn't wholly work, I know. So I remind students often that a grade is meant to reflect the writing itself: clarity of expression, cohesion, use of details, a lack of grammatical and mechanical error. Then, I try in my summary comments for each essay to affirm the power of the student's experience, while providing suggestions for enhancing the expression of that experience.

In the semester's final weeks, we shift our focus from autobiography to biography, from the self to other, although the course's underlying principle and pedagogy remains the same. As we think about biography, I challenge them to consider again the idea that every life narrative has meaning, and to find for themselves the meaning in the subjects they choose to write about. By way of example, I share my grandmother's story: a woman who lived in the same house from her marriage to her death, some sixty-five years; who never held a job outside the home; who lived by the rhythms of her husband, waking with him, cooking his meals, washing his clothes, tucking him in bed; and whose guilty pleasure was watching *As the World Turns* every afternoon for thirty-five years. Though her life seemed far from extraordinary, I talk about the meaning I discovered in her ordinariness, what studying her patterned life taught me about myself and about the ways I misjudged her.

My own lack of understanding about my grandmother provides entry into our consideration of the ways biography is a kind of interpretation, as is the very act of relating to another. Obviously, because we cannot fully know the "other," we are challenged with the task of interpreting another's actions, words, achievements and failures; we bring to that interpretation our own experiences and perceptions, much as we would in the process of reading and understanding a text. The final two writing assignments for the course require this act of interpretation: first, in an essay about how another person relates to the writer (see Appendix C); and then, in an essay about how another person relates to the world around her (see Appendix D). For each assignment, students are asked to do some research, including interviews and observations, amassing material to interpret about their subjects' lives. They must also come to some sense of the themes or principles that guide their subjects. Concurrently, students meet in their small groups to read and discuss a published biography, and the ways particular biographers interpret and shape the stories they tell. Here, I allow students to read texts conventionally understood as biography, as well as those more ambiguously defined as such, like Mitch Albom's *Tuesdays with Morrie* or Susan Orlean's *The Orchid Thief.*

Admittedly, the biography portion of the Autobiography/Biography course remains underserved, mostly because I lack the specific knowledge about biography to make this part work well. Certainly I believe the study of biography could sustain my course's objective to affirm that every life shows God's special imprint, and that every life story has value. In some ways, even, students have an easier time expressing the significance of stories that are not their own, and can readily shape meaning and purpose into the lives of those about whom they choose to write. One risk of writing biography about a closely known other, of course, is that the text can too easily become a paean to the subject's greatness, a hagiography of sorts about grandmas, mothers, best friends, lovers. Perhaps surprisingly, though, students' essays consistently contend with the complexities of their own biographical interpretations, discovering through their writing process layers of another's character they had not previously recognized: a grandfather whose stoicism masked his generosity, a friend whose kindness proved to be self-serving, a mother afraid of introspection and self-understanding. In exploring their subjects, then, I imagine these essays serve an important function for the writers, who more fully recognize the complexity, perhaps even the paradox, of human nature: that our goodness is compromised by our fallenness, and that each of us, no matter our life stories, are in need of God's mysterious grace and love.

And indeed, I discover this message again and again, in my students' biographical essays as well as in the autobiographical sketches they produced earlier. Especially as the semester progresses, and as students become more comfortable with the writing act, with their own stories, with their audience of peers and of me, their essays becoming increasingly introspective and honest. Their enhanced command of autobiographical writing almost seems to correspond with a greater depth in their writing, both in the subjects they choose to explore and in the meaning they give to that exploration. And in that depth, I often discover the theme of brokenness, of relationships to each other and to God compromised again and again by their own human frailty.

Lamott writes in *Traveling Mercies* that we may be inclined to wish from God "some permanence, a guarantee or two, the unconditional love we long for."[5] Her essays are shot through with this longing, as is the writing of my students who asserted at the semester's beginning that "nothing much has happened to me." That nothing much turns out to be a good deal more, as students produce essays of surprising intensity: about self-loathing that leads to cutting, to eating disorders, to depression; about parents suffering through cancer treatments; about working with AIDS victims or Palestinian children. Even in writing about seemingly small encounters—disagreements with roommates, a walk alone, a conversation with a stranger—students reflect seriously about life's complexities, their own emotions, their seeming limitations. Not often in ways that might be considered maudlin or sentimentalized teenage angst, but in ways that seem to me true, honest, sometimes painfully raw. And, their essays are also full of affirmation about God's powerful grace in our lives. Lamott writes that "Most of the time, all you have is the moment, and the imperfect love of people" and the "mystery of Grace."[6] Thus because my students' stories provide a consistent reminder to me of this imperfect love and of this mystery, faith integration in my Autobiography/Biography course has its own kind of reciprocity: for I too feel renewed by the written testimony to God's living, breathing presence among us.

A character in my favorite novel, Rohinton Mistry's *A Fine Balance*, has this to say about life stories: "It's extremely important [to tell your own stories] because it helps to remind yourself of who you are. Then you can go forward, without fear of losing yourself in this ever-changing world."[7] In a sense, I think, I also want my students to feel that writing their stories allows them to map where they have been, and to see where they are going; in doing so, they will have a clearer understanding of the ways God has moved, and continues to move, through their lives.

In the course's final project, a portfolio of their semester's work, students are given opportunity for this kind of reflection—and projection. For the portfolio, students are required to revise three essays they completed during the semester, in addition to crafting an analysis of their semester's writing and of what they learned about their selves, and their life stories, through that writing (see Appendix E). In some ways, the portfolio merely reinforces revision as a necessary part of the writing process, challenging students to improve the rhetorical expression of their life experiences. But more, I want students to see their portfolio as an artifact, documenting who they were and what they believed significant during their time in college.

And even more than that, I want the portfolio to be its own testimony: about the rich depth and complexity of their own lives; about what it means to have a life created and shaped by God; and about what it means to shape that life into meaningful words for others.

Endnotes

1   Were this an upper division course, I might be inclined to have students read parts of Daniel Shea's *Spiritual Autobiography in Early America* (Madison: University of Wisconsin Press, 1988). Shea's book in part traces the tradition of the conversion narrative in early American history and would provide for students the context needed to better understand spiritual autobiography's place in American literature.

2   Anne Lamott, *Traveling Mercies: Some Thoughts on Faith* (New York: Pantheon, 1999), 3.

3   Ibid., 3.

4   Of course, there have been times when student groups did not gel, most often because of personality conflicts or because a collective of shy people founded a group together. There has also been an occasional falling out during our discussions, although the most significant conflict was resolved when both students found themselves working together on our writing center staff.

5   Anne Lamott, *Traveling Mercies*, 168.

6   Ibid., 168, 143.

7   Rohinton Mistry, *A Fine Balance* (New York: Vintage, 1997), 594.

Teaching as Local Politics:

Shaping Courses to Your Students

Chris Willerton (Abilene Christian University)

A long-time English professor and administrator, Chris Willerton argues that professors must shape courses to meet the particular needs of our students. In "Teaching as Local Politics: Shaping Courses to Your Students," he explores the shaping of two "skills" courses for ACU's "mainly Texan, middle-class, politically conservative, and professionally ambitious" students. Chris received his Ph.D. from the University of North Carolina. He started teaching at ACU in 1970. He was founding director of the ACU Honors Program and oversaw its transition to Honors College. He was active for many years in the National Collegiate Honors Council.

All politics is local, said Tip O'Neill. So is teaching. The challenge of integrating faith and learning is always embodied in particular students in a particular place. As in politics, you can't transplant issues and practices willy-nilly from one locale to another. As case studies, I will describe two of my recent upper-level courses, "Literature and Belief" and "Poetry," showing how they were shaped by the clientele and the culture at Abilene Christian University. There is more to combining faith with learning than beginning each class with a prayer list and a song.

"Literature and Belief" (English 471) was launched in 1988 by my colleague Darryl Tippens partly for the sake of getting students to read Augustine. Our students were and are mostly innocent of church history and theology. Abilene Christian University was founded in 1906 by members of Churches of Christ. Like many others in the free church and evangelical categories, our members were ahistorical. The American Restoration movement (or Stone-Campbell movement) of the early 1800s aimed at throwing off "man-made traditions" and restoring the first-century church in light of God's revelation in Scripture. Consequently our students arrived with high biblical literacy and little curiosity about philosophy, theology or church history after the first century. Small wonder they had not heard of Augustine. Or Pascal or Bonhoeffer or Weil. By the 1980s, the time seemed right for Darryl to collect these writers and others into a course. Its success led the department to add "Film and Belief" a decade later. "Rhetoric and Belief" is on the drawing board. When it is in place, we will require every English major to take at least one of the three.

I have taught "Literature and Belief" three times and found it strenuous and thrilling in equal parts. I do my best to let the students' capabilities and interests drive the selection of material, the choice of assignments, etc. At least my years here have given me some data about those capabilities. When I came to the faculty in 1970, the student body was over 90 percent Church of Christ members. Lately it is under two-thirds, the remainder being heavily evangelical. The biblical literacy has declined, and our students share a lot of mental habits with others in their generation. Careerism is powerful though most students try not to consecrate it. Those who take "Literature and Belief" are not usually the careerists and not always English majors. They expect the course to contribute to their faith and to their success in resisting secular culture. The challenge of the course is to honor these affective and spiritual goals while giving due attention to the literature as literature. I try to sell an incarnational theory of art, arguing that a novel or poem is not a container for an idea but an embodiment of it. This is a stretch for the SparkNotes generation, who like "content" unencumbered by "form." But whenever they grasp the fusion of idea with form, they come a step closer to a fusion of study with worship.

Briefly, that's how I see my students' habits and priorities, and it's the basis for my choices of readings, classroom practices, and assignments. Is it a stereotype? Yes, on the days I'm not paying full attention. But most of the time I consult this profile as my "implied student" for the course. Without some generalization, we can't gauge our decisions about teaching. As Wolfgang Iser says, a writer has an "implied reader" to guide decisions about point of view, word choice, and so forth, anticipating a transaction in the act of reading. And we speak easily about an "implied audience" for advertising, political campaigns, and so on. A teacher has an implied student ("audience" would imply passivity), anticipating a transaction in teaching and learning. Whether that figure is a stereotype depends on the teacher's willingness to revise it week-by-week in contact with the actual class.

Let's proceed, then, to the readings. Here is a list of the works I currently use in the course:

- Augustine, *Confessions.* (Oxford UP, tr. Henry Chadwick)
- Buechner, Frederick. *Godric.*
- Dillard, Annie. *For the Time Being.*
- Greene, Graham. *The Power and the Glory.*
- Impastato, David, ed. *Upholding Mystery: An Anthology of Contemporary Christian Poetry.*
- Lewis, C. S. *The Screwtape Letters.*
- Norris, Kathleen. *The Cloister Walk.*
- O'Connor, Flannery. *Spiritual Writings.* A collection edited by Robert Ellsberg.
- Pascal, Blaise. *Pensees.* (Penguin)
- Weil, Simone. *Waiting for God.*

(In past iterations, I have also included Frederick Buechner's *Telling Secrets*, Diane Glancy's *Cold and Hunger Dance*, and Leo Tolstoy's *The Raid and Other Stories.*)

Obviously these books form three main groups—autobiography (Augustine, Buechner, Glancy, Norris, Weil), fiction (Buechner, Greene, Lewis, O'Connor, Tolstoy), and theology (Dillard, O'Connor, Pascal, Weil, with frequent outbursts in Augustine, Buechner, Glancy, Lewis, Norris). The Impastato anthology has poems to represent all three groups.

Let's pause now for the clamor from fellow teachers: *What do you mean, take out Tolstoy? And where's Dostoevsky? Where's Aquinas? Why aren't you including drama? I see too many women writers. I see too few women writers. Everything here is Western—what a bigoted, colonialist list. Where's Endo? In fact, where are Hinduism and Islam? How can "Literature and Belief" be restricted to Christianity? Why aren't you including films?* The answers are (a) fifteen weeks, (b) other courses, (c) the mission of this particular course. We all know that every course is a compromise. A fifteen-week semester doesn't permit assigning forty-five books, so some authors have to go. The time limit even biases me toward shorter books. A short book read carefully can be more life-changing than a long one skimmed. Moreover, I try to avoid duplication with other courses, to let students meet as many authors as possible. Having scouted my colleagues' reading lists, I omit Milton, Herbert, Bunyan, Tennyson, Browning, Hopkins, Auden, Eliot, Faulkner, Joyce, Waugh, Erdrich, Endo, and others the students will probably meet in other courses. I omitted films (though I tried a film the first time around) because we have the "Film and Belief" course. Finally, the mission of the course gives me boundaries. The catalog description is "A survey of classic literary texts concerned with faith, doubt, and Christian spirituality from Augustine to the present." I fudge the term *classic*, obviously, saying in the syllabus that I include both "recognized classics and recent works that seem likely to endure." But the other terms in the course description provide a mission that is very valuable for our school in our era. Being mostly eighteen to twenty-two years old and brought up in conservative churches, our students are much concerned with "faith, doubt, and Christian spirituality." Felt needs are great motivators of learning. As much as I would like to see a course linking literature to comparative religion, a course on literature and Christian belief should come first for our university. And I remind myself that this course is only part of the constellation in our catalog. It takes a number of courses to shape students toward any goal—biblical literary, cultural literacy, analytical thinking, international perspective, charity. Though I don't treat Hinduism and Islam in this course, our department does in the sophomore World Lit survey, and colleagues in other departments do in some of their courses. This course simply does what it can.

Given those purposes for "Literature and Belief," what path does the course take? I begin with Buechner's *Godric*, Augustine's *Confessions*, and Norris's *Cloister Walk*, for studies of individuals under the pressure of faith development; move to poems in Impastato, which are grouped by theological themes—the Cross, transformation, death, injustice, Presence, and so forth; we work in Pascal, O'Connor, and Weil before we end with Dillard's *For the Time Being*, Greene's *Power and the Glory*, Lewis's *Screwtape Letters*, and student presentations. In earlier versions of the course, which didn't have the poetry anthology, we would read Greene right after Augustine, for their similarities and contrasts. In the middle of the course, we would read Pascal and Weil after Norris, extending the unit on individuals' struggles toward faith. We would end the course with O'Connor, following Dillard's angst and complexity with O'Connor's ornery practicality.

Agreed, it's not a very tidy path. Autobiography and theology bob up in several places besides their appointed sections. But strict grouping by genre doesn't matter much. Accessibility does. It's vital, I've learned through trial and error, to start not with theology but with story. Students, like most readers, love story, and they are hungry to hear narrators (or hear about characters) with lots of emotional investment in the events. For every dozen students who have read *City of God*, thousands have read *Confessions*. By wooing the student with narrative and with personal emotion, allowing theology to enter as needed, I steal Augustine's own method in *Confessions*. Apparently many of the students, as they enter the course, bring a very personal need to see how Christianity matters, and approaching the question by narrative seems to work for them. They lock in instantly to the self-examination of Godric, Buechner himself, Augustine, and the whiskey priest. They respond strongly, too, to stories about the influence of others upon the believer, in Lewis, Tolstoy, and Norris. In Lewis's trenchant comedy, Screwtape's letters are full of diabolical advice about the influence of family, church, business associates, and romantic partners. Tolstoy examines social ambition, the soldier's code, the pressure of family expectations, and so forth. Norris writes as an outsider entering a monastery, learning why monks and nuns put themselves under holy discipline. Certainly Norris could fit among the first set of writers, being eloquent at self-examination, but her explicit project is to understand a community and to negotiate its influence on her.

Another appeal to the students' felt needs is in doing theology per se—Pascal, Weil, and Dillard—and this has to wait till late in the course, when the students have the muscle for it. In the extremes to which these writers carry their thoughts, my students find Pascal brilliant and strenuous, Weil radical, and Dillard scary. That's why the students need to work up to them. The difficulty is not only in the sophistication of the writings; it's in the ruthlessness of the demands Pascal, Weil, and Dillard make on themselves. Another reason to place these authors late in the course is the challenge of their literary forms. It takes strenuous attention to bridge fragment after fragment in Pascal, to ride the surge of Weil's arguments, and to switch constantly among the threads of Dillard's discussion of the problem of evil—birth defects, Chinese tyrants, Teilhard de Chardin, Israel, population statistics, and so on. It takes a muscular and determined reader to succeed with them, and my students have a sense of competence when they do succeed. A similar challenge in form is one reason I placed Diane Glancy's book after these the first time I taught the course. *Cold and Hunger Dance* is nearly hypertextual, jumping among anecdotes of girlhood, Cherokee history, the Bible, Black Elk's visions, and life in Minnesota. It's a marvelous book and was hard to part with, but I had to make room for O'Connor in the second version of the course.

Ironically, O'Connor lost out in the third version, being replaced by a poetry anthology. Impastato's anthology had worked for the upper-division foundational Poetry course, which I will discuss below, because the thematic grouping is stimulating, the introductions cheerful and pertinent, and the poems richly varied. It is a highly intelligent collection whose editor obviously feels a powerful spiritual vocation to serve the reader through the choices of included texts. Decade by decade, however, students have less experience with poetry. Dropping a poetry unit in the middle of autobiographies and novels was, I thought, a refreshing change-up. But anxiety among the non-English majors shot up. Many selections in Impastato are very poetic poetry—indirect, metonymic, evocative, unparaphrasable. Even the English majors have not read much contemporary poetry, and their attention spans are tattered by Web-surfing and multitasking. The students flourished with the plainer poems that told a story—Andrew Hudgins's Southern yarns, David Citino's mad monologues by Sister Mary Appassionata, Wendell Berry's anecdotes—and did finally learn to listen closely enough for Denise Levertov's and Richard Wilbur's poems. I assigned a thematic group of poems, then we discussed as a class whichever poems they had responded to best. Given the range of students—from majors to nonmajors, from graduating seniors to students taking their first advanced course—this approach proved effective, helping me meet them where they were and develop the enthusiasms they had discovered in reading. Nonetheless, it will help next time to be more selective with the assigned reading.

Closing the course with the sharing of major papers is vital. In all my courses, I end with some classroom exercise that allows me to use my punch line—"You've done well today. And let me point out that you've said things today that you *could not have said fifteen weeks ago*. You didn't know as much, and you didn't have the tools. Look what you can do now." In this discussion-heavy course, we have a strong community when we reach the last week, and sharing the papers is satisfying.

What sort of exercises help students reach their fifteen week's growth? They are nothing unusual, but I choose them with the conviction that close attention to the text and close reflection on the text build spiritual insight as well as interpretive skill. First, the daily writings. Each student comes with a half-page reflection on the day's reading, sometimes responding to an assigned question. I often read from several of these to launch discussion. This daily exercise discourages students from getting by in class with a quick skim and glibness. Scoring them 0–5 lets me signal the student about the difference between a good effort and lame one but without the threat implicit in A's, B's and C's. And a good effort, I explain openly, requires close attention to the text—really listening to the author—and sensitive reading—really listening to oneself. In many courses, they learn that integrating faith and learning means attaching a Christian moral to everything. My hunch is that it continues a trajectory they started in Sunday School and in youth groups in high school. I have to ease them out of thinking that moralizing is enough. I also have to minister to the dualists and the postmoderns (bear with my stereotypes, please). My dualists believe that the purpose of schooling is to get Right Answers and that Right

Answers get you to heaven. My postmods (who are a benign sort) figure that nothing is certain, that every religious person has an equal chance of being right, and that niceness gets you to heaven. Both kinds of thinking are simplistic, and I try to lead them from both extremes toward the middle. A score of 3 seems to set them thinking, "Maybe it's not as pat as I thought."

The second type of exercise is short papers, five of them about three weeks apart. These two- to three-page "personal reflection" papers are meant to be ambitious, requiring the student to extend or apply or challenge some idea or passage. These are the short sprints to prepare for the long run of the major paper. I use the label "personal" to warn the students away from mere English-major cleverness—"By 'personal,' I mean that you have invested yourself in the issue, not necessarily that you tell personal anecdotes."

The third type of exercise is the major paper, which is comparative, connecting two or three works from the course and incorporating research. This is the paper that caps the course, showing off whatever analytical skill and personal illumination the student has reached in fifteen weeks. I have had fourteen weeks to nudge them with daily grades and short-paper grades, so they know that risk-taking and strenuous thinking will be rewarded on the big paper. The fourth type of exercise is exams. The three exams count for only a third of the course grade, reinforcing my view that the course is more about skills than about facts. But each exam requires both. There are definitions and short discussions that require only giving back the lectures, but the comparison questions require thought.

Classroom time, naturally, is heavy on discussion. We sit in a circle and often disperse into small groups. I lecture as needed to give historical and biographical context. To help them continue the processing at home, I use Blackboard to post handouts and links to useful sites. In class and online, I often caution them about what modern readers bring to the text unconsciously. Here are two important clauses from my syllabus:

> The relation of literature to belief is dynamic: there is always a dialogue going. Therefore this is a course in pursuing questions and contemplating the answers various writers have put into literary form. The writers we will read are fearless thinkers and would not object to our testing their answers. Students should begin the course with a determination to grow in the clarity of their thinking, the range of their sympathy, and the strength of their religious conviction.

> We will treat reading as transactional. That is, treat the reader as a co-creator of the meaning of the text. People bring different backgrounds,

information, expectations, and reading tactics to a text. Consequently, each gets a different experience from reading the same text. We will consider how reading about belief can change the reader's own belief. We will discuss the need for "charitable" reading—opening oneself to the influence of the text and postponing judgments—as opposed to "the hermeneutics of suspicion" or "reading against the text." T. S. Eliot says rightly that Christian readers need an additional, spiritual set of standards when they read, but we should ask at what point in the process we should bring in those standards.

My debt to Alan Jacobs's *Theology of Reading* is obvious. His concept of "charitable reading" helps me with both the dualistic and the postmod tendencies in students. The dualist wants to judge right away, and the postmod wants to avoid judging. In the class community, they learn that judging should wait until the whole case is heard, that judging can't be put off forever, and that Christians can disagree agreeably in their conclusions.

My most satisfying method for helping the class work inductively is to "map" the day's reading. Rather than put an outline on the board and dictate one theme after another, I help the class make "maps" on the board as the discussion goes. It's a way to make them more adept as readers—able to hike across a book patiently, then turn around and see the patterns in the landscape. With practice, they begin to see the patterns as they go. Dictating theme after theme won't teach them that. Nor will plopping down on the desk and asking the class cheerily, "Well, what did you think?" Airing uninformed opinions isn't good enough.

The first time or two that we use mapping, I introduce a new selection with two or three circles on the board—major themes or topics I noticed. I ask the class whether they noticed the same things and whether they have circles to add. "How do these ideas come across?" I ask, and we begin to draw lines out to characters' names, important phrases, or sub-ideas. At the next class, I draw the main parts of the map again, and we add circles and lines. We make some circles bigger and some smaller as we figure out the author's priorities. Making a map is reassuring to the group—"We've been there. We know that much."— especially when we're reading nonlinear material. Buechner's *Telling Secrets*, for instance, criss-crosses his past instead of reporting it chronologically. His book is true to the ruminative process of memory. Some autobiographers prefer, "This happened, then that happened in the pageant of my life." Buechner is more likely to say, "This happened when I was a boy, and here's what happened years later when I finally understood it." You could teach *Telling Secrets* with an outline of its chapters. But the operative word would be "teach" rather than "learn." I'd rather the class roam a few chapters a day and decide where the mountains and valleys are. That way, the students are learning to learn nonlinear material. A map is precisely a way to see the forest in spite of the trees. Here's a simplified version of one class map of *Telling Secrets*, which we accumulated and revised over three class meetings.

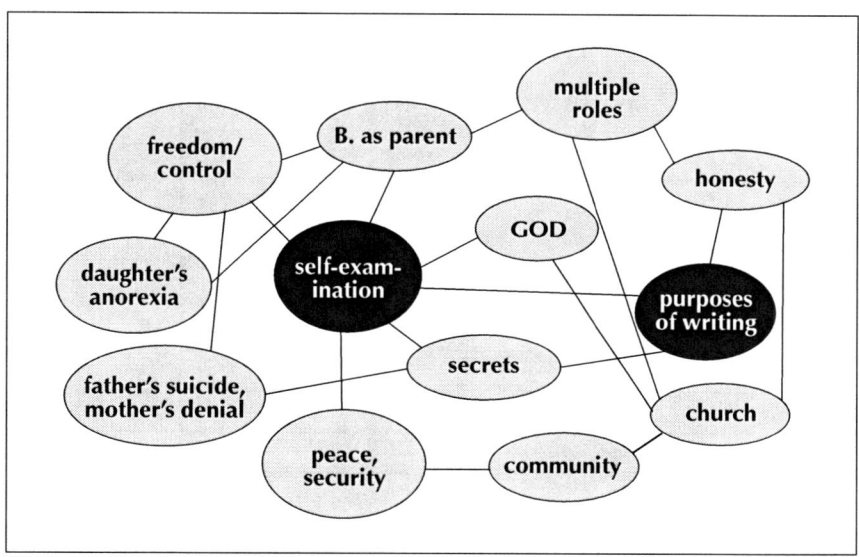

A good class discussion is a kind of surfing. It's a thrill when you're zooming along, but after the wave dies, you aren't sure just where you've been. A map or sketch on the marker board reassures the class that there has been a pattern after all—these certain topics have been the center of gravity for the author in this passage. When students catch on to making their own maps, they have a new tool for processing a discussion or thinking through a difficult author. And the group effort in making a map is an aid to camaraderie. The seasoned students (already adept with Borges and Calvino) become models for the less experienced (those accustomed to being told what every work means), and soon everyone has confidence. What does success look like? The class comes up with balloons and links more quickly, the quieter students get the confidence to contribute to the map, and the exams have clearer and better-detailed essays.

This is a good time to mention the students' responsibility for reading. The English majors moan about having too much to read (we've all been there, any time we took three advanced courses in a semester). They admit to me that they often do triage—what do I have to read, what would be good to read, what could I skip, there being only twenty-four hours in a day? The nonmajors naturally give priority to the advanced courses in their fields, so they may resort to triage, as well. I've found that the daily writings—and making a point of calling on everyone in discussion—motivate most students to get the reading done. But at the end of term, when it's time for formal feedback on the texts, I call for special candor and ask for anonymous ratings. Here's the heading for the grid I use.

	Should we keep this text in the course? (Score 4 through 1.)	How thoroughly did you read it?
	4. definitely yes 3. probably yes 2. probably no 1. certainly no	4. very thoroughly 3. routine 2. skimmed 1. only what was read in class
Augustine		
Buechner		
[list continues]		

Below the grid, I prompt them for suggestions and detailed remarks about the texts—are there others they'd suggest, etc.? A separate course-evaluation form asks them for anonymous feedback about assignments, exams, and so forth. But for judging the effectiveness of the texts, I rely on the grid. To know how to weight the praises and complaints, I need to know how well the students read each work.

Let me turn to another course that I adapted to the students as I came to understand them better. "Poetry" (English 378) is a genre course for third- and fourth-year students, and its content varies with the teacher. When my turn first came to teach it, I decided that it should be need-driven and that what the English majors needed was modern and contemporary British and American poetry. But year by year, I became aware of other needs—in political awareness, understanding of world cultures, and acquaintance with Christian poetry after Eliot. These shortcomings seem to go with our student body, which is mainly Texan, middle-class, politically conservative, and professionally ambitious. (No condemnation implied—I was cut from exactly the same cloth when I came to college decades ago.) So I have since swung the course around to deal with those needs.

176

In its last and most satisfactory version, my course rested on two anthologies, J. D. McClatchy's *The Vintage Book of Contemporary World Poetry* (1996) and David Impastato's *Upholding Mystery: An Anthology of Contemporary Christian Poetry* (1997). (At this writing, the Poetry course has rotated to another teacher. When I added Impastato to "Literature and Belief," there was no danger of using the same book in two courses.) After two weeks' study of the genre of poetry, the class spent seven weeks in McClatchy, then six in Impastato.

Through McClatchy's collection, students enter the political and personal worlds of poets in Russia, El Salvador, Nigeria, and dozens of other countries with troubled histories. McClatchy presents translations of eighty poets in six hundred pages, omitting poets from America, Canada, Ireland, Britain, Australia, and New Zealand because they are easier to find in print. To fit into seven weeks, I select twenty-eight poets from twenty-two countries.

The result is a poetic immersion in the Other. My students were surprised and troubled to learn about countries where poetry can get you killed or imprisoned. Except for a few who support the International Justice Mission, our students take little interest in foreign politics. These poems took them to remarkable new territory. Nationalism, fascism, homeland, apartheid, liberation theology, and other terms that sounded so dusty in a lecture became exciting when seen through the lives of Voznesensky, Bachmann, Alegria, Cardenal, and others. The abstract term "social justice" became vivid after they read about people who went to prison for the sake of it. Many of our students *practice* social justice—building houses for Habitat, driving for Meals on Wheels, working at homeless shelters, spending Spring Break with inner-city ministries—but they almost never use the term. "Social justice" is not part of their vocabulary in the way it is for Catholic university students, for instance. My students, I discovered, are ripe for politically committed poetry. Many of our students are vocal critics of abortion rights, and they have given some thought to conflicts between government policy and private conscience. But they don't expect to go to prison for demonstrating. As children of a secure middle class, they often frame "the cost of discipleship" in terms of not cheating on tests or not sleeping with a boyfriend. As important as such personal issues are, these students find it bracing to plunge into deeper water, studying moral quandaries under some of the world's most eloquent poets. My best teaching aids are Web sites by the poets or their activist admirers, and the BBC and CNN Web sites. The course would be weaker if we had to meet without an Internet connection and digital projector.

The issue of teaching translations should be addressed here. I warn my students that "poetic" features like alliteration, rhyme, and so forth can't be trusted in translation. They may be in the original, or they may not. I don't just confess the problems of translation, I insist on them. My favorite demonstration is to give the students copies of a Rilke sonnet, "Letzter Abend" (The Last Evening) in two translations (Herder Norton, Stephen Mitchell), telling them to return to class ready to discuss the differences. At our next meeting, they will probably have found that Mitchell is more explicit than Norton, adding words to clarify the situation, and that Mitchell does more than Norton to echo the rhyme scheme (by his use of slant rhyme) and to keep the iambic pentameter. Then we triangulate—I give out an interlinear version that follows the German word order in the English, making it easy to compare Rilke's own words to the translators' decisions. We decide that Mitchell gives image and situation priority over literal meaning and tweaks some wording for the sake of rhythm and sound. In contrast, Norton tries to be transparent and not get in the way of the English reader's seeing what *words* Rilke wrote. Norton loses in music what he gains in literal accuracy. Several in the class preferred Norton though several others thought Mitchell was more dramatic. The example stays with them as we move on in the course.

I teach the students an analogy I borrowed from a scholarly friend: a poem in its original language is an ice cube, which the translator melts down and refreezes—it's the same water (content, message) but not the same ice cube. This is why it's vital for the students to hear some poems in the original language. Preferably, read them aloud yourself, and read well. You'll establish your ownership, and you'll model the visceral pleasure of reading a fine poem aloud. You need to show that you are moved by the original, I tell them, and that you find nuances of translation intensely interesting.

These are the poets I chose from McClatchy, in the order in which we read them. I follow his example in grouping them geographically but arrange the groups for accessibility and continuity.

- Latin America: Ernesto Cardenal (Nicaragua), Claribel Alegria (El Salvador), Octavio Paz and Manuel Ulacia (Mexico), Pablo Neruda (Chile)

- Western Asia: Nazim Hikmet (Turkey), Andrei Voznesensky, Yevgeny Yevtushenko, and Joseph Brodsky (Russia), Adonis (Lebanon), Mahmoud Darwish (Palestine), Yehuda Amichai, Dahlia Ravikovitch (Israel)

- Africa: Kofi Awoonor (Ghana), Wole Soyinka (Nigeria), Dennis Brutus (South Africa)

- Central Europe: Ingeborg Bachmann (Austria), Tomas Transtromer (Sweden)

- Eastern Europe: György Petri (Hungary), Miroslav Holub (Czech Republic), Czesław Miłosz, Wisława Szymborska, Zbigniew Herbert, and Adam Zagajewski (Poland)

- Asia: Taslima Nasrin (Bangladesh), Shu Ting (China), Ryuichi Tamura and Shuntaro Tanikawa (Japan)

Impastato's anthology opens different doors for the students. His fifteen poets all write in English, allowing me to buckle down to prosody in ways that I cannot with translations. Delightfully, his book is arranged by theological theme, not by author, so that my students get a conversation on each topic. On "Sacrament," for instance, Impastato leads with Louise Erdrich, following with Richard Wilbur, David Brendan Hopes, Wendell Berry, Denise Levertov, David Craig, Les Murray, and finally Andrew Hudgins. Moreover, Impastato stretches my students to see the themes in unfamiliar manifestations. Especially with poems by Scott Cairns, David Citino, Hudgins, and Erdrich, my students keep remarking, "I hadn't thought of grace (or the cross or transformation or whatever) that way."

My students also encounter new ways of expressing belief. On our campus, English majors usually think of "Christian poetry" as the work of seventeenth-century writers, Victorians, and T. S. Eliot. Every two years or so, we have guest readings by living poets who write about faith—Li-Young Lee, Diane Glancy, Walt McDonald, Jill Baumgartner, and others. But that's hardly an acquaintance with modern religious poets. Most students' genres of choice are film and song, and their professors have to devote most of their course time to "major" authors, Christian or not. So the students are surprised to find comedy a vehicle for faith in Citino's poems of Sister Mary Appassionata and in Hudgins's drunken monologists. They are surprised to see faith borne by the huge awareness of Levertov's poems, gritty anecdotes in Erdrich, rural meditations by Berry, and fantastic speeches by Cairns's Raimundo Luz. These are ways of embodying faith that most of my students simply hadn't met.

Like "Literature and Belief," this is more a skills course than a content course. The primary skill is reading—at a much higher level than some are used to. I have already commented on students' lack of experience with contemporary poetry. So I give all the skill-building aid I can think of. Just as I drew discussion maps in the other course, I post Web links and notes on the world poetry and a running set of notes for Impastato's collection. I urge the students to be patient, giving a complicated poem several readings over a week or two. Here are statements from my syllabus:

> **A note about thorough reading: Reading changes your brain.** There is no way to fulfill your potential as a reader/interpreter/critic/ teacher unless you process lots of poems. "Process" means to read, reflect, struggle, retort, connect, compare, have doubts, have confusions, have epiphanies. If you don't read everything attentively, you cheat yourself of educational value, stall your aesthetic growth, and disappoint those who look to you for expertise.

> **How to read poetry:** Receptively and repeatedly. As modern artists, these poets range from plain to obscure. Be prepared for clear political statement, for goofy surrealism, or for anything in between. Many poems will need repeated readings. If a poem is still confusing after two readings, that's OK. Let it sit, and bring your questions about it to class.

"Poems are packed," I say. "Give things time to surface. And give your brain time to update its wiring. You are changing as a reader." Week by week, the students build their skill with contemporary poetic techniques, and my summaries become more selective. They also include more of the students' own comments. After each class, I revise or expand the notes to include the best of the day's insights. If the class comes up with three strong readings of a poem, I list all three.

Given these goals of developing as readers and as world citizens, what kind of assessment is called for? I require two main papers, each under each pages but inviting strenuous writing. The first is a comparison essay on works by two poets in the McClatchy anthology. Students compare and contrast not only the poets' worldviews or aims but also their techniques. Research material should comprise 30–50 percent of the paper. The second paper is a close reading of one poem in the Impastato anthology. Research material should comprise 20–30 percent of the paper. I define "close reading" for them as detailed examination of phrasing, rhythm, imagery, allusion, etc. as they combine to affect the reader. I reassure students that close reading will accommodate various critical systems—feminist, poststructuralist, cultural, etc.—so they can use their favorite approaches.

The way research should inform these papers always needs explaining. I encourage a sense of enterprise since a conventional recovery-of-information paper is out of the question—most poets in the course are not in the publishers' mainstream. This is no *Rime of the Ancient Mariner* paper that a student could cobble up from a single collection of explications. Still, research is required. A stream of uninformed consciousness won't do. Research material is hard to find on some of McClatchy's world poets, even with the World Wide Web, and I encourage students to use non-English sources if they have some competence in the language. This is another nudge against American students' parochialism. I've said that the reading gives them an immersion in the Other. One benefit of research is that it brings some competence and confidence in seeing the Other fairly.

As I finish discussing these courses, I imagine contact points with other essays in this volume. Some of our pedagogical challenges will be the same, and some will be different. Church history, as I've said, is a blank to many of our students, but that wouldn't be true at Lutheran and Reformed colleges. Liturgical practices that are portrayed in the novels and echoed in the poems need footnotes for my students but wouldn't at a Catholic college. International awareness and a hunger for justice are beginning to thrive at our university but have long been cultural features at some other campuses. Still, I'll wager that every group of students is parochial in its way. The challenge for their teachers is to teach to them as they are and not as the teachers assume them to be.

Bibliography

Augustine. *Confessions*. Trans. Henry Chadwick. Oxford: Oxford University Press, 1998.

The Body. DVD. Directed by Jonas McCord, performance by Antonio Banderas (Sony Pictures, 2001).

Buechner, Frederick. *Telling Secrets*. New York: HarperOne, 1992.

_____. *Godric*. New York: HarperOne, 1983.

Dillard, Annie. *For the Time Being*. New York: Vintage, 2000.

Glancy, Diane. *The Cold and Hunger Dance*. Lincoln: Bison, 2002.

Greene, Graham. *The Power and the Glory*. New York: Penguin, 2003.

Impastato, David, ed. *Upholding Mystery: An Anthology of Contemporary Christian Poetry*. Oxford: Oxford University Press, 1996.

Jacobs, Alan. *A Theology of Reading*. Boulder: Westview Press, 2001.

Lewis, C. S. *The Screwtape Letters*. New York: HarperOne, 2001.

McClatchy, J. D. *The Vintage Book of Contemporary World Poetry*. New York: Vintage, 1996.

Norris, Kathleen. *The Cloister Walk*. New York: Riverhead Trade, 1997.

O'Connor, Flannery. *Spiritual Writings*. Ed. Robert Ellsberg. Maryknoll, NY: Orbis, 2003.

Pascal, Blaise. *Pensees*. Trans. A. J. Krailsheimer. New York: Penguin, 1995.

Rilke, Rainer Maria. "Letzter Abend." In *Selected Poetry of Rainer Maria Rilke*. Trans. Stephen Mitchell. New York: Vintage, 1989.

_____ In *Translations from the Poetry of Rainer Maria Rilke*. Trans. M.D. Herter Norton. New York: Norton, 1993.

Tolstoy, Leo. *The Raid and Other Stories*. Tras. Louise and Aylmer Maude. Oxford: Oxford University Press, 1999.

Weil, Simone. *Waiting for God*. New York: Harper Perennial Modern Classics, 2000.

"JESUS THOWN EVERYTHING OFF BALANCE":

Emily Dickinson, William Faulkner, and Flannery O'Connor on the Necessity of Christian Radicalism in the Study of Literature

RALPH C. WOOD (BAYLOR UNIVERSITY)

In his essay, Ralph C. Wood argues that we must be neither smug nor must we apologize when, as Christians, we appropriate authors like O'Connor, Dickinson, and Faulkner. Our goal as Christian instructors is to serve the "reign of Jesus Christ." Ralph is the University Professor of Literature and Theology at Baylor University, where he teaches in the English and religion depart-ments as well as at Truett Theological Seminary. Ralph lectures frequently on Flannery O'Connor, Walker Percy, J. R. R. Tolkien, and C. S. Lewis; his book, The Comedy of Redemption: Christian Faith and Comic Vision in Four American Novelists (Flannery O'Connor, Walker Percy, John Updike, and Peter De Vries), *first published in 1988, is still in print today. His most recent books are* Contending for the Faith: The Church's Engagement with Culture *(Baylor University Press, 2003),* The Gospel According to Tolkien: Visions of the Kingdom in Middle-earth *(Westminster John Knox, 2003) and* Flannery O'Connor and the Christ-Haunted South *(Eerdmans, 2004). He also serves as an editor-at-large on* Christian Century.

Christian tradition knows no sharp distinction between soul and mind. When our Lord commands us to love God with all our mind and soul, he is employing a Semitic doublet that admits of no real distinction: mind and soul are virtually the same thing. When St. Paul urges us in Romans 12:2 to be transformed by the renewing of our minds, he means nothing strictly mental or intellectual. The Hebrew *leb/lebam*, like the Greek *nous*, has little to do with mere intelligence or ratiocination, with abstract thinking or academic learning. These words *leb* and *nous* are often translated "soul" and "heart" as well as "intellect" and "mind." The two qualities are utterly inseparable, as the Book of Common Prayer makes evident in its Collect before Holy Communion: "Cleanse the thoughts of our hearts by the inspiration of thy Holy Spirit." Only when heart and mind, soul and intellect, are woven into a seamless web do we become fully human: creatures made in the image and likeness of God.

My Hebrew scholar-friend James Kennedy points out that the word commonly translated "heart"—as in Samuel's telling Saul that God has found a man "according to his own *leb*"—does not refer to David's extraordinary piety but to God's extraordinary action: He has decided on David and none other. Kennedy adds that it is only when God fashions him from dust (*apar*) and soil (*adamah*), breathing into him the breath of life (*neshamma*), that man becomes a living being, a vital *nephesh*. And when Yahweh withdraws his breath—his spirit—Adam and all his descendants are indeed dead. As creatures thus fashioned from the ground, we may comically be regarded as animated mud, as dirtballs with a conscience! Blaise Pascal put the matter more politely but with the still scandalous claim that we are "thinking reeds." *Ni ange, ni bête*, said Pascal—neither angels nor beasts. Walker Percy wittily adds, however, that we are also "walking genitals," the only creatures whose sexual drive does not depend upon the female's being in a state of estrus.

The upshot is that our biblical ancestors set the standard for the entire Christian tradition by insisting on the radically inseparable relation between the outward and the inward lives, envisioning us always as embodied souls or ensouled bodies. Our conscience and character, our loves and desires—our essential identity before God and man—thus lies in the irreducible unity of our body and mind and soul and spirit. What we do with *them*—together with all of their extensions, especially our property and possessions—signals our integral and undivided nature. Nowhere other than in literature does human life become more fully realized in character and event, in plot and tone and atmosphere. This is thus an essay in Christian criticism that attends to the radically embodied character of our existence in the church and the world. First, I seek to account for the strange absence of any distinctively Christian presence in the canon of American literature—and why the contemporary evangelical condition remains exceedingly discouraging for the production of such literature. Then I will seek to show why we must take the anti-Christian and non-Christian naysayers ever so seriously, never setting them up as straw figures to be burned but rather honoring them as our worthy interlocutors. Here I will have recourse to Emily Dickinson's and William Faulkner's work, especially her poem "This World is not Conclusion" and his story "The Bear." Finally, I will advert to Flannery O'Connor as the chief American artist who teaches how to approach our difficult singular task—namely, by identifying the nihilism that lurks in the church no less than the culture, yet also demonstrating why she gives us real cause not to enter the culture wars. Christians have something much larger at stake, I will argue, than this little skirmish.

I.

It is surely a scandal that "a nation with the soul of a church," as G. K. Chesterton famously described our country, should have produced so few writers who are Christian in any substantive sense of the word. Emerson, Thoreau, Dickinson, Melville, Poe, Hawthorne, Twain, James, Frost, Faulkner— nearly all of our eminent writers are heterodox at best, atheist or even nihilist at worst. Only such major-minor writers as Flannery O'Connor and Walker Percy can be called distinctively Christian: writers whose artistic vision and work derive from the scandalous claims of God's own self-identification in the Jews and Jesus and the Christian church. The perhaps obvious answer to this conundrum is that brilliant minds gifted with artistic imagination have seen biblical faith for the snare and delusion that it is and thus have refused to make its false claims essential to their work. My counter-case is that our major writers have little substantive regard for Christianity because our churches have made it virtually impossible for them to do so. Despite our nation's inveterate religiosity—exceeded perhaps only by that of India—I maintain that the church has become virtually invisible in America. It has so fully identified itself with the American project that our artists have had little cause to heed any unique and distinctively Christian witness in the churches.

Let us first consider Emily Dickinson as an example of a writer who was unable to embrace the Faith of the church because it had become so closely identified with New England culture. She was the legatee of an evangelicalism that had made inward individual experience the crucial mark of authentic Christian faith. Not the church but the state had been entrusted with the most important outward affairs, most notably slavery and its military defense. Well before the Civil War and the frontier revivals, this arrangement had become established as the nation's unofficial religion. It left Dickinson unable to embrace Christian faith—not, I believe, because she had encountered its authentic expression and found this version wanting, but rather because she spurned what she saw in the faith as inescapable, triumphalist moralism and pietist individualism. That she rejected such moralism may have caused her to take refuge in a religious individualism, retreating into a reclusive life in order to avoid being enlisted for an allegedly Christian cause that she knew to be dubious at best, spurious at worst.

During her single year of college life at the Mount Holyoke Female Seminary, the seventeen-year old Dickinson was tutored by the school's founder, the redoubtable Mary Lyon. Like other Whig evangelicals of her day, Lyon envisioned Christianity as forming a powerful tandem with science and education for bringing about a moral revolution of the entire planet. The Kingdom of heaven was soon to come on earth—if not in the nineteenth then surely in the twentieth century, which would so certainly be the *Christian Century* that a still-existing journal was thus named. In an 1842 address setting forth this confident evangelicalism, Lyon envisioned a time rapidly approaching when all people would "act according to the principles of reason and religion," when "all that now goes into the war channel, will then be consecrated to the service of knowledge and benevolence."[1]

The key to such moral transformation lay in the idea of punctiliar salvation—the notion, namely, that one is defined as a Christian by way of a sudden emotional conversion experience. Such a dramatic inward rebirth was public proof that one had personally appropriated the gift of divine grace. A miraculous conversion was the spiritual equivalent of the physical "violations" of nature that were said to be miraculous evidences of God's existence. "In working toward the conversion of her students at Mount Holyoke," Roger Lundin writes, "Lyon divided them each year into three groups." The "Christians" were those who could testify to the certainty of their salvation experience. The "Hopers" believed themselves on the verge of conversion. The "No-Hopers," by contrast, could not attest to any drastic emotional reversal that proved their faith in Christ.[2] What had begun in the seventeenth century with the Puritan practice of the examined conscience, whereby one sought outward objective evidence of divine election, thus led in the nineteenth century to a radical spiritual subjectivism. Salvation was located not in the church's public and communal enactment of the Gospel by living out the Story of God's presence in the gathered community's practices and doctrines. Rather was it radically relocated in the solitary and inward self, and thus in a traumatic individual conversion experience that alone could attest to the efficacy of Christ's work.

Emily Dickinson was numbered on the short list of souls called the No-Hopers. They were the special targets of fervent evangelical attention at Mount Holyoke and Amherst alike. Dickinson remained one of the few holdouts. "How lonely this world is growing," she wrote in the spring of 1850. "Christ is calling everyone here [. . .], and I am standing alone in rebellion, and growing very careless."[3] That Dickinson declined to make a public profession of a tempestuous conversion experience does not mean, as Lundin clearly shows, that she was an atheist scoffer at all things Christian. On the contrary, Dickinson admitted "that I shall never be happy without I love Christ." Yet if the love of Christ were signified by an overwhelmingly subjective conversion, Dickinson knew that she lacked it. The outward doctrinal claims of Christian faith were not her chief or at least not her only worry. What vexed Dickinson were her own uncontrollable and potentially delusory emotions. To her friend Abiah Root, she thus explained her refusal to attend the Amherst revival meetings of 1850: "I felt that I was so easily excited that I might again be deceived and I dared not trust myself."[4] And if the world's wonder—especially her own poetic talent—were understood as something to be repudiated, Dickinson could not perform such a negation of what was patently good. A culturally established Christianity seeking to force Emily Dickinson's conversion could not possibly win her permanent esteem. Better than her own ministers and teachers, Dickinson saw that the Jesus of the Gospels—whom she never spurned but always honored—demands no such emotional effusions. Dickinson is to be commended rather than condemned, I believe, for daring not trust herself to the vagaries of the subjective self.

Writing again to Abiah Root, Dickinson also confessed that "I have perfect confidence in God & his promises and yet I know not why, I feel that the world holds a predominant place in my affections. I do not feel that I could give up all for Christ, were I called to die."[5] Surrendering all to Christ, Dickinson was encouraged to believe, meant that she would have to relinquish her poetic integrity if she became a professed Christian. Given this heretical dichotomy, Dickinson was surely right to refuse such a supposedly heroic act of abdication, such a gnostic denial of the good creation. In rejecting the deity of nineteenth-century Protestant piety, she did not minimize her soul's experience, as Bruce Lockerbie maintains, so much as she expanded it. Indeed, Dickinson became our most important poet of the spiritual quest, not another one of the many dreary and virtually unreadable Victorian pietists.

A poem at once sprightly and memorable, precisely because it is at once troubling and edifying, is Number 501. Here, I believe, Dickinson sets forth an arresting and perceptive understanding of the relation between faith and doubt:

This World is not Conclusion.
A Species stands beyond—
Invisible, as Music—
But positive, as Sound—
It beckons, and it baffles—
Philosophy—don't know—
And through a Riddle, at the last—
Sagacity, must go—
To guess it, puzzles scholars—
To gain it, Men have borne
Contempt of Generations
And Crucifixion, shown—
Faith slips—and laughs, and rallies—
Blushes, if any see—
Plucks at a twig of Evidence—
And asks a Vane, the way—
Much Gesture, from the Pulpit—
Strong Hallelujahs roll—
Narcotics cannot still the Tooth
That nibbles at the soul—

It is noteworthy that Dickinson does not deny the finality of *all* worlds, but only of *this* outward and visible world. There is another species of the same genus that is indeed transcendent and unbounded—namely, the heavenly and unseen world whose finality she does not doubt. Karl Barth observes that this mysterious heavenly realm is no less created than the earthly sphere, and thus that it is neither to be feared nor worshipped as divine, though it does indeed terrify and delight with preternatural wonder. In relation to his earthly environment, man is meant to see, hear, understand, and rightly have dominion over it. But with regard to the inconceivable celestial world, man remains at once unknowing and completely dependent:

> At this inner boundary of creation stands man as though even as a creature he had to represent this above and below, and thus, as a creature, to signify his place in a relationship which penetrates into the heights and depths in a quite different way from that of heaven and earth [i.e., the way of the angels and the beasts]. Man is the place within creation where the creature in its fullness is concentrated, and at the same time stretches beyond itself; the place where God wishes to be praised within creation, and may be praised.[6]

We must not claim too much for Dickinson, baptizing her as an anonymous Christian.[7] Thus would we violate the integrity both of her poetry and our own Faith. Yet we must mark the failure of pietistic Christianity to honor the mystery of the invisible realm. It attempted to make outward and visible conversion experience serve as a surrogate for—rather than a sign of—our engagement with the inward and invisible world. Insofar as we can call Dickinson a believer at all, it must be in Williams James's and Rudolf Otto's sense of the term: she venerated what Otto called the *mysterium tremendum et fascinans*, the Holy Otherness that at once frightens and attracts, both alarming and alluring, repelling and captivating us. That her pietist community wanted to bypass this mysterious middle realm between earth and God was utterly unacceptable to Dickinson. If we are to honor the true God, we must praise him (as Barth suggests) from *within* the creation, glorifying him in gratitude for this created realm that remains as unseen as melody and harmony yet as real as resounding chords. Philosophical inquiry can fathom nearly everything under the sun but this most important thing: the mystery of the Infinite. The dry speculations of airy academics thus prompt Dickinson to an agnostic "don't know." Worldly wisdom, even at best, is but riddles and conundrums. Heavenly wisdom—the engagement with this unknown world that issues in real sagacity—requires a constant grappling with the unobvious, a daily martyrdom to easy nostrums, even the contempt of both the cultured and uncultured despisers of doubt-filled faith.

Dickinson's mystical kind of faith in the unseen world also entails radical risk. It is never something as clear and certain as a proposition. It's an affair of slipping and advancing, of losing and rallying, of weeping and rejoicing. So shy of self-confidence is such faith that it blushes when asked to expound its own piety.[8] Dickinson also joins Christians in acknowledging the limits of mere experiential evidence, since it carries no more weight than a twig might bear, fruitful though it may be. She also calls us to remember that, as sinful citizens of the sinful church—the tattered bride of Christ—we receive dubious direction from the wind-blown cock atop our crucifobic churches. Though meant to announce the miracle of the Resurrection, it often blows with every wind of doctrine, even as it sometimes crows with undisciplined erotic energy.

Despite the flailing of perfervid preachers and easy believers, true faith—whether in the unseen heavenly realm or in the incarnate God—is never free from the toothache of doubt. The feel-good pharmacists of the No-God offer vain narcotics to ease the agony entailed by authentic belief. The Lord of heaven and earth will not anesthetize shallow souls with worldly finalities, even of the most "spiritual" sort. So does the lesser lord of the celestial sphere implant the molar of diffidence no less than the tusk of certainty, and they both nibble at the soul like a mouse at cheese. Emily Dickinson's deity thus bears more than a distant resemblance to the true God. For her god is utterly unlike Blake's "Old Nobodaddy," Hemingway's "Our Nada Who Art in Nada," and thus the Big Guy in the Sky whose death we ought to celebrate. Her god resembles the One who abandoned his doubt-wracked Son in Gethsemane as he prepared to mount the bloody Tree from which he would rule the world by reconciled lives rather than coerced conversions.[9]

I contend that Christian scholars are obliged to honor such faithful Dickinsonian doubt by teaching our students not to dismiss but to absorb it. A "god" who cannot be doubted is also a "god" who cannot be believed in true biblical fashion. It is noteworthy, for example, that there are many more psalms of lament than psalms of praise, and yet we have not yet sung a single "lament chorus." Nor does Yahweh vindicate Job's alleged "comforters" for insisting that Job cease crying out his protest against divine injustice. On the contrary, they are punished while Job is rewarded. Why? Not in spite of his wrestling hard with the Lord God but rather because, like Jacob, he would not turn Yahweh loose until he received something far more important than a mere theodicy—namely, a theophany, a frightening and saving appearance of God himself. There Job learns that God has many other concerns than man alone, and thus that man should not read the disasters of nature as being directed willfully and divinely at him.

Here, I believe we should also follow the example of evangelical philosopher Merold Westphal.[10] He has taught us to regard Marx and Nietzsche and Freud, not as demonic enemies but as unintended friends of the Gospel. The "god" whom they deny, Westphal rightly argues, is the "god" whom we should never have worshipped in the first place. Marx is right when he declares much of Christianity to be an opiate, a massive dose of morphine for people who want to give a comforting divine sanction to their privileged position in society. Nietzsche is right when he accuses many Christians of what he calls *ressentiment*—a fundamental animosity against life, a deep discontentment with the rough-and-tumble character of a world where the rain falls on the just and unjust alike. Freud is right when he declares that Jews and Christians often worship a nice and cuddly and friendly "god" whom they have projected onto a universe devoid of such deity.

Karl Barth is altogether right in saluting these naysayers of the "no-God." He regards the pseudo-divinity of popular Christian belief as the most pernicious of all human inventions. Belief in this merely civil deity stanches any radical transformation of either persons or communities. "The cry of revolt against such a god," says Barth, "is nearer the truth than is the sophistry with which men attempt to justify him." Yet it is ever so difficult to surrender belief in this comforting and consoling no-God who merely confirms "...the course of the world and of men as it is":

> We suppose that we know what we are saying when we say "God." We assign to Him the highest place in our world: and in so doing we place Him on fundamentally one line with ourselves and with things. We assume that He needs something: and so we assume that we are able to arrange our relation to Him as we arrange other relationships. We press ourselves into proximity with Him: and so, all unthinking, we make Him nigh unto ourselves. We allow ourselves an ordinary communication with Him, we permit ourselves to reckon with Him as though this were not extraordinary behaviour on our part. We dare to deck ourselves out as his companions, patrons, advisers, and commissioners. We confound time with eternity. . . . And so, when we set God upon the throne of the world, we mean by God ourselves.[11]

II.

Emily Dickinson is but one of the many writers whom we should esteem for taking Christianity more seriously than the church itself often regards it. Melville and Hawthorne are two other figures who are especially discerning in their analysis of our terribly twisted condition. So is Emerson to be saluted for making a wholesale rejection of Christian faith, refusing even to celebrate Holy Communion in its non-sacramental Unitarian form. But for me the non-Christian writer whose work retains overwhelming, even transformative, power is William Faulkner. Faulkner remains, in my opinion, our finest if also our fiercest literary assailant against acculturated Christianity in its Southern expression. That the church undergirded a savage system of chattel slavery was, for him, its chief failing. In disclosing the sinister quality of this institution that was so deeply linked to white Christianity, Faulkner unwittingly enables the church to repent of its sin. Yet Faulkner makes no easy moralistic judgment of so obvious an evil. The Old South was, in many ways, a wondrous place. That it produced Robert Penn Warren and Eudora Welty, Flannery O'Connor and Walker Percy, Allen Tate and Faulkner himself, is sufficient testimony to its cultural excellence. Though Percy loathed "the monstrous mythologizing" of the so-called Southern Way of Life, he lauded the region's authentic virtues: "the conservative tradition of a predominantly agrarian society, a tradition which at its best enshrined the human aspects of living for rich and poor, black and white. It gave first place to a stable family life, sensitivity and good manners between men, chivalry toward women, an honor code, and individual integrity."[12] Even so, it was a culture that rested on human bondage, and nowhere more tellingly than in "The Bear" does Faulkner expose its fiendish cruelty.

Rather than offering a tract against slavery and the segregated society built on it, Faulkner enables his readers vicariously to experience a shock of moral recognition alongside his sixteen-year old protagonist, Ike McCaslin. The boy finds himself examining an early nineteenth-century ledger kept by two of his great-uncles, Buck and Buddy. The two brothers had entered half-literate jokes in the record book as they bantered back and forth about the McCaslin family's various dealings with their slaves. The crucial entry involves a black woman named Eunice: "*Bought by Father in New Orleans 1807 $650. dolars. Marid to Thucydus 1809 Drownd in Crick Cristmas Day 1832.*" A second entry almost six months thence reads as follows: "*June 21th 1833 Drownd herself.*" Writing two days later, the second brother adds: "*Who in hell ever heard of a niger drownding him self.*"[13] What young Ike McCaslin has discovered—to his staggering horror, though it had caused only vague puzzlement to his uncles—is the cause for Eunice's suicide on the Feast of the Nativity. The day of the world's divine rebirth, we learn, had been the day of Eunice's deliberate death. What should have been an occasion for great gratitude and rejoicing was, instead, the time for final despair. On Christmas Day, Eunice had found out a truth that was beyond her bearing: her daughter Tomasina was three months pregnant. We also learn from the ledgers that this daughter Tomasina had been fathered, not by Eunice's slave husband Thucydus, but by Carothers McCaslin, the plantation owner himself. Now, twenty-two years later, this same "Tomy" had been impregnated by this same Carothers McCaslin—i.e., by her own father.

Like their forebears, Buck and Buddy McCaslin could not conceive of Negro slaves as human beings, as having their own moral integrity, as capable of suicidal rage against this most fundamental violation, and thus of killing themselves. Blacks to them were dumb chattel—objects to be sold in markets and traded in card games—having little more dignity and worth than an ox or a mule. Yet the brothers' mention of Eunice's self-murder, six months later when her daughter Tomy died in childbirth, reveals that Buck and Buddy were not totally opaque to the truth. They were haunted with a dim and inchoate sense of guilt, with a moral burden that would become a deadly weight only a generation later in young Ike McCaslin. For in discovering that Eunice had taken her own life in an act of sheer metaphysical renunciation—repudiating a system so evil that it could allow the father of a slave child to summon this same slave daughter to his bed of carnal lust and to father yet another child on her—young Ike also repudiated his plantation legacy. Rather than becoming a wealthy cotton farmer, he has elected to live as a landless itinerant carpenter—not unlike the Nazarene carpenter's son who declared that his Kingdom was not of this world.

Young Isaac McCaslin had been given his deepest moral formation in the annual deer and bear hunts that he had enjoyed with his kinsmen along with Sam Fathers, the Indian master of these annual ventures into the wilderness. There Ike had undergone a deep initiation into the most fundamental mysteries—especially the sheer gratuity of the natural world in all of its beauteous wonder and feral fierceness. Yet the high holiness of the woods is being ever more rudely desecrated by the acquisitive instincts that prevail in the town. And so Ike determines to preserve the virtues of the primitive hunt over against the vices of so-called civilization. Rather than perpetuate the evils that he has inherited from his McCaslin ancestors, he will break the chain of violence and exploitation and greed. He will make atonement for the sins of his fathers.

Ike cites the book of Genesis as giving humanity its original summons to become stewards and communicants with the land, not its domineering owners and arrogant proprietors. Man was created, Ike argues, "not to hold for himself and his descendants inviolable title forever, generation after generation, to the oblongs and squares of the earth, but to hold the earth mutual and intact in the communal anonymity of brotherhood" (GDM, 257). Despite Cass Edmonds's utter incredulity at Ike's decision, the youth renounces his plantation inheritance for the sake of the universal human verities that Keats voices in his "Ode on a Grecian Urn":

> *He was talking about truth. Truth is one. It doesn't change. It covers all things which touch the heart—honor and pride and pity and justice and courage and love. Do you see now?* (GDM, 297)

Cynical Cass will never discern the metaphysics and thus the morals of the hunt. Yet Faulkner seems also to have had his own doubts about the efficacy of Ike's act, even though Ike repeats the ringing rhetoric of Faulkner's Nobel Prize Address that lay more than two decades in advance.[14] In fact, Faulkner parodies nearly every aspect of Ike's sterling act of moral repudiation. For example, Hubert ("Uncle Buck") Beauchamp had left the young Ike a legacy of thirty gold pieces in a silver cup. Quite apart from the demeaning allusion to Judas's similarly sized guilt-money, Buck had rapidly reduced the value of the legacy by borrowing against it even before Ike was born. Finally, he took the silver cup itself, leaving in its place only a tin coffee pot filled with copper coins and worthless I.O.U.s.

Ike's valiant moral protest—his attempt to preserve the high morality of the hunt, if only in the inner sanctum of his own solitary self—proves increasingly bootless. When his wife learns, for example, that Ike has refused his inheritance, she refuses all sexual intercourse with him. Without property, Ike can never become a responsible paterfamilias. Thus does McCaslin become a fatherless and ne'er do well carpenter—"not in mere static and hopeless imitation of the Nazarene" (GDM, 309), but rather as a new kind of racist himself. We learn in "Delta Autumn" that, because Ike had repudiated the plantation that had rightfully fallen to him, it has been taken over by Cass Edmonds' son Roth, a ruthless *roué* who treats its black inhabitants far less humanely than Ike might have done. Indeed, Roth has formed a sexual liaison with the octoroon great-granddaughter of Tomy's son Turl, fathering a son on her. Roth tries to silence the mother of his child with a monetary payment that he makes Ike himself deliver. But the elderly Ike who was once the defender of Negroes and the courageous critic of their exploitation is scandalized to discover that this nameless woman wants Roth not to pay her off but to marry her. In a burst of racist fury, Ike urges the young Negress to wed a fellow black and to move back to the North: "Maybe in a thousand or two thousand years in America, he thought. But not now! Not now! He cried, not loud, in a voice of amazement, pity, and outrage: 'You're a nigger'" (GDM, 361). This woman of such negligible importance as to have no name responds with a critique of Ike that brings his supposed moral revolution to less than naught—indeed, to shame and ignominy: "'Old man,' she said, 'have you lived so long and forgotten so much that you don't remember anything you ever knew or even felt about love?'" (GDM, 363).[15]

This dour conclusion to the Ike McCaslin stories may seem to indicate that Faulkner is a profound moral realist who shares something of Reinhold Niebuhr's suspicion of an ethical idealism which naïvely and self-righteously refuses to make necessary compromises with fallen human nature. Yet there is something far darker animating Faulkner's vision. What Nietzsche called the will-to-power is intrinsic to human existence, Faulkner suggests, and it operates in the woods no less than the town. For if the hunters did not kill their prey, they could not live. If blacks are not made slaves, some other race or group will just as surely be subjected to human bondage, whether legal or cultural. The institution of property merely systematizes this urge that the hunt spontaneously expresses. Unless we assert ourselves against nature, mastering it to our own will and use, we cannot survive even as animals, much less as humans. To be human is thus to own and to control and to kill. To have an ego is to be an egotist; it is to subdue others to our own interest. It is not only an ennobling human tragedy that Faulkner displays in his fiction, therefore, but also the brazen will to power in a Hobbesian-cum-Darwinian world wherein all make war against all.

It follows that communion with the numinous spirit that animates both the heavenly and earthly realms, both the invisible and the visible worlds, filling humanity with a mystical longing for truth and beauty and goodness—that this vague mysticism cannot serve as the basis for human transformation. For Faulkner, there is neither a divinity nor a community able to liberate human life from its endless internecine struggle of wills. We are left with a bleak and withering solace. It is to be found only in an irrevocable sense of loss and guilt—in the futile pangs of conscience—to which we are doomed as alienated and isolated creatures. "Knowledge of one's estrangement, and the unwillingness to make one's peace with it," writes John Sykes, "is in Faulkner's world the highest achievement of moral man."[16] Ike McCaslin is a noble and admirable failure, we must conclude, but he is also the inevitable failure that, in Faulkner's world, every human creature is destined to become. In no way does this dour fact lessen the worth of Faulkner's work. On the contrary, we owe him an unpayable debt for posing the sharpest possible critique of Christianity by offering the keenest and most drastic alternative to it—a vision of human life as having a history entirely of our own making, a history at whose core there is a furious and resounding clash of wills signifying nothing.

III.

Flannery O'Connor famously declared, in speaking of William Faulkner's work, that she could recognize the Dixie Limited when it came roaring down the rails, and thus that she got her little mule and wagon off the tracks as soon as possible. Rightly if thus comically did O'Connor confess the grandeur of Faulkner's fiction as compared to her own modest efforts. Neither in artistic style nor historical sweep does O'Connor's work approximate anything akin to his. Yet it is noteworthy that O'Connor did not describe Faulkner's literary locomotive as the Dixie *Express* but rather as the Dixie *Limited*. Faulkner's fiction constitutes no literary "express" because it quite literally does not "press out" a moral vision that is capable of personal and social enactment. This is not to deny, of course, that Faulkner strikes a certain balance between opposing forces: between the psychologically trapped Joe Christmas and the morally struggling Byron Bunch, between suicidal Quentin and enduring Dilsey, even between the rapacious entrepreneur Flem Snopes and the humble business-man V. K. Ratliff.

Though Faulkner's struggling souls never succeed, they are nonetheless ennobled in their defeat. Yet while Ike McCaslin is imbued with a moral ide-alism that demands the transformation of both himself and his racist society, he is helpless to enact it. He has no moral community either to inspire or to sustain his moral vision. On the contrary, Faulkner deliberately undermines Ike's sterling ethical ideals by demonstrating their inherent futility. Ike ends, as we have seen, by perpetrating a racism of his own. Thus is Faulkner's fictional universe suffused, not only with metaphysical nullity, but also with an inher-ently *limited* moral vision that denies the possibility of radical transformation, whether personal or social. One task of Christian criticism is to name such limits, even while honoring the literary grandeur that enshrines them.

Though Flannery O'Connor brings her characters to drastic judgments of their moral and religious vacuity, these "moments of grace" usually come at the moment of death. Such drastic confrontations are not for the sake of a grue-some delight in gore but for the sake of religious clarity instead. "When you can assume that your audience holds the same beliefs you do," Flannery O'Connor declared in one of her most celebrated pronouncements, "you can relax a little and use more normal means of talking to it; when you have to assume that it does not, then you have to make your vision apparent by shock—to the hard of hearing you shout, and for the almost-blind you draw large and startling figures."[17] O'Connor was not referring to her secular audience alone as need-ing to be startled into attention; she was no less worried about her Christian readers. "If you live today," she wrote to Elizabeth Hester, "you breathe in nihil-ism. In or out of the Church, it's the gas you breathe."[18] Though she had no desire whatever to compete with Faulkner—knowing well that his talent was immeasurably greater than hers—she discerned that her fiction would need to embody a radical answer to the implicit nihilism of his work if it were worth any credence at all. The nothingness that Faulkner willingly and consciously embraced, as she saw with uncanny prescience, infects almost the whole of modern American culture, ecclesial no less than secular.

O'Connor was especially impatient with the glib sophistication of the elite who, without wrestling with the doubt that vexed Emily Dickinson and William Faulkner, sought refuge in a complacent humanism. At a New York dinner party hosted by the poet Robert Lowell and his then-wife Elizabeth

Hardwick, the novelist Mary McCarthy was present along with O'Connor and others. McCarthy would later proclaim her emancipation from the church in *Memories of a Catholic Girlhood*. Here she was content to opine that she still found the symbolism of the Eucharist to be useful for her fiction, though of course she didn't believe a word of its hocus-pocus. The ordinarily quiet and unassertive O'Connor—who rarely spoke to strangers unless first addressed, and then only with a shy hesitance—made a notoriously acid reply: "Well, if it's a symbol, to hell with it."[19] The shocked response recorded by the other dinner guests must have been similar to the pattern described by William Buckley. If you mention God at a New York dinner party, said Buckley, you will be stared at; and if you mention God twice, you will not be invited again.

From the very beginning, O'Connor set her work against the grain of her culture and time. Not at all for the sake of any kind of Christian obscurantism was O'Connor a contrarian. Quite the opposite, she discerned that something far more radical and drastic would be required if both the church and the world were to be rescued from the abyss of Nothingness. Unlike advocates of the civil religion that was aborning in the 1950s, that would triumph by the end of the millennium, and that continues to rule much of evangelical America in the early twenty-first century, O'Connor regarded *dogma* as a salutary rather than a pejorative term. Thus did she make her upper-case confession: "My stories have been watered and fed by Dogma" (CW, 930). She rejected the common view that dogmas divide while ethics unite ("deeds, not creeds"), since doctrines are supposedly focused on esoteric matters, and thus are not amenable to practical use. O'Connor declared, quite to the contrary, that the creeds are meant precisely to unite Christians, however much we may remain divided about moral matters. The creeds are compressed narrative summaries of God's self-identification in Israel and Christ; and as such they are vehicles "of freedom and not of restriction" (CW, 943). "Dogma is an instrument for penetrating reality," O'Connor insisted. On another occasion she added that "Christian dogma is about the only thing left in the world that surely guards and respects mystery" (MM, 178).

O'Connor does not make mystery a synonym for puzzle or riddle or conundrum—those things that balk the mind and stifle understanding. Nor was it a convenient locution for vaguely spiritual concerns. Here she is close to Dickinson, while delving much deeper—not merely into the invisible world but into the divine realm itself. "To St. Paul and to the early Christian thinkers," writes one of her favorite Old Testament scholars, Claude Tresmontant, mystery is "on the contrary the particular object of intelligence, its fullest nourishment. The *mysterion* is something so rich in intelligible content, so inexhaustibly full of delectation for the mind that no contemplation can ever reach its end. It is an eternal delectation of the mind." The more deeply we penetrate mystery, the greater our ignorance grows. "Mystery isn't something that is gradually evaporating," O'Connor wrote to the skeptical Emory student (and future prize-winning poet) Alfred Corn. "It grows along with knowledge" (HB, 489).

It also develops only with fierce struggle, for O'Connor was quick to recognize that Christian faith can never be instrumental to any other good, no matter how noble. The Gospel can never be employed as a mere means to some allegedly greater end—not even for such noble causes as economic justice, the recovery of family life, or peace between warring tribes and nations. This explains why, though she supported Martin Luther King, Jr., she could never be a fervent enthusiast for the civil rights movement. She rightly saw that, once the races were integrated, we would still be bedeviled by the crookedness of the human heart. Hence her unshakeable conviction that the Gospel is not a mechanism or vehicle for anything else, especially the culture wars. It is, instead, the very basis for the drastically alternative community that God is seeking to create for the salvation of the whole world—i.e., the maculate and whoring Bride of Christ called the church.

O'Connor is not naïve about the church. She had little patience with "mass" Catholics who receive the weekly sacrament without its making any discernible difference in their lives. "The Church for them," she wrote, "is not the body of Christ but the poor man's insurance system."[20] When once asked what kind of Christian she would become if she were not a Roman Catholic, she replied, far from jestingly, that she would join a Pentecostal Holiness church. Belief for Flannery O'Connor must be radical or it is not belief at all. Faith is not another item in the laundry list of one's loyalties: it is all or nothing at all. Thus did she confess that she was "a Catholic (not because it's advantageous to my writing but because I was born and brought up one) and at some point in my life I realized that not only was I a Catholic but that this was all I was, that I was a Catholic not like someone else would be a Baptist or a Methodist but like someone else would be an atheist" (CW, 930).[21] O'Connor had no patience for a merely polite piety. She admired Camus and Sartre and Faulkner because they took God seriously enough to deny his reality.[22] O'Connor's God-botherers resemble an atheist in a Peter De Vries novel who cannot forgive God for not existing. Yet O'Connor's atheists, whether Christian or secular, are usually unable to elude the divine Pursuer.

One of O'Connor's most memorable characters, The Misfit from "A Good Man is Hard to Find," is another of her God-botherers who sees that the real issue is not humanism or civil religion or any of the other substitutes for radical Christianity. He is an ex-Christian who, having felt the Abrahamic knife at his own throat, has embraced the nihilistic life of mass murder. He is a serial killer before they became the vogue. And so he is appalled that Jesus raised the dead. This bringer of death is profoundly offended that the Giver of Life cannot be dismissed as a mere holy man or eminent ethical figure, but must be adjudged as either the incarnate God or else a wholesale fraud. Unlike the psychopathic Misfit, the Grandmother is a proper lady who would gladly reduce Christian faith to sociology or culture or personality development if, in so doing, she could save her own life. She proves to be a good Christian atheist in the sense memorably specified by John Wesley when he said that we are practical atheists whenever we live as if God does not matter. The Grandmother's self-assurance is so complete that she believes she can manage not only her own life but her family's lives, as well. She also believes that she can convince even this serial killer to spare them all. In a crescendo of desperate defenses, she assures The Misfit that he is a good man, that he is not mediocre, that he should pray for Jesus to help him. In a last maniacal attempt to save herself, even at the cost of her own soul, the Grandmother denies her own Laodicean faith, declaring that perhaps Jesus did not raise the dead. Undeterred by these frenetic acts of self-protection, The Misfit kills her in cold blood and with cynical clarity: "She would of been a good woman," he observes with perfect redneck grammatical truthfulness, "if it had been somebody there to shoot her every minute of her life" (CW, 153).

O'Connor offered a witty clue to the comedy implicit in this seemingly gruesome story—which also entails the heartless execution of the Grandmother's son and daughter-in-law and three grandchildren, one of them an infant—when she observed that, while a lot of folks get killed in her work, nobody gets hurt. No one is made to cringe while anticipating a horrible death, or to suffer abominable tortures. Instead, the Grandmother's otherwise nondescript son and daughter-in-law muster a surprising dignity as they face their own and their children's deaths. And the Grandmother herself, though brutally slaughtered, is not spiritually injured. The Misfit murders her, instead, as he recoils in horror from her confession of their deep kinship. He pumps bullets into her chest only when she touches him on the shoulder in an outrageous act of mutual identification: "Why you're one of my babies," she cries. "You're one of my own children" (CW, 152). In this single saving gesture that costs the Grandmother her life, she at last drops all of her fearful self-justifications, all of her vain attempts to stay alive at whatever price. Finally she tells the truth: she is not a good woman, he is not a good man, they both are in terrible trouble, and they both need radical help.

It is a perfect climax first anticipated when The Misfit first confronts the Grandmother. For she confesses her essential kinship with this calloused killer: "His face was as familiar to her as if she had known him all her life but she could not recall who he was" (CW, 146). The Misfit is her *Doppelgänger*, her shadow, her second and secret self. This is not to say that the Grandmother is a monster of malevolence. Like nearly everyone else, she is a well-meaning but self-serving person—an ordinary Christian atheist. Her life rests on nothing more solid than her desire for respectability. She wears a hat and gloves when traveling so that, if found dead beside the road, she will be recognized as a lady. She fantasizes about taking her family to see a plantation mansion with white columns and a secret panel. She sees a naked Negro child standing in the door of a shack, not as a child living in abject poverty, but as "a cute little pickaninny." Convinced that her own way is always best, she manages to prevail in all family disputes.

Yet her conscience is sufficiently pained at having lied about the antebellum mansion that, in a sudden upsurge of emotional guilt, she indirectly causes their car wreck. The problem is that Grandmother has no deeply ingrained moral and religious character; she is a genteel and unacknowledged nihilist. When faced with the threat of death, therefore, she is willing to deny her faith in the hope of saving her life. The Grandmother is a woman who lives by her own lights, though they provide little illumination of her sinful condition. She is Flannery O'Connor's portrait, not of *l' homme moyen sensuel*, the average worldly person, but of the average Christian soul living amidst the compromises and deceits of ordinary life with a blithe obliviousness to the Nothingness opening beneath her. Hence her capitalized generic name: she is not one of our grandmothers; she is one of *us*.

The Misfit had perhaps once found himself in the Grandmother's place: a man seeking the easiest path, avoiding all trouble, staying out of harm's way. But at some indiscernible point, his good intentions ceased to suffice. He began to cut corners and to trim edges, until he gradually came both to commit and to justify evil deeds. The Misfit is thus a mirror of the Grandmother, a man who might well have the face of her own child. Seeing at last his desperate plight, she can also see how much it is like her own. Such shared sinfulness is what The Misfit dare not confess, and so he guns the old lady down with three quick shots.

Though the Grandmother enunciates no overt faith, she seems to make what ancient Christian tradition called "a good death." She dissolves a lifetime of complacency and conceit in a brief acknowledgment of her Adamic solidarity with her killer. Her divinely happy ending is perhaps figured in her final posture. Sinking down to death in her puddling blood, she is not wrought with anguish or regret; instead, her legs are "crossed under her like a child's and her face [is] smiling up at the cloudless sky" (CW, 152). O'Connor leaves her ending open to conflicting interpretations: the Grandmother can also be construed as having remained as spiritually childish in death as in life. Yet the cruciform legs and the beatific expression and the inviting heavens suggest that she has died in a state of grace.

It must be confessed that few readers have discerned the Grandmother's saving gesture of grace without O'Connor's later explanation: "Her head clears for an instant and she realizes, even in her limited way, that she is responsible for the man before her and joined to him by ties of kinship which have their roots deep in the mystery she has been merely prattling about so far. And at this point, she does the right thing, she makes the right gesture" (MM, 111-12).[23] As a still maturing writer, O'Connor would not again make the moment of self-awakening so obscure, even though her endings would remain no less disturbing. They leave us with a chilling sense of our own complicity in the evils that her characters often commit.

If the Grandmother's final state is ambiguous, The Misfit's is not. He is a confessed nihilist who, unlike her, has wrestled hard with the God of the Gospel. His unbelief is as thoughtful as her piety is unreflective. We learn, from his reported confession to a prison psychiatrist, that he has been reared as a Bible-believing Baptist. Having never heard of Sigmund Freud, The Misfit responded with a wondrous literalism to the psychiatrist's suggestion that his homicidal acts were products of an unconfessed Oedipal desire to slay his father. The Misfit will have nothing of such reductionist psychology. In his brilliantly cornpone way, he denies that he is a victim of his unconscious drives: he is, instead, the proud agent of his own will-to-power:

> It was a head-doctor at the penitentiary said what I done was kill my daddy but I known that for a lie. My daddy died in nineteen ought nineteen [an unusual year, to say the least] of the epidemic flu and I never had a thing to do with it. He was buried in the Mount Hopewell Baptist churchyard and you can go there and see for your-self. (CW, 150)

The Misfit rejects the faith of his fathers because he's a good materialist, though he's far from knowing it: he will not credit ancient events that he cannot empirically verify. Since he was not present to witness Jesus's miraculous acts, he therefore will not believe them. Yet his literalism also has its merits: it will not permit him to make the typical modernist disjunction between Jesus's message and his miracles—as if one could keep the former as moral truth while discarding the latter as crass superstition. The Misfit refuses this convenient dichotomy between the human and the divine. Jesus's power over physical death, he knows, is the mark of his power over spiritual death. Christ's raising of the dead constitutes a command for The Misfit also to be transformed: to surrender his proud sufficiency and to embrace the love of God and neighbor. From the fundamentalist sermons of his Baptist boyhood, The Misfit knows that he must either gladly seize or bitterly reject Jesus's invitation. There is no safe middle way, no accommodating alternative to the drastic extremes of belief and unbelief, no bland neutrality between Jesus Christ and absolute nothingness:

> "Jesus was the only One that ever raised the dead," The Misfit continued, "and He shouldn't have done it. He thown everything off balance. If He did what He said, then it's nothing for you to do but thow away everything and follow Him, and if He didn't, then it's nothing for you to do but enjoy the few minutes you got left the best way you can—by killing somebody or burning down his house or doing some other meanness to him. No pleasure but meanness," he said, and his voice had become almost a snarl. (CW, 152)[24]

The Misfit has pushed the logic of his unbelief to its dreadful conclusion. He sees, as O'Connor often observed, that ours is not a culture of moral progress and evolutionary development but the culture of death. The final alternatives, The Misfit discerns, are not religion and science but the gospel and nihilism. Like Ivan Karamazov, he wants to return his ticket to the arena of life. But unlike Ivan, The Misfit has chosen nothingness as the substance of his being rather than a mere theoretical possibility. He is determined to offer scandalous signs of his spiritual offenses. In practicing his nihilism, The Misfit is not tempted by anything so small as theft. He is a murderer rather than a robber because, as he confesses, "Nobody had nothing I wanted" (CW, 150). To have stolen desirable objects would have been to acknowledge the goodness of things other than his own sovereign self-will. The Misfit relishes, instead, the deeds of annihilation: murder and arson and cruelty. They alone are able to display what Nietzsche called *Wille zur Macht*, his naked desire to overpower others by means of his nihilistic will.

Yet The Misfit is a civilized Nietzschean, a courteous killer whose manners match those of the Grandmother. He is embarrassed, for example, that he has no shirt to wear in the presence of women, having shed his prison uniform in making his escape. The Misfit always addresses the Grandmother as "Lady," and he always uses a proper "Yes'm" and "Nome" in responding to her. O'Connor was a stout defender of such outward politeness, but not when it serves to obscure the canker of soft-centered sentimentality. The Misfit's misery lies, he believes, in his failure to meet the expectations of society. He has failed to conform to the world's standards, and thus to "fit in," to live the balanced and well-adjusted life that perhaps the prison psychiatrist had urged upon him.

For all the brilliance of his fundamentalist nihilism, The Misfit fails to see that it is not Nietzschean nonconformity but Christian eccentricity that he needs: to acquire another Center than the world's hub, to become a fool for Christ's sake, to be re-formed in the image of the Cross. Gradually, therefore, he slides into whining self-justification. At first he admits that he is not a good man but a guilty convict, but finally alleges that he cannot even remember his evil acts and thus that he does not deserve to be punished for them. "I call myself The Misfit," he said, "because I can't make what all I done wrong fit what all I gone through in punishment" (CW, 151). Brave Nietzschean will-to-power thus ends in solipsistic victimology. If only he had been present at Jesus's miracles, The Misfit explains, "I would have known and I wouldn't be like I am now" (CW, 152). The Misfit is a closet Platonist in his belief that knowledge equals virtue and ignorance equals sin: he wants merely to *know* the truth, not to *do* it. Thus is the Misfit's voice choking with self-pity when the Grandmother extends him her surprising gesture of solidarity. And as soon as he kills her, the red-eyed murderer wipes his glasses, fogged as they are with a terrible tenderness toward himself. O'Connor discerns what our churches and culture have both failed to mark: that the alternative to the hard realism of the Gospel is not an equally hard nihilism but a squishy self-pity. Sentimentality, she said, is to Christianity as obscenity is to art—it is a kind of pornography, an unearned feeling of either sweet solace or bitter.

If our teaching is to have any real trenchancy and purchase, it will have to be rooted in a Christian radicalism such as O'Connor so memorably enfleshes in her fiction. On the one hand, we will need to confess that we Christians often have ourselves to blame when the world turns away from the Gospel either by neglect or rejection. So poorly have our churches provided the world a drastically alternative way of life that our best writers have had cause to refuse any privileging of Christianity in their work. On the other hand, we will also praise them for having shown us what is right and good about a skepticism that, in the case of Emily Dickinson, refuses all false versions of the Gospel. Her poetry also enfleshes a mystical faith in the world of the unknown and unknowable. Thus do Christians have due cause to embrace Dickinson's work, even its spiritual incompleteness. So do we owe to William Faulkner unbounded gratitude for revealing the horrors of a culture built on the subjection of an entire race to their allegedly Christian masters, even if he remains despairing about any permanent remedy to the perpetual domination of the weak by the strong.

Only a non-defensive kind of Christian radicalism is sufficiently confident to affirm the work of the Spirit in these worthy interlocutors and antagonists. There must not be a whit of smugness in our appropriation of the great canonical non-Christian texts of our literary tradition. There is no such smugness to be found anywhere in Flannery O'Connor's work. Yet neither is there a whiff of apology. She dedicated her life to the singular proposition that must also be ours as Christian teachers and students: If we are faithful to the God of Jesus Christ and his church, we will always be honored—whether in being persecuted and resented for having maintained our integrity, or else in being welcomed with joy by both our friends and antagonists.

Endnotes

1 Quoted in Roger Lundin, *Emily Dickinson and the Art of Belief* (Grand Rapids, MI: Eerdmans, 1998), 37.

2 Ibid., 40–41.

3 Ibid., 52.

4 Ibid., 49.

5 Quoted in D. Bruce Lockerbie, *Dismissing God: Modern Writers' Struggle Against Religion* (Grand Rapids, MI: Baker, 1998), 41.

6 *Dogmatics in Outline*, trans. G.T. Thomson (New York: Harper Torchbooks, 1959), 63.

7 "I'm ceded—I've stopped being Theirs" (#508) is the poem in which Dickinson most clearly elevates her poetic vocation over the dubious demand of the church that she repudiate the world. Like Virgil crowning and mitering Dante at the end of the *Purgatorio*, Dickinson enthrones herself with the diadem of Artemis, virgin goddess of the new moon, baptizing herself not in the name of the Father, Son, and Holy Ghost, but with the honorific of the highest art, poetry:

> Baptized, before, without the choice,
>
> But this time, consciously, of Grace—
>
> Unto supremest name—
>
> Called to my Full—The Crescent dropped—
>
> Existence's whole Arc, filled up,
>
> With one small Diadem.

Poems quoted in notes are from Emily Dickinson, The Collected Poems of Emily Dickinson, ed. Thomas H. Johnson (New York: Back Bay Books, 1976).

8   The same holds with conversion to Christian faith properly understood. When someone asked Karl Barth to recount his salvation experience, he replied that it occurred on a Friday afternoon in the year A.D. 34, when Christ was crucified. Our great and small and necessarily ongoing conversion experiences are but distant appropriations of this one saving Act.

9   Dickinson understood, with Ivan Karamazov, that without faith in God, ethics hover over an abyss. Hence her willingness to embrace the moral equivalent of false fire (ignis fatuus) rather than to rob the moral life of its transcendent basis:

> Those—dying then,
> Knew where they went—
> They went to God's Right Hand—
> That Hand is amputated now
>
> And God cannot be found—
>
> The abdication of Belief
> Makes the Behavior small—
> Better an ignis fatuus
> Than no illume at all. (#1551)

10   Merold Westphal, Suspicion and Faith: The Religious Uses of Modern Atheism (Grand Rapids: Eerdmans, 1993).

11   The Epistle to the Romans, 6th ed., trans. Edwyn C. Hoskyns (New York: Oxford University Press, 1968), 40, 44.

12   Signposts in a Strange Land, ed. Patrick Samway (New York: Farrar, Straus & Giroux, 1991), 51.

13   William Faulkner, Go Down, Moses (New York: Modern Library, 1955), 267. Further references will be designated GDM.

14   "I decline to accept the end of man. It is easy enough to say that man is immortal simply because he will endure: that when the last ding-dong of doom has clanged and faded from the last worthless rock hanging tideless in the last red and dying of evening, that even then there will be one more sound: that of his puny inexhaustible voice, still talking. I refuse to accept this. I believe that man will not merely endure: he will prevail. He is immortal, not because he alone among creatures has an inexhaustible voice, but because he has a soul, a spirit capable of compassion and sacrifice and endurance." Qtd. in The Faulkner Reader: Selections from the Works of William Faulkner (New York: Modern Library, 1959), 4.

15   Although Faulkner never permits his narrator to cast blame on Ike for his moral abdication, he did so in an interview with Cynthia Greer when she declared Ike to be her favorite Faulkner character: "Well, I think a man ought to do more than just repudiate. He should have been more affirmative instead of shunning people." Greer's interview is reprinted in Lion in the Garden: Interviews with

William Faulkner, eds. James B. Meriwether and Michael Millgate (Lincoln: University of Nebraska Press, 1968), 225.

16 John Daniel Sykes, Jr., *The Romance of Innocence and the Myth of History: Faulkner's Religious Critique of Southern Culture* (Ph.D. dissertation, Charlottesville: University of Virginia, 1986), 201–2. Sykes has shown that Faulkner's Christ figures are meant to shock and outrage his readers, whether in their bizarre difference from received images of Jesus or in their painful similarity to the church's authentic Christ. On the one hand, Faulkner creates deliberate caricatures of Christ in order to wrench Jesus free from the moralism, and especially the racial bigotry, to which Southern Protestantism has held him captive. On the other hand, he also fashions overt likenesses to Christ in order to convict white Christians of their hypocrisy in failing to follow his example. In both cases, Faulkner's Christ figures are meant to discredit what he perceives to be the stifling culture religion of his region. It is noteworthy, however, that Faulkner is much more convincing in portraying a monstrous Christ such as Joe Christmas of *Light in August* than in limning an earnest Christ such as the Corporal in *A Fable*. The Corporal is almost pathetically unconvincing, so obvious are the parallels of his life to that of Christ. Sykes argues that, despite his unquenchable religious yearning, Faulkner was never able to overcome his inveterate nihilism.

17 Flannery O'Connor, *Mystery and Manners: Occasional Prose*, eds. Robert and Sally Fitzgerald (New York: Farrar Straus & Giroux, 1970), 34. Future references will be designated MM.

18 *The Habit of Being: The Letters of Flannery O'Connor*, ed. Sally Fitzgerald (New York: Farrar Straus & Giroux, 1979), 97. Future references will be designated HB.

19 *The Collected Works of Flannery O'Connor*, ed. Sally Fitzgerald (New York: The Library of America, 1988), 977. Future references will be designated CW.

20 Qtd. in Williams Sessions, "'Then I discovered the Germans': O'Connor's Encounter with Guardini and German Thinkers," unpublished essay.

21 Here, as in so many other things, O'Connor stands near to Walker Percy. Anyone living in an age as morally and religiously intolerable as ours, said Percy, has the right to demand "a gift commensurate with the offense": "This life is much too much trouble, far too strange, to arrive at the end of it and then be asked what you make of it and have to answer, 'Scientific humanism.' That won't do. A poor show. Life is a mystery, love is a delight. Therefore, I take it as axiomatic that one should settle for nothing less than the infinite mystery and the infinite delight; i.e., God. In fact, I demand it. I refuse to settle for anything less. I don't see why anyone should settle for anything less than Jacob, who actually grabbed aholt of God and wouldn't let go until God identified himself and blessed him." From "Questions They Never Asked Me," in *Signposts in a Strange Land*, ed. Patrick Samway (New York: Farrar, Straus and Giroux, 1991), 417.

22 The only reference to Emily Dickinson in O'Connor's letters comes in a second-hand report that her mentor Caroline Gordon had "discovered a streak of diabolism in Emily" (CW, 1172). I suspect that Gordon had read Dickinson's mockery of the no-God of New England pietism as secretly demonic, when in fact it was quite justified. As we have seen, Dickinson's esteem for the invisible

and unknowable world (but not for the God who is it Maker and Finisher) makes her work sub-Christian but hardly diabolical.

23 O'Connor explains in a letter why The Misfit shrinks from the old lady's touch: "Grace is never received warmly. Always a recoil ..." (CW, 1150).

24 The many well-intended corrected versions of "thown" betray a fundamental deafness to rural Southern speech.

"Take Nothing for the Journey Except a Staff":

Teaching Fiction Workshop

Albert Haley (Abilene Christian University)

Albert Haley offers a very personal view of the many difficulties of the creative writing workshop in which the "village of self-expression" is often the only destination; instead, Al argues that budding writers need a time of "discipleship" with a master teacher who can guide and mentor the student through the particular pitfalls faced by writers today. Al's goal for the stories of his students is nothing less than to affect the larger world. Currently the Writer in Residence at Abilene Christian University in Abilene, TX, he was raised in Alaska, graduated from Yale University, and in 1993 completed an MFA from the University of Houston. His fiction has appeared in the New Yorker, *the* Atlantic Monthly, Rolling Stone, *and* Image: A Journal of the Arts & Religion. *He is also the author of two books,* Home Ground: Stories of Two Families and the Land *(Dutton, 1978) and* Exotic, A Novel *(Dutton, 1982).*

I'd like to begin with an exercise that I suppose is every storyteller's birthright. I'd like to imagine for a moment—

There's a grassy field and an empty stadium. I stand still in the center of it all. From my vantage point I see a series of perfectly thrown or hit balls that arc through the air, the many feet that churn the green grass. I hear the roar rising in the stands.

Now I turn to an empty factory and place myself amidst the machinery. With care I move close to wheels that will turn and belts that will convey.

Again, in my mind I conjure what is to come: the clanking and the overall hum; the sheer, blasting, mechanical force of relentless productivity on the march.

Last, I move behind a podium in a hall where shouting supporters will soon appear. Already I can hear the much-anticipated speech that will be delivered and how the thronged mass cheers, making a genuine spectacle as they wave signs in the air.

Our society seems to have settled ideas about activities that are of significance. We focus on the blur-speed distraction of sports, the breathlessly reported pulse of the economy, and the intrigues and travails of politics. In fact, the antiquated medium I just turned to this morning (called a "newspaper") is replete, as always, with stories from these exalted realms.

By contrast, the setting a teacher faithfully heads toward is filled with much less drama or even sensory input. Our work is done in a world of drab institutional desks or tables, white boards on the walls, and perhaps a smattering of technology thrown into the mix. Add students and something significant is supposed to happen, though it will quite likely never make it into the breaking news or appear illuminated on a scoreboard.

When I think about my specific job, that of teaching students to fashion something of value through the creative use of words, the images I receive are even more humbling. However dynamic I may try to make our little workshop, I know that the actual writing will be done later in the most prosaic corners of our busy world: in a library carrel, in a fast-food joint, in a dorm room sometime deep in the pocket of night after young revelers on the hallway have settled down.

What is this room where I teach all about? Why is it so much more difficult to visualize what needs to be done here than it is to see in the mind's eye the scoring of points, the emergence of gleaming, machined parts from the factory, or to hear that rousing speech and witness ballots going into the box? I can't say, but at least I have an idea of what I seek. I believe in the possibility of blank pieces of paper that fill up with words to become a story, delivering truth to readers in some way, small or large, that changes a part of them forever.

My ambitions are high and there is no shortcut to achievement. As I tell students from the beginning, the world of literature does not have an affirmative action plan for writers, Christian or otherwise, and this is as it should be. All of us must write in such a way as to meet, or exceed, the standards set by the best writers of the past and present.

The main question is, how are we going to get there?

Hitting the Road

Writing a story of publishable or near-publishable quality is the goal I set forth in fiction workshop. Though striving for such a lofty thing sometimes astonishes students who thought they signed up for a course the chief aim of which would be to express themselves, I do not back down. Hopefully, we're going to write the kind of short story that features fresh characters who find themselves in interesting situations that test them. Its language and narrative structure will complement one another so that form supports and underscores content. By the time the story reaches its end, it will have conveyed something to the reader about the realities and complexities of life without coming right out and saying it, subtlety being its hallmark.

For a beginning writer to achieve all this is the equivalent of learning to juggle a series of multi-colored balls, not only keeping them up in the air, but demanding that they whir by in a certain pleasing order—*Here comes the red, the green, the blue.* This is why the potential for failing to achieve our goal is so high. Storytelling is a difficult art to master, and unless the teacher can find ways to assist the apprentice jugglers, not only will a chaotic exhibition emerge with balls flying all over the classroom, but someone (*look out!*) might very well get hurt. Little surprise, it could be the teacher.

Honestly, there's nothing more demoralizing and painful to handle than an onslaught of typical undergraduate fiction. Left to their instincts and limited means, students will take my optimistic vision—there's a storyteller in nearly all of them, just waiting to be released—and transmute it into tangible dreck. Even the most gifted and experienced student is capable of writing awful stories, the kind that will make the teacher want to rise up and flee the room and locate the nearest incinerator pile where, after burning the evidence, he can start anointing himself with ashes. Worse, other students are as likely as not to judge their peers' deficient work to be acceptable and maybe even "great," naively assuming that its worth is bound up in the sincerity of the effort.

This is the point at which I start to think about Jesus and his disciples.

Anyone who reads the Gospels with something approaching an open mind realizes that a rather obscure rabbi taught his twelve closest followers a great deal. Enough to change the world. What is easy to forget is that it took Jesus time, and the Twelve certainly didn't make it easy for him. Given the challenges Jesus faced with his own students, I've often thought it might be possible to learn a thing or two from his teaching process.

I begin with a picture of some of the disciples' low points. A soaked and humiliated Peter thrashing in the waves after he thought it would be a good idea to walk on water like the Master. The failed casting out of the evil spirit in a boy while Jesus and the inner circle were on the Mount of Transfiguration. James and John wanting to call down fire from heaven on unrepentant villages.

It seems to me that these episodes amount to lived-out versions of dreadful stories composed by Jesus's earnest but essentially inept charges. Though these men had the best of intentions and threw all their energy into their tasks, they produced "work" that was sketchy, incoherent, or melodramatic and cliché, not to mention theologically and emotionally out of tune.

On the other side of that first-century coin is the progress the same men sometimes made. I remember how Jesus commissioned the Twelve to go into the villages and cities and perform miracles (Mark 6:8–10), and when they returned there was a good report given with evidence to confirm it: They had preached that people should repent, they had driven out "many demons," and they had anointed with oil "many sick people" and healed them.

What was the difference between the disciples as confounded dunderheads and the disciples who hit the road and swept through those villages like some fresh breeze gusting renewing energy into shadowed places and dusty crannies? I have to think it was who they were looking to. Their approach to the so-called "limited commission" contrasts sharply with the other times when the disciples conjured ideas on their own and seized the initiative (behaving, as we'd say today, "proactively" or engaging in "self-expression"). When the latter model was followed, they emphatically failed. However, when Jesus set the task, created boundaries, provided instructions, and further, offered the Holy Spirit to accompany his followers in constant support, the Twelve gave birth to marvels.

If one revisits the beginning of the limited commission, at the heart of Jesus's directions was that the disciples "take nothing for the journey except a staff." Think about this. We carry more with us in the car to make a trip across town—drink, snack, cell phone, music player, umbrella, jacket, and of course a purse or wallet. Jesus's stringent requirement forced the Twelve to rely upon whatever the situation at hand presented to them. By stripping the disciples of their own resources, Jesus paradoxically prepared them to be at their best. Even as they stood apart from Jesus they would have to lean on him. In his name they would need to seek out sympathetic individuals who could provide food and shelter. Stripped of money and accessories, they literally had nothing to offer in return except news of the Kingdom of Heaven. Thus, they remained in the relationship of disciples looking to a master. They could never displace Jesus with their own feats of self-reliance.

In a similar fashion, beginning writers need to set aside their personal baggage consisting of preconceptions about what they wish to write and how to write it. Instead, they would do well to listen to an older, experienced teacher, wise in the ways of writing. It's important: The teacher guides their writing.

This means that students need to feel that they can receive more from their teacher than a few line edits and some brief overview comments, efforts that amount to not much more than the whistle blowing of a dispassionate referee. What students really need is a partisan, a coach who is with them, wanting them to succeed before a manuscript even emerges. They need a writing "master" willing to risk being intrusive, who gently suggests what are the most creative stories they might pursue and those that are best avoided or abandoned. They need to feel their teacher's enthusiastic and no-nonsense presence so they remain focused on the fact that they are capable of finding the ultimate prize. It's especially important that the teacher helps them set their sights on this prize at the most difficult times—when they've done the equivalent of going off to a distant village and they are now all alone with just an irritatingly white sheet of paper that's not giving up any of its secrets to them.

What apprentice fiction writers really don't profit from is being told, in the name of creative freedom, to go off and blaze their own trails and "sign up to bring a story to class to be workshopped when you have it." The aspiring wordsmith with endless horizons and too little mentoring is a writing accident waiting to happen. Unfortunately, in our time this cause-and-effect relationship hasn't been widely recognized.

One-Car Rollovers and the Other Wrecks of the Writing Life

Because the project of writing fiction must rely heavily upon that mysterious thing we call "creativity," it is often thought these days that creativity can only be promoted if the teacher is not interjected too much into the early process. To avoid at all costs smothering creativity, workshops have arisen from coast to coast where the main approach (in every genre) is for the student to go home and, with bracing self-autonomy, write about whatever he or she supposedly feels inspired to pursue. After that, the teacher receives the manuscript and helps the class critique it. This is the "workshop method" made popular by the Iowa Writers Workshop, a veritable institution that has produced some of our best writers in recent times. Make no mistake; I believe the workshop method is imminently suitable for graduate students who are already experienced writers. It more often than not delivers useful assistance when it comes to the revision of the writer's story. But as most writing teachers will acknowledge, workshopping stories by undergraduates produces hit-and-miss results. In a misfiring workshop, we're soon up to our ears in stapled pages of the aforementioned dreck with the daunting task of going around the table and each tactfully commenting upon it. This problem is compounded by the fact that students have an instinctual fear of failing at writing something of substance. This causes them to set their sights rather low. They choose familiar topics or cliché subject matter for their stories. They become the equivalent of freelancing disciples who, left to their own devices, dash off to the nearest, most familiar town where they secretly hope little will be required of them.

This navigation error is not the fault of the workshopping method. It's a problem that lies with what comes *before*. Before anyone should even think about invoking the word "workshop," I believe undergraduates in a fiction writing class ought to be "discipled" in the craft of writing. This means teaching them the basic elements of fiction writing for as much as the first two-thirds of the semester. After that they will be ready to workshop their stories during the remaining time and profit from hearing how an audience of peers receives their best efforts.

My own preference is to teach about the crafting of sentences, the deployment of details, narrative voice, the rounding of characters, the role of conflict, point of view, and modes of beginning and ending, all as a prerequisite for my students writing their first short story. Besides craft lectures and writing exercises, we undertake a classroom analysis of published short stories by great writers from whom one can learn the techniques we've been talking about. Knowing from personal experience how difficult it is to compose something that proves a satisfying story with no missteps along the way, I do everything possible to prepare students in the shallow end of the pool before we do the ultimate—hold our breath and jump into water well over our heads.

Even with all the advance preparation, students are still not quite ready to write their first story. There is one thing left to discuss, the topic that is least talked about at the public university or in graduate creative writing programs, even the highly rated one I attended some years ago. I believe it is the ultimate question for any writer, particularly a writer of faith. This missing item is, "What should one write stories about?"

Contending for the Content

In the eyes of many, story content is an impertinent thing for the teacher to question or weigh in on. It smacks of interfering with the creative process and, worst case, could lead to foisting upon young writers the teacher's own censoring agenda or ideology. However, as Christians we can look at this differently. The teacher who brings up the issue of subject matter is merely trying to help each student see which village he or she can most profitably enter. After all, there's usually no need to go where others have already tread. There's also a danger in turning the other way and going to places that are inhospitable to the writer. What we want is a desirable literary geography, places in the terrain of the imagination where the writer will feel most challenged and offer in response his or her particular version of writing gifts that reward readers.

What this amounts to is a consideration of motive. Is the writer going into the village because she feels comfortable and can self-indulgently enjoy herself there? Or is she taking a more difficult road and going into a particular village for the sake of the people who live there and the opportunity to get to know them and tell their stories? If the writer does not write with the correct motive, the odds are not good. I can't overstate my view: *Poorly chosen content, not mechanical weakness, is usually the single greatest source of bad writing.*

Every writer today faces a terrible temptation that grows worse in an age of celebrities and media-driven emphasis on the cult of the individual. It is the temptation to write selfishly. When this happens, one is misled into believing that writing is simply a matter of mapping out a preferred destination for oneself. Call it the village of self-expression. This kind of writing can become an exercise in melodramatic rendering of one's own likes and dislikes or flinging around pet phrases and ideas or paying tribute to favorite writers or genre works through poor imitation.

Of course, I don't believe unfiltered self-expression is bad per se. Journal writing, for example, can have a verifiable therapeutic effect for individuals. What I believe is wrong is when one conflates self-expression with art. That is, one believes that something that appears to be of interest to oneself, and is expressed strictly at the level of one's personal standards (whatever those may be), merits the lasting attention of others. Such writing might be presentable to your mother or sympathetic roommates, but as soon as a writer makes the move to show work to a larger audience the demands change. The reader's interest isn't aroused by the fact that the writer has honestly expressed himself or herself. The writer is irrelevant as far as the reader is concerned. The reader only wants to know *what's here for me?* And readers, if they are good readers, will have expectations based on other writers they have encountered. Will you entertain me like Dickens with his extravagant plotting and eccentric characters? Will your characters move me like Raymond Carver's utterly believable, struggling, antiheroes of the lower middle class? Will you shock me with your insights into the dark recesses of the human heart the way Toni Morrison does? Will your prose glitter and free-style and catch air like that of Joyce, Faulkner, or Arundhati Roy? In other words, the literate, intelligent reader I want my students to write for has an acquaintance with literature that over the ages has erected certain standards. These are *high standards*; otherwise, the whole idea of having standards would be ludicrous and anyone who felt the urge to put words on paper could be declared a writer.

Here then is our motive. We're trying for one semester to write for the ages. Our models are the authors whose books will remain on the shelves of the library. We seek not to merely entertain or express but to do the greater thing—go into the sorts of villages and cities where God, working through us, can perform whatever miracles are needed.

How terribly ambitious and high minded this is! I'm reminded of an Iowa graduate to whose university workshop I once spoke. He was familiar with my views on the uses of fiction and he introduced me as, "This is Mr. Haley. He thinks stories can change the world." Then he chuckled. I was perplexed at the time as to why he thought I held to a humorous notion. I had not yet realized how common it is in the literary community for writers to be technically skilled but behave as agnostics toward their own work. Such writers don't have all that much faith in fiction. I imagine in the eyes of that writer I was a tad old-fashioned in aligning myself with those who believed that bringing stories to people could possibly affect some of them in a lasting way. But why not believe this? Why go through all the labor of putting down words if we leave everyone indifferent, unchanged, or only amused?

As for the sticky subject of genre fiction—writing that desires simply to entertain through plot rather than illuminate via development of character—I've found that it can get in the way of "writing for the ages." This is a problem because upwards of a third of my class habitually chooses genre fiction as their preferred form of elective reading material and, not surprisingly, they want to compose in this vein themselves. Despite this, I insist that all students try to write literary (i.e., character-driven) short stories for the entire semester. Sometimes this causes shock. Whenever this happens I remind them that if they can succeed at the most demanding form of fiction (the literary short story, many writers attest, is more difficult to execute than a novel), once they exit the workshop they can go back to writing genre works with excellent results. Through writing literary short stories they will have learned to place a new emphasis on character and a refined prose style. This will make their genre fiction rise above the general pabulum churned out by writers seeking to replicate some formula for a bestselling horror novel, romance, fantasy, or thriller.

The Other Half of the Story

Art, if taken too seriously, is a form of idolatry. No story in the world has in and of itself ever fed people or bound up their wounds. Writing is serious business, but it's hard to imagine it being on par with events where life and death hang in the balance. I came to this conclusion when after several years I realized that I was perceived by a few students to be unreasonable or overly committed on their behalf. They felt that I'd pointed them to a perilous mountain and demanded that they climb it, yet they saw before them only crumbling handholds, a dire situation that was exacerbated by a limited desire to work their way to the top. Surely they would lose their grip and tumble. Thus, they wanted to know: Prof. Haley, why can't it just be a *hill*?

I don't want students to feel that they are in extremis. In reality, there is no disgrace (nor a high-altitude freefall) involved in writing a not-so-great story as long as one has tried one's best. The worst that awaits these students when they find themselves back on the ground is a hard-earned "B" and memories of how intensely exhilarating and surprising the semester was for all of us.

The funny thing about giving students a challenge, though, is that once they get over their initial dismay, they sometimes kind of like it. They never expected this class would be downright hard. They thought everything would be guided by intuition and the flutter of the Muse hovering nearby. The words would come easily, and invariably they would be good. But serious writing asks them to draw upon strength they perhaps have never suspected is within themselves. They begin to see that if they revise enough, their manuscripts significantly improve. There is a reward in this. Fellow students start talking about their productions the same way they talk about stories in their literature anthologies, noting the complexities and how they deal with truth and mysteries. In short, the hard trek can be worthwhile. They can complete the climb and arrive at a place where compelling and lasting stories are told.

Limits Leading to Freedom

My students are free to explore just about anything, but the qualifier "just about" is crucial. I provide guidelines that include certain limitations, and these are spelled out in the syllabus. Only once has a student asked, "Isn't this censorship?" This was a verbal challenge for which I was actually grateful. It offered a chance to explain something important: Sensible censorship can be good for us. There's no need to fear reasonable limits. In fact, each of us personally practices censorship every day and regards it as a way of maximizing our pleasure and well-being. We censor certain foods that we refuse to eat because they're bad for us or we just don't like them. We censor who our confidantes are. We censor, hopefully, whom we're willing to marry. In other words, we set for ourselves limits to what is possible.

To follow Jesus, and to be writers who wish to do good work that honors his call to serve one another and love our neighbor, we need guidelines beyond the usual standard of striving for aesthetic excellence. Our collective outlook must include the fact that we cannot, in the name of creating what we suppose to be "art," deny the reality that humans have been made in the image of God. I tell students that to allow writing to indulge in breathless reportage of blood-drenched violence, torture, rape, graphic sexual acts, insane ravings and so forth, is to give readers a distorted view of humanity that implies that the *imago Dei* doesn't exist. If beginning writers provide no balance to this kind of dark gaze or become morbidly obsessed with evil to a nihilistic point that leaves no hint of light, then they have failed to present stories that correspond to a Christ-centered view of creation. Humans are not to be celebrated as nothing more than instinctual animals preying on one another. A story that asks readers to side with terrorists or serial killers or batterers of women or even happy libertines has discipled itself to the wrong master.

The other material I take a cautious view toward has nothing to do with issues of morality and immorality. It's simply a "questionable zone" designed to protect all the writers in the workshop. There are certain areas that young writers may not yet be mature enough to explore. Writing about these subjects could cause them personal distress that outweighs any benefit to the world at large. And, even if the authors are able to write about these things with artistic objectivity and control, their stories may cause problems for other workshop members who are not prepared for poignant presentations of sin and its unvarnished consequences. I'm thinking of students who might make fiction out of their own history of sexual victimization, questions about gender identity, addiction, undergoing an abortion, or other struggles. It's important to make clear that the workshop cannot serve as group therapy where we conjure stories as thinly disguised confessions in order to receive sympathetic reactions to our flaws. There are other venues on campus for working toward mental health and spiritual improvement. My first obligation is to protect each writer's personal life rather than let others, in a worst-case scenario, jump to the easy assumption that a particular student's story is disguised autobiography and fodder for pity or gossip or some inept on-the-spot counseling. For these reasons, I read every story in advance of its being workshopped, provide editorial comment to the author, and, if necessary, meet with him or her to

218

discuss concerns about content. If I believe the story isn't the best one for the workshop to see, I insist that the writer workshop a different one.

Aside from that, my students can write about anything. I prefer, though, not to leave them bereft of a hint or kindly suggestion. Most students are looking for ideas for stories and therein lies an opportunity. The teacher can encourage them to find stories in certain realms that seem to be under-reported in our times. The teacher can also warn them that other settings, characters, and situations have been much done in recent literary fiction, even to the point of becoming cliché. What I'm hoping to do with this advice is to point out the more distant villages and cities, even the obscure ones, that have until now been overlooked or not much visited. It is my hope that this will result in what every editor is longing for, a refreshingly original story.

The first step in finding this kind of story is to move at least ten miles away from all the bad ones that may have occurred to you to write. Every teacher can easily make a list of what he or she thinks has been the subject matter of the worst student stories they've seen over the years. Do this and then share the list with the class. Don't forbid these sorts of stories, just point out their dubious track record and the fact that a student will have to work especially hard to mold an effective story out of this kind of material. Without a doubt, at the top of my own list of "bad stories" is the one that takes place at college with college students as protagonists. I'm not completely sure why, but it is very difficult for even published writers to write a story with an academic setting that anyone other than a fellow academic could care about enough to make it to the end. Too often I encounter a species of student autobiography spun into fiction that results only in tiresome navel-gazing that has somehow been mistaken as an apt way of carrying out the dictum "write what you know about."

Besides making the list of "bad" ideas for stories, it's equally valuable to direct students to promising material for their stories. The teacher can make this other list, writing it on the board or placing it on a handout. The list should be presented not in a mandatory tone, but in the spirit of "Don't you think it might be interesting to read a story about this for a change?" The students are free to ignore the list. More likely they'll be stimulated to add ideas of their own. The main thing to inculcate is not a prejudice for or against certain material but to emphasize the concept that *what* you write about really matters and is a major determinate of writing success.

One item I've kept on my "what to write about" list is the life of believers. I happen to believe the Christian fiction writer is in a position similar to ethnic minority writers a few decades ago. Within the boundaries of literary stories, Christian characters have been scarce to nonexistent, yet all of us know that in real life Christians occupy as significant a place in the community as anyone else. This is not to say that we ought to write about Christians because it is a way of witnessing on behalf of Jesus. The purpose of placing a fictional version of Christians into a story is not to proselytize. When a Christian character is portrayed, he or she ought to exist to help the author and reader understand a bit of life through that particular and (to many people) peculiar set of eyes.

Writing about Christians, I think, is more easily talked about than done. I've noticed that it's difficult for a single short story (as opposed to a novel) to sustain the weight of characters who are believers. I've theorized that this is because more is involved in creating an accurate portrait of a confessing Christian than characterizing someone by, say, their skin color or regional identity. It's not a matter of a few lines of description or dialogue or working up an accent. Each believer comes with a complex belief system that is familiar only to people within the Christian culture. This is not such a problem if you want to write for other Christians, but if you wish to enter the overall world of literature, you may end up baffling many readers. For that reason, young writers might look to the example of Flannery O'Connor. She tended to make some but not all of her characters explicitly Christian (or at least church-going and Jesus-talking). To make her stories work, she invented a shorthand for their religious experience that helped the nonreligious enter the story. O'Connor's believers were not complicated Catholics like herself; they were crazy, Southern fundamentalists, a concept many readers could quickly grasp. Then, if they had ears to hear, careful readers might learn about the actual faith that sustained O'Connor herself.

Speaking of Flannery O'Connor, goodness knows we've been a long time without one like her, but I tell myself I must be realistic in my expectations. Writing well about the religious life usually requires time to mature in the faith. A writer who is eighteen to twenty-two years old may not be ready. This is what most of my students decide, and they go on to write stories about other things. Someday, however, they may try to write about this endlessly fascinating subject matter, and I eagerly await the results.

To the Coffee Bar

I began these thoughts by imaginatively walking through some different spaces, then ending up in the classroom. I'd like to conclude by removing us from that topography of desks and white boards and driving over asphalt for a couple of miles until I park, get out, and open another door and—

As soon as I walk inside I smell what has lured me here. It's the dark odor of fresh ground beans and shots of espresso that insinuates itself all the way into the rafters overhead. Nearby patrons are clicking computers. Others have books open and are reading or chatting softly. How amusing that the most caffeinated place in the world is an island of calm. I can't think of any locale I find more muted and civilized. This is exactly where I feel like ending this period of rumination about what I do semester after semester.

A grande latté, please.

And now we can sit down. With your permission I'll pull from my pocket a few scribbled notes containing short advice that did not fit into the preceding. If this were a DVD, these items for your consideration might be the bonus features. You may decide to skip them or choose to visit them another day. It's up to the user and I won't be offended either way. I have my hot drink, its milky foam is delightfully plush, and I'm sitting by the window in the sunlight. What more could I ask for? So here goes.

Remember, he who has seen me has seen the father: Every human being starts out "suffering" from a syndrome whose chief symptom is that he or she is overwhelmingly creative. This normally undiagnosed condition is called "childhood." Our innate desire to make new things, fed by an easy access to the imagination, is a God-given attribute. However, for most people, creativity becomes something they are taught to view as impractical and dispensable in the face of supposedly more important matters in life. They are soon cured of it. For Christians, I think it is worse since beginning with the Reformation there is a long history of churches viewing the arts as the broad pathway to heresy and immorality. In fact, the greatest difference I have noticed between my days teaching at a public university and the students I now have is that the Christians are less reflexively creative or likely to have sought out on their own serious art of any kind, especially the works of contemporary writers. Taking this into account, I present my beginning writers with a theology of creativity (supported by biblical texts) that offers a mandate for Christian artistic expression. I start with the fact that from the first intonation of "Let there be ..." God is the Creator par excellence. He makes all the wildness of creation and caps it off by creating us in His image as fellow creators. Then comes Jesus and through him we really see God in action. It's quite startling.

For Jesus the status quo doesn't work, and he does not mind breaking the news to its proponents. Taking risks and crossing boundaries are all part of how Jesus lives, and it is what he expects from his disciples. Jesus's approach seems to me closer to that of an artist than a politician or business person or scientist. His way of revealing truth is not a matter of calculation or controlled processes. Instead of neatly organizing existing information and reaching a logical conclusion, he offers up epiphany-styled breakthroughs, usually in the form of stories he tells. With that in mind, I want students to develop an exploratory openness when they write rather than staying close to the safe and familiar out of fear of giving offense to fellow Christians. When they create with this kind of freedom, they are able to bring their best fruits to God and their fellow humans.

Eat with sinners: If Christian writers expect to have an effect upon the world through their published work, they must be aware of the high standards set by the best literary writers and then produce work that measures up to them. This means they would do well to become familiar with more than just the classic short story writers of the past. A good anthology of contemporary fiction can place before students the sort of short stories being published today in high quality magazines and journals. I will be the first to admit that this takes some students on an uncomfortable journey. Contemporary fiction has increasingly made use of once forbidden language, sexual situations, and unsavory human behavior. I believe this is less a reflection upon the writers than the type of society they find themselves writing about. Be that as it may, the teacher will do well to develop an approach that helps students face even a story they don't like and extract from it the very real strengths of the writer. This is not the same thing as commending the story's darkness or some of the material dealt with. The value of working through these tough stories is that it reminds us that Jesus did not allow the superficial moral qualms of the Pharisees and their kind to stop him from "eating with sinners." If we can't first eat with those who think differently than us, listening and learning from the overall culture in the form of its best writers, then we are naïve to think that the world will ever hear the voices we would like to raise.

Be faithful in little and then you can be trusted with much: I like to spend the early part of the semester with short writing exercises, a practice that students seem to enjoy. It builds confidence. They write a character sketch with a goal that after reading their words I could pick out in a crowd the person they just described. In another assignment, they construct a setting in a way that stimulates all of the senses. There's a two-page scene exercise in which they must create two characters who meet and one of them experiences an internal conflict. To make students stretch, I turn to the "sentence exercise." They write 20-30 discrete sentences with the goal that each sentence evokes possibilities beyond what the sentence is nominally asserting. (Hint: "The sky was blue . . ." doesn't work; "There had been a time in his life that he was happy whenever he saw a sky so blue," is getting there.) Once students have practiced these building block aspects of the short story, they are ready to attempt erecting a complete structure. Then I can say, "We're switching from three hundred words to three thousand."

Repent, repent: Writing a story involves swimming in oceans of forgiveness. A weak passage that needs to be cut, an off-key word or an unclear image, a two-dimensional character, the flaws are both great and small. Such indiscretions amount to at least seventy times seventy, and each instance requires the recognition that because I am human, I am sometimes weak and I fail, yet *I am not condemned for it*. Forgiveness is real grace for a writer; it's what can keep him or her going. However, this kind of forgiveness never means identifying mistakes in the manuscript and blessing them. With the offer of forgiveness must come the desire for repentance. The writer always corrects. And keeps on correcting. I tell students the legend of how Raymond Carver revised a story upwards of thirty times before he was ready to publish it. If one starts talking to successful writers, this is not as legendary or unusual as it sounds. Extensive revision comes with the territory, and we should start demanding it of ourselves. Once students see how serious I am about this facet of writing, it is exciting to watch the results as they revisit their work and substantially improve it. Revising is an important part of making our high standards a reality. Students learn that no piece of fiction in first draft form is ever ready to be submitted to a magazine or even shown to a workshop. After the initial draft, the writer needs to let the work "cool," then take another look to see what works and what doesn't, then finally get down to revising. Soon it becomes a matter of personal pride. Students wouldn't think of showing the workshop a story without making some of the changes I've suggested during my initial editorial screening. Indeed, this is my favorite part of workshop, to point out to the class what the first draft of the story was like when I saw it and how the writer has gone on in the days since to improve it and make it ready to be presented to others.

"Only the writer and I know how far this story has come," I say, and I can't help it. I smile just a little because this is the prize, this is the longed for good report of their working very hard.

THE POLITICS OF *ADAPTATION*:

Teaching R-Rated Films on a Christian Campus

ELEANOR HERSEY NICKEL (FRESNO PACIFIC UNIVERSITY)

Eleanor Hersey Nickel describes the experiences of teaching the R-rated film Adaptation *to two different groups of students in Literature and Film. The first group—including many male Communication majors—loved the film uncritically and found it difficult to consider their faith and values as possible points of critique. The second group—made up entirely of female English majors—found the film distasteful and offensive. These two groups of students exemplify two major problems with faith integration in the Christian college classroom, and a clever film with "adult content" can be surprisingly useful in challenging both audiences. Eleanor belongs to St. James Anglican Cathedral and chairs the English Department at Fresno Pacific University, a Mennonite Brethren university in Fresno, California. She has published many articles on Hollywood film, television, and popular fiction.*

I am responsible for making a homeschooled Christian man look at Gwyneth Paltrow's naked body. For the first time in his life, this innocent student watched an R-rated movie, *Shakespeare in Love*,[1] for my class and was confronted with graphic sexual images that most of us would take for granted,[2] but that shocked him into stopping the DVD. His personal Christian beliefs were that he should not watch this film. This was the first time I ever taught Literature and Film, as an independent study before I launched the course as a regular offering. When the student came to his regular meeting with me, he told me that he had chosen not to finish the film and expressed concern about continuing on with the course if he would be required to watch other sexually

explicit scenes in the future. I had designed the syllabus while I was still a graduate student at a public research university, beginning with various adaptations
of *Romeo and Juliet* and continuing through the centuries to contemporary literature. Without thinking of the possible reactions of conservative Christian
students, I included *Shakespeare in Love* because it cleverly combines two modes
of adaptation: a historically authentic performance of *Romeo and Juliet* embedded within a fictional analogy of the plot in Shakespeare's own life. But this student's reaction stopped me in my tracks. Are there really men in their twenties in
California who have never seen this kind of film? Did I commit a sin by asking
him to watch it? This experience introduced me to the challenges of teaching
the other R-rated film on the syllabus, Spike Jonze's *Adaptation*.[2] Fortunately, I
quickly learned some strategies that allowed me to avoid shocking and offend-
ing the student while still allowing him to engage with the film's innovative techniques, which I then applied in the regular classroom. My two radically different
experiences teaching *Adaptation* have shown me that Christian professors have
nothing to fear from R-rated films, since they can challenge both those who
blindly appreciate secular films and those who refuse to watch them.

Many would ask: why do you have to teach R-rated films? Aren't there
plenty of good PG films that show the same film adaptation techniques without the nudity, the drug use, and the f-word? The fact remains that *Shakespeare
in Love* and *Adaptation* reach a level of sophistication that I have not found
in more family-oriented films. The first time I saw *Adaptation*, soon after its
release on DVD, I knew that I had to include it in a future course on Literature
and Film. The screenplay is by Charlie Kaufman, who is considered one of the
most original writers in Hollywood based on such bizarrely unique films as
Being John Malkovich[3] and *Eternal Sunshine of the Spotless Mind*.[4] The main
character is Kaufman himself (played by Nicolas Cage) and the plot focuses
on his attempts to adapt a nonfiction book by Susan Orlean called *The Orchid
Thief*. Kaufman is feeling the pressure from the success of *Being John Malkovich*
and struggles to find a creative angle that will also treat this rambling narrative
about orchids with respect. While he is suffering from writer's block and tear-
ing up draft after draft, his twin brother Donald (also played by Cage), decides
to become a screenwriter and attends a class by a screenwriting guru named
Robert McKee. Using the most formulaic Hollywood contrivances, Donald
writes a thriller named *The 3* and becomes wildly successful, further contribut-
ing to Charlie's downward spiral. Charlie eventually hits on the idea of writing
a screenplay about his own attempts to write the screenplay, creating a hilarious
meta-narrative. However, Charlie panics and decides to hand the script over to
Donald to complete. The film then switches modes and becomes (presumably)

Donald's Hollywood version of the script: Susan Orlean falls in love with her subject John Laroche, they both become drug addicts, Donald is killed in a car wreck, and Laroche is killed by an alligator, followed by a happy ending in which Charlie finishes his movie and finally gets together with the woman he loves.

Like most truly postmodern texts, this film sent me straight to the internet. Was there really an author named Susan Orlean and a book called *Orchid Thief*? I will never forget the moment that I typed the book title into Amazon and saw the blue cover of *Orchid Thief* pop into view. This was a *real book*! Who agreed to this? Didn't the author get offended? Is there a real Donald Kaufman? (The film credits do include him.) This sent me to the favorite website of all film teachers, *Internet Movie Database*,[5] and I eventually discovered that the story of Kaufman struggling to write the screenplay is real, but the twin brother is fictional.

Two years later, in summer 2004, I taught the independent study version of Literature and Film as a "pilot" and prepared a syllabus for the first regular course offering in Spring 2005. Still fascinated by Kaufman's film, I removed two of the texts from my original graduate school syllabus and made *Orchid Thief* and *Adaptation* into the final texts of the course. I spent several weeks reading Orlean's book, researching the background of the book and film, and creating lesson plans. Fortunately, the student in my independent study alerted me to a danger that I had not seen—which is somewhat surprising, since I had been teaching at Fresno Pacific for several years. Apparently I still suffered from the same malady as many of the Communication majors at my university, effectively turning off my "Christian perspective" when I watch movies, absorbing multitudes of nude scenes and curse words without even noticing them. I am very grateful to this student for his honest response to *Shakespeare in Love,* which allowed me to make important changes to the syllabus that I was creating. Fortunately, since I am trying to cover the history of film, most of the adaptations in the middle of the course were made prior to the 1960s and, therefore, contained little objectionable content. *Adaptation* was the only other R-rated movie. Because I respected my student's choice not to expose himself to such images as a young, single Christian man trying to live a faithful lifestyle, I chose a couple of scenes from the film that contained no mature content. He read the book and watched these scenes, which were enough to give him a sense of the film's genius without further disturbing his sense of ethics. Since I also allow students to choose which films to write about, he also avoided having to write a paper about *Adaptation*.

This experience caused me to do some soul-searching, resulting in the decision that I am not interested in forcing students to watch scenes that make them uncomfortable, primarily because I recognize that my experiences with the church are markedly different than theirs. Although my family is Episcopalian, we attended Methodist and Congregational churches after our move to rural Vermont. My church experiences were typical of New England—I was encouraged to believe in God, to pray to Jesus, and to live a moral lifestyle, but nobody ever pointed out any possible tension between the church and the world. The church fit seamlessly into the world, and my liberal, Baby Boomer, single mother saw no reason to shelter me from the media. Episcopalians are known for their intellectual approach to the faith and their relatively "worldly" values, which include drinking alcohol, dancing, and using reason and scholarship to approach the Bible. While I faithfully attended church, I listened to the same music and watched the same television and movies as my friends, very few of whom were believing Christians.

This upbringing encouraged me to create a firm and unquestioned boundary between the Bible I read and the movies I watched. This worldview was challenged, fortunately, when I attended Gordon College, the only nondenominational Christian college in New England. There I encountered a startlingly evangelical world in which most of my peers were conservative Baptists who never watched R-rated movies or dated non-Christian peers. However, the English curriculum at Gordon at that time did not include much film, so while I did learn to "integrate faith and learning," a favorite phrase of the college, I did not think very deeply about integrating faith and film. Of course, attending public graduate schools did not help either, since my professors were mostly atheists, and I managed to hold onto a theologically naïve view of film all the way into my first years as a Christian college professor.

The students at Fresno Pacific come from a variety of backgrounds, since we do not require them to be Christians: some have never been to church, while others come from families which are only nominally Catholic or Protestant. Yet many come from conservative, evangelical homes and attend churches that I had never heard about until I moved to California—Foursquare, Assemblies of God, Evangelical Free. Many of their parents homeschooled them or sent them to Christian schools and discouraged them from watching secular films. These students have a radically different approach to popular culture than I do, which our more experienced professors have learned to accept. I found out that the professor who teaches Film Studies allows students to watch an alternate film if the content is objectionable to them. Since he teaches at night and shows the films in class, this includes allowing students to get up and leave. My situation is easier. I have a 50-minute time slot, so the students watch the films on their own, removing any peer pressure from their decisions.

Recognizing that my students need to be given genuine choices about their level of engagement with the R-rated films, I added a crucial paragraph to my syllabus describing the "Adult Content" and giving students the option of completing alternate assignments. On the first day of class, I now read this policy along with the rest of the syllabus, which has had a very positive effect. None of the twenty-six students who have taken the regular class have talked to me about any discomfort with the films, although I assume that some of them have quietly avoided watching them and have simply opted for other paper choices. Unlike the independent study, the larger class allows students to remain silent if they wish, and I choose only non-offensive clips to show in class. Yet the paragraph seems important because it not only warns students about potentially offensive material, but gives them permission to stand by their values, which I sometimes wish had been part of my own upbringing as well. Some images that I saw as a child have so horrified and haunted me that I genuinely wish that I had never seen them. Although it is a practical advantage for me to be able to watch graphic violence and nudity while I am keeping myself up to date with the latest developments in cinema, I also acknowledge that none of us are immune to sinful thoughts that can arise from indiscriminate viewing.

Once this paragraph was included in the syllabus, I created the lesson plans, beginning with *Orchid Thief*. For those who might be considering adding these texts to a Literature and Film course, I can report that Susan Orlean's book has been a tremendous hit among my students, without containing any offensive material. In a genre that resembles journalism and creative nonfiction, Orlean writes about her experiences in Florida investigating a man named John Laroche who had been arrested for stealing orchids. This investigation, which originated as a story for *The New Yorker*, led Orlean on a journey to discover why people are so passionate about orchids that they will risk their lives to get them. The orchids begin to symbolize the kind of passion that gives meaning to human life. Kaufman highlights one of the key quotes in *Adaptation*: "I don't even especially *like* orchids. What I wanted was to see this thing that people were drawn to in such a singular and powerful way."[6] Now that I think about it, Orlean's book could be used as an interesting example of the fruitless search for meaning in anything other than God, although I have never taught it that way. The book ends on a note of disappointment and longing, as Orlean once again misses seeing the rare and famous ghost orchid in bloom, suggesting that the meaning of life, like the ghost orchid, is always finally "fantastic and fleeting and out of reach."

The most interesting thing about this book is its ability to create a passion for orchids in nearly anyone. Knowing that I am no gardener, I never did more than look carefully at the orchids at Lowe's while I was shopping for lawn furniture. However, the first time I taught the course, a young Hispanic man actually went to a meeting of an Orchid Society in Fresno and came back with orchids. He did have an ulterior motive for visiting the group, since his fiancée's father was a member of the society, but the whole class listened with fascination as he described the meeting. The passion for orchids became more powerful in the second, all-female class. When I went to one student's birthday party a few weeks after the end of the spring semester, she confessed that she had been talking about orchids so much that her fiancé pulled over to an Orchid Barn when they were traveling to the Bay Area and bought her several orchids. I found this hard to believe, since this student is somewhat of a hippie and seemed unlikely to own such an elitist flower. Sure enough, she brought out these gorgeous flowers, which the former members of the class all examined. This student later dropped out of college due to a lack of motivation, but she writes me letters saying that she has been attempting to grow orchids on her desk at the insurance agency where she works.

Rather than capitalizing on the potential for discussions of faith in relation to this story (how could we make someone interested in Jesus the way Orlean makes us interested in orchids?), my first lesson plan focuses on the difficulty of making the book into a film in any traditional way, since it has no real plot and focuses on Orlean traveling around Florida talking to various orchid lovers. Students then spend several days writing screenplays for specific scenes in the novel. By this point in the course, they have had some practice (using real screenplays as models) and have learned that it is much harder to write using only dialogue and descriptions of camera shots than they ever thought.

For the first exercise, small groups of students write screenplay versions of the scene in which Orlean talks to orchid collector Lord Mansfield at an American Orchid Society gala. Since the scene centers on dialogue, the exercise should be easy, but the trick is to translate Orlean's dry humor to film. For example, it is hard to adapt this quirky description: "His wife had impressed me in the receiving line because she was so pretty and her hands felt like baby powder."[7] However, Mansfield gets increasingly drunk during the scene, which can be accomplished on film, and the episode ends with a bittersweet line of dialogue from Mansfield that can be lifted right into a screenplay: '"I have a son who is thirty-nine and I'm sure he wants to get his hands on my orchids. I think he's quite eagerly waiting for me to die."'[8]

Once the groups have written their screenplays, I type them all into a Word document that I can project on the screen. Many groups' scenes fall flat because they simply copied the dialogue and did not insert their own forms of humor, allowing them to see how difficult it is to translate the humor of literature into that of film. Yet the opening of one group's screenplay demonstrates their increasing sophistication at setting the scene:

> INT. MANSION
>
> Focus on orchid petals, pull back to whole flower in glass case. Warning sign: "Do not touch the glass." Pull back more to entire room—add noise and soft music to background.
>
> Susan Orlean, looking a little out of place, walks to a table. Bumps into a man trying to get to her table. Many tables are in the way, as well as orchid displays. She is underdressed.
>
> Focus on a man standing against the wall: shiny, white hair, black plastic eyeglasses, trim build. He's holding an American Martini. Sean Connery.

Other groups succeed at inserting purely visual forms of humor, such as the one who made us all laugh by having Mansfield ask Orlean what species she collects, followed by a "shot of Orlean's dying orchid."

Following this exercise, groups must add a scene that is not in the book, but could be part of a film. These scenes tend to be much more successful, which helps to convince students that it is okay for films to depart from books in order to make their own works of art. (Many English majors enter the class with the idea that a film adaptation should not change the book, and they often claim that the screenwriting exercises opened their minds on that issue.) In one scene, Orlean visits a group of senile orchid collectors at "Shady Acres Retirement Home," allowing the writers to have some fun with fake species names:

> MAN WITH LOONEY TUNES SHIRT
> You know I found *paphiopedilum fairriearlum* when I was in Guatemala. . . 'course back then we didn't call it the. . .
>
> MAN WITH "I'M WITH STUPID" SHIRT
> (interrupting)
> And *you* know for damn sure that *I* found *paphiopedilum fairriearlum* in Ecuador. I found it with the help of the Pompeiiquenemas' High Chieftan for over 25 years.
>
> MAN WITH STAINED WHITE T-SHIRT
> (interrupting)

Huh? Orchids?

After discussing all of their screenplays, I show the scene from the *Adaptation* screenplay in which Orlean goes home to visit her husband and friends, preparing them for the idea that Kaufman will be inserting quite a few new scenes.

On the final day of the *Orchid Thief* unit, we discuss the ending of the book and the theme of "adaptation," as students in small groups discuss how Orlean sees constant change and evolution in flowers, in the state of Florida, in the Seminole tribe, and in her own life. This allows for some discussions of faith, since the book mentions Charles Darwin's fascination with orchids as examples of the evolution and mutation of species. Students seem to find this exercise helpful as they acknowledge that adaptation is a part of life, despite the popular Christian sentiment that since God is unchanging, we should approach our lives (and the Bible) with an eye toward stability, tradition, and authoritative meaning. Many students at Fresno Pacific were raised to believe that Darwin's ideas are wrong and evil, so this conversation tends to provide a wider perspective.

After this two-week unit, students watch *Adaptation* on their own in preparation for the three class periods devoted to the film. This is where the contrast becomes very clear between the students in my classes in 2005 and 2007. In 2005, I had thirteen students, eight men and five women. Most of the men were Communication majors, who tend to be more liberal, more enamored of the media, and more interested in film; the women were all English majors, who tend to be slightly more conservative, more skeptical of the media, and more interested in literature. The night before the first class period devoted to the film, students began posting on the course's online message board, for which they received extra credit. A male English major began the thread. While I have corrected a few spelling errors in these quotes, I have preserved all of the students' wording and punctuation:

> Holy crap, i just finished watching the film, and i must say that it was brilliant. I've heard mixed things about the movie, but i am so glad that I got to watch it in the context of this class, and having read the book. i just love that donald is writing the typical thriller screenplay, and that's what charlie's film becomes! so freakin' cool.... people who haven't read the book i don't think can have as good of an understanding of what went on screenplay-writing wise with this film. just the whole concept of orlean and laroche being in love, her whole book being a sham, the ghost orchids containing a drug,

> laroche never did internet porn....haha! it took cheesy action/thriller plotlines to make the rest of the film! and the classic ending with characters changing, people dying and the cheesy pop song....so freakin' brilliant, its kinda blowing my mind right now.

The student's enthusiasm is obvious, as well as his high level of comfort with the R-rated elements of the film, as in the phrase "internet porn....haha!"

This response was not unique to the men, since the second post was written by a female English major—a homeschooled student from a conservative family:

> Oh my goodness, I can't tell you how great this movie is...wow. So funny. Every time 'Donald' came onscreen I would start laughing. I'm laughing now thinking about all the funny things he does. Charlie has this hilarious dry humor that is great too. I absolutely love the beginning voice-over (which is like myself-complaining about my flaws) and the subsequent voice over throughout the movie (even when the professional screenwriter says not to)! I like how when Charlie finally decides to ask Donald for help in his screenplay, it seems like Donald "takes over" the movie and seems to be writing it almost, with all the suspense and killing and affairs. This might sound morbid and callous of me, but I almost died laughing when the alligator (or croc) bites LaRoche. hahaha. I also love the English Professor joke...

Other than the contrast between "Holy crap" and the more orthodox "Oh my goodness," the responses are very similar. In the third post written before the opening class session, another female English major raises some concerns about the portrayal of women but ends on a positive note: "I do really like this film for many, many reasons. But I don't really like how they changed (at least in my mind) Susan's character. It makes the film very funny and interesting, but it makes me sad for her...but she agreed to it, so if she doesn't care, then it has to be ok. But no matter what, the screenwriting is brilliant."

On the first day of class discussion of the film, I open with a lecture about Kaufman's career and which parts of the film are factual and fictional. For example, screenwriter Robert McKee and orchid thief John Laroche are both real and accepted their portrayals in the film, Charlie Kaufman is actually thin, married with children, and has no twin brother. I also read excerpts from online interviews with Susan Orlean, in which she graciously accepts the film's portrayal of her as a drug addict and adulterer. Then I show the same ten-minute clip that I recommended to the independent study student, which shows the basic structure and characters without any sexual scenes or offensive language. The discussion focuses on how *Adaptation* defies any previous category of film adaptation and creates a new one, which I label "meta-adaptation." The lesson plan does not focus on whether the film is good or what it might have to do with Christian faith, although I'm sure that my enthusiasm is clear during the lecture.

The second class period allows for more critical reading of the film, although from feminist and Marxist theoretical perspectives rather than an explicitly Christian one. Since I teach the required literary theory course in my department, I bring in critical approaches whenever I can. I begin by showing a short clip (again, with no offensive language) in which Kaufman tries and fails to get up the nerve to approach Orlean and then gets pressured by his male chauvinist agent to complete the screenplay more quickly. This clip naturally leads into a discussion of gender, which I tie into the articles about film adaptation that we discussed at the beginning of the semester. According to my lesson plan, we discuss this clip in relation to "feminist adaptation theorists' complaints about male screenwriters destroying women's novels. What is the value of showing, with clearly erotic overtones, a man's 'faithfulness' to the text as an act of desire for the woman writer?" The second half of class applies a Marxist perspective to the same clip, again as noted in my lesson plan: "How does this film represent economic considerations as an impact on film art? What does it say about the Hollywood marketplace?"

It is interesting that students did not discuss either of these critical approaches on the message board. Apparently, on the first day of discussion, I mentioned the fact that I don't like the ending of the film. The message board postings immediately took up that topic, beginning with a male student who was willing to consider a negative reading: "Yeah this movie is genius. I think that this class really played a role in how much I liked it. I like Charlie's other stuff too, though. I loved the movie, but I am not quite sure about the end. It works, but just barely. I think that I am in the same boat as Eleanor. I will be excited to hear the class discussion on Friday." Yet the two students who initially raved about the film defended the ending, the woman claiming that "the movie could not have ended differently" and the man agreeing that since he likes the joke, "the ending is satisfactory for me."

By the time we got to the last class period, which focuses on the ending, students had already made their opinions clear. Perhaps in an effort to play devil's advocate, I expressed my frustration with the fact that the film ends in the midst of Donald's mainstream Hollywood version of the story rather than returning to Kaufman's "real" experiences. The cheesy love scene and the song

"Happy Together" are obviously meant to be tongue-in-cheek, but still seem anticlimactic after such an edgy film. Students defended the film vigorously in class, and their message board postings afterward focused on a joke that appears after the credits of the film, a quote from Donald's fictional thriller *The 3* and the words "In Loving Memory of Donald Kaufman," which led into a discussion of whether it would be funny for someone to make *The 3* into a real movie.

It may seem like there was very little integration of faith and learning in this experience, and I probably could have done more with overt discussions of faith. However, I still think that the unit on *Adaptation* was very successful, as it challenged the students' almost excessive love for the film and reminded them that we need to approach all films with a critical eye. The student's comment that "I think that this class really played a role in how much I liked it" also suggests that more conservative students might have broadened their experiences by learning to appreciate a secular film that they probably would not have watched on their own. In sharp contrast to the student in my independent study, they seemed to embrace the opportunity to discuss an R-rated film. *Adaptation* certainly worked brilliantly as an example of postmodern manipulation of the traditional film adaptation categories, which tend to focus on levels of "faithfulness" to the original. At the end of the semester, students gave speeches analyzing their own choice of film adaptation, demonstrating that they had learned that there is more than one way to be "faithful" to a book. Perhaps they also learned that there is more than one way to be faithful to God when you're at the movies.

The second time I taught Literature and Film, I had a class of thirteen female English majors. I used the same lesson plans for *Orchid Thief* and *Adaptation* and expected my students to enjoy the film as much as the previous class. With hindsight, I realize that I probably gave this group inflated expectations for the movie, which might have contributed to their more cynical reading. Perhaps not surprisingly, this group was quick to recognize the film's problematic portrayal of women and sexuality. Since many of my female students claim that they are not feminists (despite my ongoing efforts to contextualize the term), this discussion was framed as a Christian critique as much as a feminist one.

The first message board post was written after our initial class discussion, in a thread that a student entitled "Disgruntled Adaptation":

> So it sounded like there were quite a few people today who were violently opposed to the Adaptation of "The Orchid Thief" and while I

agree that it is totally different from anything I could possibly have expected, I have less of a problem with it than I was anticipating. I think our attempt to adapt certain scenes and how difficult those were really opened my mind to accepting other forms of adapting the novel. It was impossible to do a regular transposition, and you have to admit (well maybe not) that it was absolutely brilliant in its uniqueness. Panic is a great motivator! lol! Have any of you softened toward it?

Despite this call for the other women to "soften" their attitude, the next writer insisted that she was not comfortable with the film's portrayal of sex:

I actually liked the movie, especially now that I understand the perspective switch in the end. The only thing that really bothered was the amount of sexuality that was totally unnecessary in my opinion. I don't think they helped advance the plot, the characters, or the appeal of the movie at all. Aren't there better, classier ways to show that Charlie was lonely and sexually frustrated than multiple masturbation scenes? I sort of understand the Susan-Laroche sex scene, and it was relatively tame, but even that could have been more tasteful. I think Hollywood is taking advantage of increasingly greater freedom of content and becoming flat-out crude. I think there is still something to be said for subtlety and tact.

The reference to masturbation scenes is interesting because they are fairly subtle. Until I read the screenplay, I had not realized that Kaufman was supposed to be masturbating when he stared longingly at the photo of Orlean (played by Meryl Streep) on the back cover of *Orchid Thief*.

Not only did these students pick up on this sexual innuendo, they launched into a surprisingly frank online discussion. Two factors probably contributed to this: there were no men in the class, creating a kind of "safe space" for women who knew one another well, with a female professor who had established a reputation for being comfortable with controversial material. Students also tend to be more likely to discuss taboo subjects online than in the classroom, where I can't imagine such a conversation occurring. The third writer agreed that she "felt betrayed" by the sexual component of the film and asked: "Was his message that you have to throw in this kind of stuff for the movie to be liked in today's world?" The next student claimed: "I too was turned off by the sexual dynamic of his and Susan's relationship in the film. It cheapened their characters, in my sight." Yet she also admitted that she was starting to calm her "previous hostilities" to the film and that she wanted to watch it again before making a final judgment. The next student defended the film, but admitted that "the one thing that did bother me was kaufman's... let's say... fantasy 'encounters' with EVERY woman in the movie. that was definitely over-the-top, and i could have gone without that. i guess it's just kaufman's way of completely putting us in 'his' male mind, but some things are better left unexplored."

At this point in the discussion, students attended the second class period of the unit, in which I discussed the feminist and Marxist analyses of the film. Of course, I pitched this lesson very differently, since I now knew that I was dealing with students who felt hostile and betrayed by the film. (This is one of the great benefits of online discussions.) Rather than criticizing the film from a feminist perspective, I told the students about the previous group's appreciation for it and suggested that Kaufman's lust for Orlean could be perceived as flattering, since he is so over-awed by her much greater competence as a writer.

Soon after class, a fairly conservative, sweet-tempered woman wrote a post filled with an uncharacteristic number of errors: "okay, i have to start by saying that the whole kaufman fantasy thing 'glorifying women' is crap!!! if you were going to argue that he... did his thing as a tribute to susan b/c he is awed by her, you'd have to convince me that he was 'in awe' of the waitress who served him pie." After considering the potential feminist argument that the film embraces women's sexual power over men, she ultimately rejects it: "so, i guess this whole sick fantasy thing had potential to be a feminist argument, but it wasn't done in a way to make it that way, in fact, i find it offensive. so there."

The nine posts that follow represent constant shifts in the argument, as students debate whether open representations of sexuality are healthy or damaging to women. At first glance, these posts may seem just like those written on a secular campus. However, I suspect that my students only felt free to engage in this discussion because they knew they were among other Christians. A more liberal student claims:

> I'm wondering why everyone thinks the masturbation scenes are so disgusting. From people's comments, it sounds like most of you think that masturbation is something that is gross and that people should be ashamed of. Why?

> In response to Donald's crude remark about him and Caroline ("a little push, push in the bush"), I was offended for about three seconds. I think there's a reason Caroline laughs, though: men aren't the

only ones who enjoy sex, and this scene shows that women can (and should) look forward to going home to their significant other.

Another student responded with a very thoughtful, long post that reflected as much thinking about sexuality in the life of single Christian women as about the film. She begins: "It's not that I think sex is bad, and I could see why some would argue that masturbation is a healthy release of sexual frustration. And I realize women enjoy sex too... I just don't think it is a compliment to a woman when she becomes the object of masturbation in this film or when she's only referred to in a sexual manner."

A student who works as a resident assistant in a dorm agreed, focusing on this type of movie's influence on young Christian women:

> I work with about 20 sophomore girls as an RA this year, and it's really surprised me how much the "woman=sex object" attitude affects women, even within the FPU bubble. The way they think about their bodies ("I need to lose 20 pounds, or I'll NEVER get a boyfriend"), the way they dress ("But if I don't wear a low-cut shirt, the guys will never notice me"), and the way they push their boundaries in relationships ("If you don't do that kind of thing, guys will just go find a girl who will") all point to the "I am only as good as the pleasure my body can give" attitude.

Yet the next student pointed out that "movies like Tomb Raider and American Pie are more degrading to women than this one" and another agreed that "I don't know if it's because I watch a lot of R rated movies that i'm maybe less aware of the feminism outrages of this movie." Yet the next writer challenged this perspective: "We watch so many movies today that include sexually explicit images that are degrading so that when we see the next image it's just accepted as 'the norm.' My niece could probably watch this movie and not be offended or corrupted and she's 10, people. It isn't a good thing to just accept this kind of thing."

The next post is one of the most poignant to me, as the student once again relates the discussion to her friends' everyday experiences with men:
i will admit that i am a little sensitive on the masturbation subject, mainly b/c i had a good friend who found out her first "boyfriend" (they only went out for like a week) was only getting to know her b/c he wanted her to give him pics. of her to masturbate to... he didn't care about getting to know her at all, and he wasn't passionately in love with her- they'd only known each other a month. my friend was very confused and hurt (not to mention her feelings that guys only saw her as good for sex), and i can clearly remember her voice when she called me (in tears) about the whole thing.

The final post ends the discussion thread with a balanced perspective: "Although I know masturbation can relieve sexual tension, I really didn't feel that it needed to be put into the film."

So what did *this* experience have to do with the integration of faith and learning? Perhaps my more conservative colleagues would be shocked by this online discussion, although eight of the thirteen students voluntarily contributed to it. But I would argue that this unit was just as successful as the previous one. Several of these students were more like the one in my original independent study, unlikely to watch R-rated movies and generally distrustful of the secular media. The fact that they watched the film more than once, adjusted their opinions, and debated its merits allowed them to engage *Adaptation* with the kind of sophistication and detail that is often required in "real life," for example when parents have to decide what kind of material is appropriate for their children. The online discussion of sexuality also seemed rare and valuable to me, especially because I had nothing to do with it. I do not write on the message board at all, allowing the students complete control over that medium, and I usually do not refer to it in the classroom. Christians in their twenties need to be thinking about these issues, and the fact that they were so honest with each other demonstrates that Fresno Pacific has been successful in creating the "community" that we constantly advertise. I joked at the end of the *Adaptation* unit that I wished I could combine the 2005 students with the 2007 students for some kind of mixer, and then I would finally have both perspectives represented. Yet if I had not experienced this drastic shift in response to the film, I would not have been inspired to think so deeply about these issues.

How will I teach *Adaptation* in 2009? One element that I plan to incorporate much more fully is an article from the *Journal of Religion and Popular Culture* that I happened to run across at the very end of the 2007 semester, Matthew Anderson's "*Adaptation*: The Self-Proclaiming Rhetoric of Charlie Kaufman and of the Apostle Paul."[9] I found this article just in time to photocopy the first page and hand it out to students as an example of a Christian perspective on the film, but they did not look convinced. Next time, I will try to be even more deliberate and explicit in relating the movie's issues to the students' faith, partly by discussing Anderson's claim that "Kaufman's strategy unconsciously parallels the rhetorical practice of Paul, who also successfully 'wrote himself into' his narrative" (par. 3). I also imagine myself sharing the article you are reading now the next time I am teaching *Adaptation*—a self-reflexive move that is surely in the spirit of Charlie Kaufman.

Endnotes

1   *Shakespeare in Love*, DVD, directed by John Madden (Miramax, 1998).

2   *Adaptation*, DVD, directed by Spike Jonze (Columbia, 2002).

3   *Being John Malkovich*, DVD, directed by Spike Jonze, (Gramercy Pictures, 1999).

4   *Eternal Sunshine of the Spotless Mind*, DVD, directed by Michael Gondrey (Focus Features, 2004).

5   Internet Movie Database, http://www.imdb.com/ (accessed 20 September 2008).

6   Susan Orlean, *The Orchid Thief* (New York: Ballantine, 1998), 82.

7   Ibid., 83.

8   Ibid., 85.

9   Matthew Anderson, "*Adaptation*: The Self-Proclaiming Rhetoric of Charlie Kaufman and of the Apostle Paul," *Journal of Religion and Popular Culture* 13 (2006).

WHO TEACHES LIKE HIM?:

Job 36:22

DIANE GLANCY (MACALESTER COLLEGE)

In "Who Teaches Like Him?" Diane Glancy (Cherokee) offers her lyrical and reflective account of being a Christian professor of literature and creative writing at Macalester College, a school that severed its founding ties with the Presbyterian Church along with its initial mission as a Christian institution of higher education. Diane is the author of over thirty books of creative writing, including Pushing the Bear: A Novel of the Trail of Tears *(Harcourt Brace, 1996),* In-Between Places *(Arizona, 2005), and* Asylum in the Grasslands: Poetry by Diane Glancy *(Arizona, 2007). Her work has won the American Book Award, the Oklahoma and Minnesota Book Award, and the North American Indian Prose Award. Diane has also served several terms as the Five Civilized Tribes Playwright Laureate. After retiring from Macalester College in 2005, Diane re-settled in Kansas City so that she might be close to her grandchildren.*

I want to begin with John Wilson's statement in "Stranger in a Strange Land, Alternative History,"

> Christianity is the ultimate alternate history. . . . The Creator of the universe sends his son, who is also God himself, to Earth to be born of a virgin. The son grows up, is crucified, and rises again from the dead, somehow conquering death itself. Then he ascends to heaven, sending the Spirit—who is also God (there are three persons, but one God—perfectly clear, no?)—to dwell in and re-form all those who

follow him. And the world, the broken world that we know so well from our histories and our newspaper, is changed, once and for all.[1]

This *is it* for me in one short statement. I stand on Christianity broken into different meanings, and groups in disagreement with themselves, and Christianity not exactly clear but open to interpretation, hard-to-believe Christianity, easy to poke holes into, aren't there a hundred questions about the Red Sea, Jonah and the whale, Christ himself, his death and resurrection, all of which have been doubted, explained their way around, ridiculed? Yet Christianity, Bible Christianity, literal Old and New Testament Judeo-Christian Christianity is still the center of my life. Certainly, it is still at the center of God's.

For nearly seventeen years I taught at a secular college where this vital information of Christ's death on the cross and his resurrection was ignored. I wondered why I was there—When I prayed, the only answer I received was, sit down, be quiet, do your work.

I know there are churches that are not sure the cross is central to the Christian faith. I know there are books that diminish the fullness of Christ—defuse him, in other words. This past year, I visited churches in Kansas City to find where I wanted to belong when I retired from my college at the end of the 2005 academic year. I heard sermons on *re-envisioning* God. I know Christianity is fractured with interpretations and denominations and groups within groups. Yet it is the living, vibrant light for my feet. For me, Christ's death and resurrection is the core of my being. I would be afraid to *fiddle* with that, or to count on anything other than that. It seems to me to be the message of the Bible. I have gone to church all my life. This is not something I've known since yesterday.

I suppose I'm an evangelical Christian who doesn't evangelize, at least in class, in committee meetings and on campus in general. I remember a few times in class stating that Christianity was the basis of my belief, but usually it didn't come up.

Macalester College, originally Presbyterian in its roots, *cut ties* with its religious tradition. I taught creative writing and Native American literature in the English Department there. I guess I felt my Christianity in the spirit of the classroom—a place where trust was built so students could make comments, share opinions, and read their poems, stories, essays, scripts. Small classes are a part of the college—maybe twelve in each writing class—twenty in Native American literature—sometimes a few more—if I agreed. In the many genres of writing I taught, we worked at reading and discussing the text—usually Best American Poetry or Short Stories or Essays. We had writing exercises that we read in class—unless the student chose to pass. Then we got into workshopping—bringing copies for everyone—the authors read their work—they had to be silent as they listened to comments—afterwards they thanked us for our critical comments—then they could respond, answer any questions that had been asked, or clarify what had not been understood. Where did Christianity come into that?

In Native American Literature, we read depressing novels about alcoholism, disenfranchisement, abandonment. Characters without names, who felt invisible, inarticulate. Questions come up—What do we live for? . . . . "According to the fundamentalist Bible belt, to make a decision for Jesus Christ. In a traditional Indian way, it is to survive, to struggle for survivance (Gerald Vizenor's word, which is survival with meaning), to move from being a human being to a Human Being with responsibility to one's family, tribe, land."[2]

The point of entry into my faith is in my writing more than teaching. In the essay that follows "July" in *In-Between Places*, I talk specifically and experimentally about my faith. The essay, "Transmotion," begins, "The holy has always seemed unholy to me. Or at least ordinary in the central Great Plains of America where I've lived. In Protestant, Holy Ghost country. A hidden place. A place as though it weren't there. A place streaked with the vapor trails of passing planes." The essay ends with a litany:

> Lord of Transformation.
> Lord of the Road.
> Lord of Cattle.
> Lord of Buffalo.
> Lord of the Far Horizon.
> Lord of the Roily Sea.
> Lord of Wind.
> Lord of Cloud.
> Lord of Northern Lights.
> Lord of Cold.
> Lord of Tongues.
> Lord of the Ear Drum.
> Lord of the Prairie.
> Lord of the Tornado.
> Lord of the Rock.
> Lord of the Oasis.
> Lord of the Flood Gate.
> Lord of the Fox.
> Lord of the Fish Net.

Lord of Transmotion.
Lord of the Well.

Once in a while I read from my work in class, but not often. In preparation for final projects, I would read from the manuscript I was working on that semester and my words of faith were there. But it is when I give talks and readings, at other colleges and conferences, I feel free to share my faith. *The Only Piece of Furniture in the House*; *Fuller Man*; *Designs in the Night Sky*; *Pushing the Bear*, a novel of the 1838–39 Cherokee Trail of Tears—all these had Christianity built into their history. One of the major themes in *Pushing the Bear* was conjuring against Christianity—conjurers were something like the magicians of Egypt—there were animal transformations—workers of magic—then there was Reverend Bushyhead—a Cherokee converted to Christianity. I have stood by his grave near Tahlequah, Oklahoma. He had to explain God—how could there be a God as they walked the removal trail— four hundred miles through four winter months?

Christianity also brings separation. The early missionaries divided up the tribes. The Indians who went to punitive boarding schools want nothing to do with Christianity.

I have taught at a small liberal arts college that did not acknowledge God. The chaplain had to be all things to all people, and at inaugurations of presidents and commencements and other academic ceremonies, I heard platitudes as we came together before some undefined or unnamed being. The faith I know, the Christ as my Savior, the death of Christ on the cross for my redemption, was not wanted. I was the faculty sponsor of MacChristian, a group of Christian students who seemed to make it through each school year. They often saw more of their differences than their similarities as Christians. Yet they often said they would not have made it without each other.

When students wrote an article ridiculing God, blaspheming was more like it, I wrote an editorial in the school paper.

I think it was in the spirit of the classroom—where I felt my Christianity. The room had been prayed over—it was an accepting atmosphere—and I had a lot of troubled students.

Christians were disrespected or not recognized. Yet Christianity is the basis of my life—God's love for the world and his work of propitiation. Christianity can be social justice, belonging to a certain denomination. I recently was on a panel with a Catholic and a Unitarian. And we all were *Christian*. I have heard the theories. What is the latest? Jesus was married and had a child. It isn't scriptural. I have heard the questioning. Did Christ actually die on the cross? Was the Red Sea a reed sea? Was Jonah really in the whale? I don't know. Those questions have never bothered me. For me the Bible is literal.

Christ is the way, the truth, the door, the life, the map for my road, the lifter of my head. He is my certainty and resilience.

Maybe those Macalester years were the whale's belly. I was closed up in God. Yet I regret the lack of witnessing I did. I feel failure in that area.

There are forces of good and evil at war. We live in a world that takes the death of the son of God on the cross to redeem. There is much at stake in our lives: eternal separation from God. There is a choice set before us—do we want to be wheat or do we want to be tares?

What amazing information is in Christianity. I who was born in sin can enter the kingdom of God by faith in the death of Christ for the propitiation of my sin. I who was separated am now joined to the heavenly kingdom by faith in the son of God who has washed me in his blood.

Recently, I've been reading in the books of Kings. Why am I reading this, unrelated as it is to my contemporary life? But there is II Kings 13:20-21: "And the bands of the Moabites invaded the land, and as they [the Israelites] were burying a man, they spied the band of Moabites, and cast the dead man into the sepulcher of Elisha, and when the man was let down, and touched the bones of Elisha, the man revived, and stood up on his feet" (KJV). Which was most distressing? Impending doom from the Moabites or the resurrection of this man they are trying to bury? It is a situation I know well. The Moabites are attacking. Have the Moabites ever done anything but attack in their many different forms? And we're here at a funeral, burying a man, and we have to get rid of him quickly because we see the Moabites coming, and we lower the man into the first sepulcher we can find, which is the old prophet, Elisha's, and the corpse touches his bones and suddenly the man we're trying to bury comes alive and probably wants out of the sepulcher right away! And he will step out of the grave to also see the Moabites coming. Does someone have an extra sword? What do we do with this ridiculous situation? This threat of death and destruction and resurrection at once—the absurdity of it all. I have been in one Moabitish situation after another. I have let down my bones into the Bible and they touch the holy words, those old prophets, and I am revived.

Endnotes

1   John Wilson, "Stranger in a Strange Land, Alternate History," in *Books & Culture* (Nov/Dec 2004), 7.

2   From the first essay, "July," in *In-Between Places* (Tuscan: Arizona Press, 2005).

Appendix A

Two Chief Elements of the Romantic Worldview or Ideology

BRUCE BOECKEL

- The Romantic view of "Man" or Humankind: Man is basically good, at least at his Romantic core, in his "heart" and in his feelings. Most people, especially uncorrupted children, at least mean well. They are more prone to unintended error than to willful evil or deceit (including self-deceit).

- The Romantic view of Civilization: Civilization is basically corruption, a putting on of "artificial" manners and mores, a decline from the innocence and goodness that come *naturally* to individuals (when they are children) and to societies in their original state (when they are "primitive").

As an educated person, you should think *critically* about Romanticism's ideological claims. Otherwise, you are allowing yourself to be programmed by an *unexamined* ideology.

As a *Christian*, you should consider whether these claims are consistent with the "knowledge of God" or whether they are among the ideological "authorities and potentates of this dark age," the shadows that hang over the minds of those who cannot "grasp" or "judge" (Eph. 6:11-12 reb).

> **Warning:** Deciding whether an ideological claim is consistent with Christian belief is often not as straightforward as you might suppose. At one level, Christian teaching is that human beings have fallen into sin and are by nature sinful. The Romantic claim that "Man is basically good" thus sounds like a direct rejection of Christian teaching.

However, Christian teaching itself isn't quite so one-dimensional. Consider the contrasting Christian beliefs below:

> **Negative:** After the Garden of Eden, humankind is "depraved" and fallen into sin.

> **Positive:** Man and woman are created "in the image of God."

How can a Christian view of human nature hold both of those principles in mind and in tension? Holding in mind this more complex version of Christian teaching, we should then ask the following questions:

- Does the Romantic vision of Man contain some insights that I am willing to consider or affirm?

- Is it possible that Romantic writers emphasize "natural goodness" so much because they are reacting against something? Are Romantic writers trying to counterbalance an over-emphasis on human "depravity" in the culture of their time, including the Christian culture of their upbringing?

- Does the Romantic author in question really embrace the "Romantic vision of Man" in such an unequivocal way? Are there moments and passages in the author's writings that show him or her agonizing over this "Romantic vision of Man," finding that it falls short as an explanation of social or personal experience? Is the author willing to entertain and present thoughts and incidents that seem inconsistent with Romantic ideology? Are such passages the marks of unfinished, inconsistent thinking? Or are they examples of courageous open-mindedness and genuine self-criticism?

Appendix B:
Critical Compass Questionnaire
Chad Engbers

I hand out the following questionnaire the day before discussing the critical compass in class. When teaching the compass—either in PowerPoint or on the blackboard—I leave the numbers off the axes until we have thoroughly covered the concepts. At that point, I add the numbers and invite students to locate themselves on the map: the sum of their answers to questions 1 and 2 places them on the vertical axis; questions 3 and 4 place them on the horizontal axis. Although students gravitate toward the middle of the grid, it is mathematically impossible for them to end up in the exact center.

Name: _____

What is the best piece or pieces of literature you have ever read? This can be anything: a novel you read over the summer, a poem you read in high school, a book you were read as a child—anything. List the work(s) that you yourself honestly esteem above all others.

Please answer each of the following questions as thoughtfully as you can. Use the literature listed above as an example if that is helpful, but feel free to think of other literature, too.

The answers to each one form a continuum, from one extreme to another. In this context, extremes are okay! All of the options represent valid positions actually held by sane literary scholars. Choose the one that is closest to your own opinion.

1. What kind of writing is most appropriate in a high school or college English course? (Do not simply choose the kind of paper on which you have been most successful; choose the one that, in the abstract, represents the most appropriate way of approaching literature.)

    1. Explication papers—objective papers that simply explain the meanings and symbols

    2. Thesis-driven essays that argue a particular interpretation with copious textual support

    3. Response papers that are mostly opinion, but with a few references to the text

    4. Private journal writing

2. What is the best part about English classes?

    1. Literary terminology (e.g., alliteration, rhyme scheme, ode, pastoral elegy). This would be intriguing even if the literature were entirely irrelevant to the real world.

    2. Literary terminology is the best part, although it is also usually important to discuss whether or not literature is relevant to the real world (either now or when the text was written).

    3. A 50/50 blend of literary terminology and real world relevance (either now or when the text was written).

    4. Discovering how literature is relevant to the real world is more important, although literary terminology can occasionally help with that discovery.

    5. Discovering how literature is relevant to the real world. If I wanted to deal with technical terminology, I would have become an engineering major.

3. What is most important to your understanding of, say, Hamlet?

1. Lots of information about historical context (e.g., when and why it was written, how it compares to other literature of the period, etc.). I don't care if the literature applies to our own time.

2. Lots of information about historical context, and some application to our time.

3. A little information about historical context, but more emphasis on possible applications to our time.

4. I don't really care about historical context; I'm mostly interested in whether or not the literature gives me anything useful for living in the twenty-first century.

4. Which of the following statements best describes good literature?

   1. It can only really mean what the author intended it to mean. Other interpretations are possible, but if they contradict authorial intention, they are wrong. Hamlet cannot truly be said to have a meaning other than the author's own opinions.

   2. The author might have had several meanings—possibly even contradictory ones—in mind. This group of meanings is the range of legitimate interpretations.

   3. It is a dialogue between the author and the audience. If the author puts no meaning into it, an audience will get nothing out of it; but readers cannot help interpreting a text from their own points of view, so the ultimate meaning is some combination of author's ideas and those of the reader.

   4. It means different things to different readers, and it is likely that the author did not fully understand all of the legitimate meanings in the work. There are, however, a few limits to plausible interpretations. (E.g., Hamlet cannot be about World War II.)

   5. It means whatever a reader thinks it means. If Hamlet makes me think about World War II, then the play is—at least for me—about World War II.

Appendix C
Autobiographical Sketch Assignment
MELANIE SPRINGER MOCK

Because very few people could write a meaningful autobiography in a semester's time, you will not be required to construct an autobiography of your whole life for this class. Instead, as we discuss autobiographical representations of the self over the next few weeks, you should be thinking of moments in your life that might reflect or represent your self in its totality—or that represent your self as it once was.

In three four to five page (minimum) autobiographical sketches, you will be asked to narrate these moments in your life, conveying to your readers the special importance of this moment in defining your self. We will be discussing the conventions of autobiography and of how one might draw another into his own experiences through writing; you will be expected to use these conventions in your narratives.

Material for your narratives can be culled from your journal or from your reflective responses, if you wish, or from exercises completed in class. You are basically free to write about any experience you feel compelled to explore, although stay away from trying to tackle too much: better to write about a smaller event in your life (one that took minutes but had lasting impact) than about a larger event (one that took years, and so of course had lasting impact). Consider as well the truth you want to convey to your readers—what take away value might the piece have for them? How will reading about your experience enhance their own selves, their world, their relationship to others and, possibly, to God?

If you are stuck for ideas, consider writing about:

- An epiphany or turning point in your life, when you suddenly realized something about your self or your world that you had not considered before.
- An instance when you experienced some form of prejudice, when you were treated a certain way because someone else prejudged who you were.
- An important relationship you had with a family member, friend, or acquaintance, and how that relationship helped you find out more about your self as well as the other.
- A journey or trip you took that challenged you to learn more about another culture as well as about who you were.

- A trying moment in your life, such as an illness, the death of a loved one, financial insolvency, the loss of something important to you.
- A time in your life where you experienced some emotion intensely, be it fear, sadness, joy, despair, etc.

Appendix D
Reading and Writing Tutorials
Melanie Springer Mock

The small size of this class, and its structure, will allow for some individual exploration, study, and writing. To facilitate this exploration, you will be asked to read three book-length autobiographies and one biography of your own choosing, based on your own interest.

In groups of three or four, you will be asked to pick a text to read and discuss together. Every week, I will meet with one group (rather than with the entire class) to discuss the autobiography/biography you have read. During that tutorial, you will need to be prepared to answer the questions listed below about the text under consideration; you will also need to turn in a two page reflection of the autobiography you have read. You will not know beforehand what questions I might ask about the text, or which direction the conversation will head. The best way to be prepared for these tutorials, then, is to read the book closely and consider how you might best answer questions posed to you. For this portion of the tutorial, you will be evaluated singularly on your preparedness and the thoughtfulness of your contribution to the conversation. Although a group member's lack of preparation will not hurt your grade, it might hinder the flow and ease of conversation, and so the quality of the tutorial.

Additionally, during the tutorial we will be looking more closely at the autobiographical texts you are working on; therefore, you will need to bring completed, or nearly completed, drafts to the tutorials. We will spend part of the time, then, critiquing each other's work and providing constructive suggestions for revision. For this part of the tutorial, you will be evaluated singularly on your preparedness (bringing drafts to the table) and on your willingness to offer your peers constructive criticism for revision.

These are some questions you might want to consider as you read the text you have selected:

- Consider the varying ways men and women stereotypically choose to write about their life's experiences. Does this text follow the typical gender patterns of autobiography that characteristically appear?

- How do you believe the writer's present self influences what he will write about his past? How does his present understanding of his life affect what he will say about his past experiences, and how he represents those experiences?
- Does this text follow the typical pattern of a conversion narrative?
- How would you describe the text's structure? Does that structure help make the writer's life experiences clearer to understand? Or did you find the structure a distraction to the story the writer was trying to tell?
- What metaphors of the self does the writer use in her autobiography?
- Is there a hero in this life story? If so, who is the hero? Who is the antagonist?
- Do you feel that the writer is, in any way, walking a thin ethical line— or has the writer, in any way, transgressed the ethical considerations of autobiography?
- Do you see a coherent self in this text? Or does the author seem to have a confused understanding of self?
- Is there a dark side to the self in this text? If so, does this change the way you feel about the author?
- How do you feel about the author after reading her text? Do you feel as if you know her? Do you admire and respect her? Or find her life story in some way unworthy of respect?
- What is the most compelling scene in the text? Why did you find it so compelling?
- Is this a text you would recommend to others? Why or why not?

Appendix E
Auto/biographical Essays
MELANIE SPRINGER MOCK

This biographical essay will require a blend of the autobiographical skills you have mastered, and of the biographical skills you will learn to master. For this four to six page essay, you will write a biography of someone in your life, but as that person relates to you. In many ways, this will be a biography of a relationship, rather than merely of a person. For example, you may choose to write about the relationship you have with your grandpa, and how that relationship has changed and grown over time. The essay may well end up being more about you than the subject about that you are writing; or, it may well end up being more about the subject than about you.

Your first task, then, is to pick a person you want to focus on. You probably should know this person well, and should have forged some kind of relationship with your subject; of course, some of our most profound moments occur when we interact with someone we don't know well, but who changes us nonetheless. Your subject does not have to be someone with whom you have a warm and fuzzy relationship; the best texts will have some level of conflict and complexity, just as do most relationship.

For this essay, you have several options. You could tell a straightforward chronological essay, describing an event that exemplifies your relationship with this person. Or, you could focus on several events that showed the emergence of your relationship, and of its complex components. Or, you could choose one of the other discourse modes you will learn about, including a segmented essay, to explore the different aspects of your relationship.

Whatever method you choose to tell your story, you will be evaluated on the clarity of your expression; the cohesion of your essay; its use of detail to show your relationship rather than just tell about it; your ability to imply what you have learned or understood about the relationship; and the lack of grammatical and mechanical errors.

Appendix F
Biography Assignment
Melanie Springer Mock

This semester, our attention has been centered on chronicling your own lifetime experiences in several autobiographical forms. In each essay the self as subject remained constant, even as you were writing about your relationship with another. Now, our focus on the subject of life writing shifts away from your own self to another, as you chronicle the lifetime experiences of a different person.

Therefore, in a five to seven page essay, you will be asked to step beyond your own experiences to explore the life experiences of another subject of your choosing. I *strongly* urge you to choose someone you know or could know, rather than a figure about whom you can only find information in books. If you write a biography using material merely gathered from what other people say, you will have little opportunity to write anything new or unique, or to bring another person to life in an intriguing way—for yourself, or your readers. You will no doubt find this assignment most meaningful if you choose someone about whom you are interested, and/or to whom you feel some sort of affinity:

a relative, a close friend, a neighbor, someone in your community. At the same time, you should have the critical distance to make this more than a paean to another: even the greatest people have flaws and make mistakes in their lives.

Your task is to make your subject's life compelling and meaningful, an exemplar of sorts for your readers. This is possible with any subject, as every life is unique, every life compelling. Even the seemingly most mundane people have no doubt accomplished something, seen something, dreamed about something, other readers will find interesting. Find that "something," and bring it to life for your readers. That said, your essay should not be a compendium of facts (born on such and such, died on such and such, yada yada). Instead, you will want to find a theme, an extended metaphor perhaps, through which you can figure your subject's life. Focus on that one aspect of this life; make it central in your essay.

This assignment will no doubt require some research. You may wish to shadow your subject for a day to capture his actions, figures of speech, the ebb and flow of his daily life; you most likely will interview your subject and those who know her; you may ask to look at pictures, letters, journals, or other items that document your subject's life.

You will be evaluated on your ability to do this, to provide cohesion to the seemingly disparate parts of your subject's life; you will also be evaluated on the clarity of your thought and expression, as well as on the lack of grammatical and mechanical errors in your text.

Appendix G
Portfolio Assignment
MELANIE SPRINGER MOCK

The portfolio is a compilation of your best work in autobiography and biography this semester. In a way, the portfolio is like a book which represents you: your self, as you write, as you interact with the world around you. The portfolio will be due by Friday, April 25, at 10:00. After that, I will take off three percentage points for every day the portfolio is late; you will need to complete the portfolio for sure by April 28 at 5:00 if you hope to receive a grade for this course.

Your portfolio will include:

- A title page listing pertinent personal information as well as a title which characterizes your portfolio and your life writing this semester (something creative, more than "My Portfolio" or "My Semester's Writing").

- A table of contents providing an order to what is in your portfolio, but not necessarily the page numbers for those items.
- A two to three paragraph (minimum) preface detailing the contents of your portfolio, especially why you chose the essays to revise that you did, as well as specific revisions done for each essay.
- A two to three page autobiography of your self as a writer; a rough draft of this essay will be written during class.
- Revisions of three pieces you completed for this class. Be aware that revision means more than changing grammar and spelling errors. Instead, you will need to follow suggestions proffered by your peers and by me as you consider ways to improve your essays.
- Anything else you think will enhance your portfolio: drawings, poems, colored dividers, pleas for a better grade, a twenty dollar bill.

In addition to these ingredients listed above, I would like rough drafts of the pieces your revised, as well as the evaluated piece with my comments. If you do not include this "paper trail" in your portfolio, you will not receive complete credit for your work, even if you essays are revised to perfection.

Your portfolio will be evaluated by the quality of the essays you include; the depth and breadth of the revisions you make to each essay; the inclusion of each component; the quality of your preface and autobiography; the lack of grammatical and mechanical errors in final products; and organization and neatness.

Printed in the United States
221907BV00002B/2/P

9 780891 125365